Peace Enforcement

Peace Enforcement

The United Nations Experience in Congo, Somalia, and Bosnia

Jane Boulden

Westport, Connecticut
London

Library of Congress Cataloging-in-Publication Data

Boulden, Jane, 1962–
    Peace enforcement : the United Nations experience in Congo, Somalia, and Bosnia / Jane Boulden.
        p. cm.
    Includes bibliographical references and index.
    ISBN 0–275–96906–1 (alk. paper)
    1. United Nations—Peacekeeping forces—Congo (Democratic Republic) 2. United Nations—Peacekeeping forces—Somalia. 3. United Nations—Peacekeeping forces—Bosnia and Hercegovina. I. Title.
    KZ6376.B68 2001
    327.1′72—dc21   00–064952

British Library Cataloguing in Publication Data is available.

Library of Congress Catalog Card Number: 00–064952
ISBN: 0–275–96906–1

First published in 2001

Praeger Publishers, 88 Post Road West, Westport, CT 06881
An imprint of Greenwood Publishing Group, Inc.
www.praeger.com

Printed in the United States of America

The paper used in this book complies with the Permanent Paper Standard issued by the National Information Standards Organization (Z39.48–1984).

10 9 8 7 6 5 4 3 2 1

For David

Contents

Preface

This book has its origins in the work done by a small group of people with whom I worked in the late 1980s and early 1990s. Self-titled the "core group," this mix of academics and practitioners examined and debated proposals for improving the UN role in dealing with international peace and security in light of the changing international environment that came with the end of the Cold War. Meeting under various auspices, and in a variety of locations, the group often focused on the possibility of greater use, or revival, of some of the provisions of Chapter VII of the United Nations Charter.

A United Nations that used force more often and did so in situations short of full-scale enforcement but beyond the peacekeeping tenet that force would only ever be used in self-defense was, by the time of the enforcement action against Iraq in Kuwait, a more likely possibility than it had been for many years. But there were many unanswered questions about using force in this way, including whether or how such a use of force fit with the provisions of the United Nations Charter, and what kind of implications using force in this way would have for operations on the ground. The idea was very quickly put to the test in Bosnia and in Somalia, two very difficult operations authorized by the Security Council in the early 1990s. Dubbed peace enforcement, after the proposal for peace enforcement units in An Agenda for Peace, these operations provided the United Nations with practical experience of the concept even while the theory was still being defined and debated.

The idea behind this book was to look at those operations in an effort to determine what the experience tells us about using force in this way. What is achieved by peace enforcement? What should be done differently next time? Is this a useful or even desirable option for the United Nations? In addition to the operations in Bosnia and Somalia the book examines the one, often forgotten, Cold War example of peace enforcement, the UN operation in the Congo in the early 1960s. Although the United Nations has authorized peace enforcement operations in other conflicts, these three case studies provide the only examples where the United Nations has engaged in ongoing military operations in peace enforcement operations. Together, they provide a useful base of experience from which to draw some conclusions about how peace enforcement works and whether or not it is a useful tool for the United Nations in dealing with international peace and security problems.

Much of the work for this book was done as a doctoral thesis, very sporadically, between 1995 and 1998. I am very grateful to my thesis supervisor, David Haglund, for his helpful comments, his patience, and his support during and after the thesis process. Douglas Bland and the Security and Defence Forum of the Department of National Defence provided me with the opportunity to visit Bosnia in the spring of 1998. The interviews, seminars, and discussions during that trip proved to be a real catalyst for my thinking about the ideas discussed here. I am also indebted to Douglas Fraser and James S. Sutterlin for their extensive and very helpful comments on various drafts of the manuscript. Thanks are also due to Liz Mullan who carefully proofread the final manuscript, and to editors Heather Staines and Heidi Straight at Greenwood Publishing for their interest, patience, and support throughout the editing and production process. In addition, I am grateful for the considerable assistance I received from the staff at the Dag Hammarskjöld Library at the United Nations, and at the UN Archives. The discussion and ideas of colleagues in the "core group" as well as in the Canadian government's working group on developing a rapid reaction capability for the United Nations contributed a great deal to my thinking. As always, as the author I take full responsibility for any errors, inaccuracies, or omissions in the text, and the opinions and judgments expressed are solely my own.

Finally, the writing of this book took place during a period of deep grief. The strong support and love of family and close friends made it possible to begin to think about life and work again, and to inch my way, however erratically and painfully, through the writing process. In that sense this is their book as much as it is mine.

Jane Boulden
Kingston, Ontario
July 2000

Abbreviations

ANC	Armée Nationale Congolaise
CENTCOM	Central Command (US)
EC	European Community
ICFY	International Conference on the Former Yugoslavia
ICJ	International Court of Justice
ICRC	International Committee of the Red Cross
IFOR	Implementation Force
JNA	Yugoslav National Army
MNF	Multinational Force (Haiti)
MSC	Military Staff Committee
NAC	North Atlantic Council
NATO	North Atlantic Treaty Organization
NGO	Nongovernmental organization
OAU	Organization of African Unity
ONUC	United Nations Operation in the Congo
QRF	Quick Reaction Force (US)
ROE	Rules of Engagement
RRF	Rapid Reaction Force
SFOR	Stabilization Force
SNA	Somali National Alliance
SNM	Somali National Movement
SPM	Somali Patriotic Movement
SRC	Supreme Revolutionary Council
SRSG	Special Representative of the Secretary-General
TNC	Transnational Council
UNAMIR	United Nations Assistance Mission for Rwanda
UNAMSIL	United Nations Mission in Sierra Leone
UNDP	United Nations Development Program
UNHCR	United Nations High Commissioner for Refugees
UNIDIR	United Nations Institute for Disarmament Research

UNITAF	Unified Task Force
UNOSOM	United Nations Operation in Somalia
UNPA	United Nations Protected Area
UNPROFOR	United Nations Protection Force
UNTAES	United Nations Transitional Administration for Eastern Slavonia, Baranja, and Western Sirmium
USC	United Somali Congress

Chapter 1

Introduction

On 31 January 1992, the United Nations Security Council met at the level of the heads of government for the first time. The meeting was evidence of a new era for the Security Council, one in which the superpower rivalry that contributed to years of stalemate and Cold War politics was replaced by a Security Council in which permanent members could agree to work together on issues relating to international peace and security. These were euphoric times for the United Nations. Not only had the shadow of Cold War rivalry been removed from the organization, but there was also a definite willingness, even determination, among member states to use the United Nations to its full potential. In chairing the Security Council meeting of the heads of government, the Prime Minister of the United Kingdom, John Major, articulated those feelings: "The world now has the best chance for peace, security and development since the founding of the United Nations. I hope, like the founders of the United Nations themselves, that we can today renew the resolve enshrined in the Charter—the resolve to combine our efforts to accomplish the aims of the Charter in the interests of all the people we are privileged to represent."[1]

In the wake of the successful military operation that pushed Iraq out of Kuwait in 1991, and along with the new optimism and commitment to using the United Nations evidenced at the Security Council heads of government meeting, came a new willingness to use the United Nations more forcefully than during the Cold War. By the end of 1992, the Security Council had authorized UN involvement in two difficult conflicts—the collapsing Yugoslavia and the ongoing civil war in Somalia. And, in each of these conflicts the Security Council authorized a use of force beyond that utilized in traditional peacekeeping but short of the full-scale use of force authorized in the UN–sponsored actions in response to Iraq's invasion of Kuwait.

The purpose of this book is to examine the use of force by the United Nations in situations that fall between traditional peacekeeping operations and full-scale enforcement measures as provided for in Article 42 of the United Nations Charter. The basic question that the book is seeking to address is: Does it work? What does the UN experience with using force in this way tell us about whether or not this is a useful approach for dealing with international peace and security problems?

In addressing these questions, the book takes a lessons-learned approach to three case studies. The goal is to develop a set of lessons that can be utilized by the United Nations, and by extension, its member states, in considering and authorizing future operations of this type. How or should the Security Council's approach change next time? What issues need to be addressed in authorizing such operations? How does the nature of the mandate affect what happens on the ground? What can we learn about how these types of mandates are implemented in order to ensure that such operations will be more effective next time? Should there be a next time?

In order to address these questions, we need to know why and how the Security Council made the decisions it did about the use of force, how those decisions were implemented in the field, and then whether what happened in the field corresponded to the Security Council's intentions. To this end, a detailed case study approach is used to determine what the Security Council intended (how the use of force mandate came about) and what actually happened when the mandate was implemented in the field. This approach is based on the assumption that in order to improve the decision making and implementation of possible future operations of this type it is necessary to have a thorough understanding of what the Security Council intended to happen and what actually did happen.

PEACE ENFORCEMENT

The authorization of the use of force by the Security Council in situations that fall into the grey area between full-scale enforcement measures and traditional peacekeeping situations has come to be known as peace enforcement. The "grey area" between peacekeeping and enforcement has its roots in Article 40 of the charter, which authorizes the Security Council to take "provisional measures" that are "without prejudice to the rights, claims, or position of the parties concerned." [2] The term "peace enforcement" is taken from Secretary-General Boutros Boutros-Ghali's proposal, in An Agenda for Peace, for the creation of peace enforcement units.[3] The media and the general public almost immediately adopted the term to describe UN operations in Somalia and Bosnia even though the operations were not of the kind proposed by the secretary-general. The secretary-general's peace enforcement proposal was specifically related to enforcing cease-fires, rather than using force for a variety of goals short of full-scale enforcement, but this distinction has long since fallen by the wayside. The term "peace enforcement" has, therefore, come to be widely used to describe UN operations where force is involved short of full-scale enforcement operations, such as the UN response to the Iraq-Kuwait war, but more than traditional peacekeeping operations.[4]

The purpose of peace enforcement operations, as the term is used here, is to bring about or ensure compliance with some aspect of a Security Council mandate or an agreement among the parties. These operations are in a grey area between peacekeeping, linked to Chapter VI of the charter and enforcement, from Chapter VII, because they share characteristics from both types of operations. Like peacekeeping, peace enforcement is meant to be impartial in nature. Unlike peacekeeping, but like full-scale enforcement measures, peace enforcement operations do not necessarily require the consent of the parties involved (see Table 1).

The UN peace enforcement operations examined in this book have the following characteristics:

- they are authorized under Chapter VII of the UN Charter;
- therefore, the use of force beyond self defense is authorized;
- they are intended to be impartial; no judgement is made as to the claims or positions of the parties to the conflict and the action is not taken against any one state or party, as is the case with full-scale enforcement responses; and
- the consent of the parties to the operation is desirable and may be present when the operation begins, but it is not a requirement.

Table 1
The Peacekeeping to Full-Scale Enforcement Spectrum

Peacekeeping	Peace Enforcement	Enforcement
Impartial	impartial	not impartial
consent required	consent desirable but not required	consent not required
self-defense	self-defense plus specific use of force authorization	full use of force authorization

Consent

A characteristic of these operations is the probability of the absence of consent from one or all of the parties to a conflict. The absence of consent can take various forms. A lack of consent may be the consequence of a lack of government, or because a party initially gives its consent and then withdraws it, or as a result of a determined policy against UN involvement. In some instances, the leadership of a party to the conflict may give consent, but that fact may not be communicated to all elements of a group or not all elements of the group may agree with the leadership's decision.

Impartiality

The concept of impartiality is a key aspect of peace enforcement operations. The question of whether or not the United Nations is behaving impartially is applied in this analysis at two separate but linked levels. First, there is the question as to whether the Security Council mandate is impartial. At the second level is the question as to whether the implementation of the mandate is impartial.[5] What does it mean to be impartial? The *Oxford English Dictionary* defines "impartiality" as "not favouring one more than another; unprejudiced, unbiased, fair, just, equitable."[6] This definition coincides with provisions of Article 40 of the charter, which says that provisional measures taken by the Security Council "shall be without prejudice to the rights, claims, or position of the parties concerned."

POLITICAL DECISIONS, MILITARY MEANS

The charter of the United Nations gives the Security Council "primary responsibility for the maintenance of international peace and security" (Article 24). In carrying out that responsibility, the Security Council has a spectrum of responses available to it under the provisions of Chapters VI and VII of the charter. The decision to respond to a given situation is a political one. The decision as to how to respond—which mechanisms available in Chapters VI and VII to use—is also political. In deciding to respond, the Security Council may authorize the use of military force as a way of ensuring the implementation of a mandate. It is a fundamental assumption of this analysis that the Security Council's "political" choices relating to the mandate of a mission—what measures should be taken and how they should be carried out—drive the military operations it authorizes.

THE CASE STUDIES

Three case studies are examined in detail: the United Nations Operation in the Congo (ONUC); the United Nations Operation in Somalia II (UNOSOM II); and, the United Nations Protection Force (UNPROFOR) in the former Yugoslavia. These three cases are chosen because they represent the only examples of the UN use of force to compel compliance involving sustained military operations. The Congo case is the only example of this kind of action during the cold war and makes the point that the idea of using force in this way is not a post–Cold War creation. As such, it also provides a good counter case to the post–Cold War examples of the Somalia and Bosnia operations.

In each of these cases, force was used to achieve different objectives. In the Congo, the use of force was authorized to prevent civil war and ensure the withdrawal of foreign military personnel. In Somalia, force was authorized to allow for the delivery of humanitarian aid and to implement a political reconciliation mandate. In the former Yugoslavia, force was authorized for the enforcement of a no-fly zone, the protection of safe areas, and the delivery of humanitarian aid.

Although these operations had different objectives, all three had mandates involving an authorization of the use of force to compel compliance with certain goals established by the Security Council. The three operations also involved major sustained multinational military operations. This is a critical criterion since one of the purposes of this book is to examine the experience of the actual use of force, as opposed to, for example, the threat to use force. The Security Council has authorized other peace enforcement operations—the French-led Operation Turquoise in Rwanda; the UN multinational force in Haiti; the post-Dayton Peace Accord missions in the former Yugoslavia; the security force in Kosovo; and the operations in Sierra Leone and the Congo—but they are not included in this study because they did not involve sustained military operations and/or because the conduct of the operations was carried out by some other organization or group of states.[7]

Each case study chapter is divided into four sections. The first section provides a brief description of the background to the conflict and the context in which the operation occurred. This establishes the reasons for the decision by the Security Council to become involved in the conflict and outlines the situation in which the UN mission is operating. The second section describes the mandate for the operation in order to establish how, why, and on what basis force was authorized. The approach here is twofold. The section traces the evolution of the mandate from the first Security Council action on the issue to the decision to use force. It then focuses on the decision to use force, outlining the nature and goals of the decision—how and why the Security Council decided to authorize force and what it hoped to achieve. In this way, an understanding of the Security Council decision-making process as a developmental and responsive process is established.

The third section of the chapter addresses the implementation of the mandate. This section begins with a brief overview of the rules of engagement for the use of force in the operation. This provides an indication of how the authorization to use force is translated into military guidelines in the field. The analysis then focuses on the actual use of force, following the efforts to implement the mandate and the results. The final section draws on all of the analyses and discussions to outline the key lessons and issues that are raised by the experience.

An exploration of the use of force issue necessarily touches on any number of other aspects of the operations—the policies of major powers, the implications of the goals of the operations, and the nature and events of the conflict itself—all related, interesting issues. The case studies, however, focus very specifically on following the use of force issue. They do not, therefore, tell the full story of the operations examined although much of the story of the conflicts and the reactions of the international community are touched on in this process.

The three case study chapters are preceded by a discussion of the provisions of the UN Charter that give the Security Council the power to authorize the use of force. This chapter describes the legal provisions made in the charter, examines how and why these provisions were rarely used during the Cold War, and then outlines the post–Cold War debate and attitudes about the UN peace and security mechanisms and how they should be used. The concluding chapter pulls together the lessons and issues raised in each of the case studies and draws some overall conclusions about the use of force by the UN in situations beyond traditional peacekeeping but short of full-scale enforcement.

The examination of the case studies reveals that there are a number of common characteristics and issues associated on the one hand with the types of choices the Security Council makes in these situations (mandate issues), and on the other hand with the kinds of problems and issues that arise in carrying out these operations (operational issues). In delineating these mandate and operational issues, the conclusions help to clarify the types of issues and problems that are likely to arise in future operations. This information should help inform the policy making process for future operations and thereby contribute to their success. There remains the broader question of whether or not peace enforcement can be said to work. Is it a viable tool for the international community in dealing with issues of international peace and security? The case studies demonstrate that the idea that it is possible to remain impartial in situations where force might be and is used is the central issue in determining whether or not peace enforcement is a viable option. In addition to developing the specific lessons relating to operational and mandate issues, therefore, the conclusions also address the linkage between impartiality and the use of force and what this means for the future of peace enforcement.

NOTES

1. S/PV.3046, 31 January 1992, 7.
2. The drafters of the UN Charter intended the article to be "provisional"—that is, that it could be used as a stopgap measure in situations where it was thought that it was important to create a pause and allow time for negotiation and other measures. For previous use of Article 40, see United Nations, *Repertory of Practice of United Nations Organs,* vol. 2 (New York: United Nations, 1982), 386–388.
3. In the late 1940s, immediately after the creation of the UN Charter, the term "peace enforcement" was sometimes used to describe the Chapter VII enforcement provisions based in Article 42. Use of the term ceased when the effect of cold war politics virtually eliminated the possibility that the Security Council would authorize such measures.
4. Not everyone agrees with the idea that there is a spectrum of responses available to the United Nations and that peace enforcement is an acceptable option for the United Nations. For example, Charles Dobbie, the author of the British army's field manual on UN operations, takes a "consent is everything" approach to UN operations. He argues that there are two kinds of operations available to the Security Council, one in which consent is present—peacekeeping—and one in which it is not—enforcement, and that there is no middle ground between them. See Charles Dobbie, "A Concept for Post–Cold War Peacekeeping," *Survival* 36, no. 3 (Autumn 1994): 121–148. Also see *Wider Peacekeeping, Army Field Manual,* Vol. 5, Operations Other Than War, part 2 (London, Her Majesty's Stationary Office, 1995). For comparison to *Wider Peacekeeping*, see the U.S. field manual: United States, Department of the Army, *Peace Operations*, FM 100-23, 30 December 1994. The manual defines peace enforcement operations separately from peacekeeping. Don Daniel and Bradd Hayes argue that there certainly is a middle ground between peacekeeping and enforcement. They propose the term "inducement" be

used to describe the middle ground. They define inducement as "a process of persuading, bringing about or causing" where the role of the mission is "to convince all concerned to assent, even if only grudgingly, without conducting widespread and sustained combat operations against anyone." Don Daniel and Bradd Hayes, "Securing Observance of UN Mandates through the Employment of Military Force," *International Peacekeeping* 3, no. 4 (Winter 1996): 105–125. Also see John Gerard Ruggie, "The UN and Collective Use of Force: Whither or Whether?" *International Peacekeeping* 3, no. 4 (Winter 1996): 1–20 (all of the articles contained in this issue of *International Peacekeeping* were later published as an edited volume: Michael Pugh, ed., *The UN, Peace and Force* (London: Frank Cass, 1997)); Adam Roberts, "The Crisis in UN Peacekeeping," *Survival* 36, no. 3, (Autumn 1994): 93–120; John Mackinlay and Jarat Chopra, *A Draft Concept of Second Generation Multinational Operations*, 1993 (Providence, R.I.: Brown University, 1993); and Elgin Clemons, "No Peace to Keep: Six and Three-quarters Peacekeepers," *New York University Journal of International Law and Politics* 26, no. 1: 107–141.

5. Adam Roberts and Marrack Goulding also make this distinction. Adam Roberts notes: "In UN peace-keeping, impartiality is no longer interpreted to mean, in every case, impartiality between the parties to a conflict. In some cases, the UN may, and perhaps should, be tougher with one party than another or give more aid to one side than another. . . . Yet there are important elements in the notion of impartiality that should not be lost, including the idea that the UN represents a set of interests, values and tasks that are distinct in some respects from those of any one belligerent. . . .'impartiality' may have come to mean not impartiality between the belligerents, but impartiality in carrying out UN Security Council decisions." See Roberts, "The Crisis in UN Peacekeeping," 115. Also see Marrack Goulding, "The Evolution of United Nations Peace-keeping," *International Affairs* 69, no. 3 (1993): 451–464.

6. *The Shorter Oxford English Dictionary on Historical Principles*, vol. 1 (Oxford: Clarendon Press, 1991), 1028. Note that the concept of impartiality differs from that of neutrality, which is defined as "a neutral attitude between two contending parties or powers, abstention from taking any part in a war between other states. . . .The condition of being inclined neither way"; and *The Shorter Oxford English Dictionary on Historical Principles*, vol. 2 (Oxford: Clarendon Press, 1991), 1399.

7. The Security Council gave the two UN–authorized, NATO–run operations that followed the Dayton Peace Accord in the former Yugoslavia—the Implementation Force (IFOR), followed by the Stabilization Force (SFOR)—authorization for the use of "all necessary measures" in carrying out the mission (Security Council Resolution 1031, 15 December 1995; Security Council Resolution 1088, 12 December 1996). Equally, the UN Transitional Administration for Eastern Slavonia, Baranja, and Western Sirmium (UN-TAES) constituted a peace enforcement operation in that the mandate was authorized under Chapter VII and UNTAES officials had the ability to draw on IFOR military support if needed. After the NATO air campaign against Serbian forces in Kosovo, the UN Security Council authorized the creation of a Kosovo Force (KFOR) to establish a secure environment and deter hostilities (Security Council Resolution 1244, 10 June 1999). In all of these cases the actual use of force has been minimal. The UN-authorized operation in Haiti also qualifies as a peace enforcement operation. On 31 July 1994, the Security Council invoked Chapter VII and authorized the creation of a multinational force and the use of "all necessary means" to bring about the transition from the illegal military regime to the democratically elected government in Haiti (Security Council Resolution 940, 31 July 1994). Under U.S. leadership, a large military mission known as the Multinational Force (MNF) was prepared. At the final hour, as a result of an agreement brokered by former president Jimmy Carter, the military regime relented and agreed to leave, paving the way for the elected government to take over and for the unopposed landing of the MNF. In June 1994, the Security Council authorized a French-

led operation in Rwanda to provide security and humanitarian relief for displaced persons, refugees, and civilians at risk in Rwanda (Security Council Resolution 929, 22 June
1994). The operation, known as Operation Turquoise, acted as a temporary measure in
support of the UN Assistance Mission for Rwanda (UNAMIR) until contributions from
UN member states brought UNAMIR to its desired maximum strength. This operation is
not considered here because the use of force was carried out primarily by France and the
operation was militarily limited. After the violence associated with the election in East
Timor, the Security Council authorized the creation of the UN transitional authority there
under Chapter VII (Security Council Resolution 1272, 25 October 1999). In Resolution
1289, 7 February 2000, the Security Council added a Chapter VII "necessary means"
authorization to the UN Mission in Sierra Leone (UNAMSIL) in order to ensure security
of the disarmament program and at key installations. In the Congo, the Security Council
authorized the use of force for the protection of UN personnel and facilities and to ensure
freedom of movement for UN personnel (Security Council Resolution 1291, 24 February
2000).

Chapter 2

The Legal and Political Background to Peace Enforcement

THE UNITED NATIONS CHARTER

Faced with the failure of the League of Nations and the disintegration of international relations into World War II, the great powers set out to develop a new collective security organization, this time one that would be strong enough and comprehensive enough to be the focal point for state actions and discussions on issues of war and peace. Negotiations on the design of the new organization began in 1942 and were led by the United Kingdom and the United States. With respect to the security provisions of the UN Charter, the drafters took as their starting point the lessons of the league and the experience of World War II. The League of Nations experience demonstrated that if states were simply left to their own devices to provide forces and support to redress a situation, the response would be minimal. This created a sense that any enforcement system must be mandatory. The successful cooperation of the allied powers during World War II led the charter drafters to conclude that the most effective way to ensure international peace and security was to have the great powers working together to combat aggression. The ideas for a mandatory system of enforcement, run by the great powers, were derived from these experiences.[1]

The international peace and security provisions of the charter are contained in Chapter VI, Pacific Settlement of Disputes, and Chapter VII, Action with Respect to Threats to the Peace, Breaches of the Peace, and Acts of Aggression. Chapter VI outlines the obligations of states and the powers of the Security Council with respect to the peaceful settlement of disputes. States that are parties to any dispute likely to endanger international peace and security are required to "seek a solution by negotiation, enquiry, mediation, conciliation, arbitration, judicial settlement, resort to regional agencies or arrangements, or other peaceful means of their own choice" (Art. 33 (1)). The Security Council can call on states to undertake these actions, can investigate any dispute, or, at any stage, may "recommend appropriate procedures or methods of adjustment" (Art. 36

(1)). If states fail to settle a dispute by the various means outlined, they are to refer the dispute to the Security Council. The Security Council will decide whether to recommend other procedures or methods, or to recommend terms of settlement.

CHAPTER VII

Chapter VII further strengthens member states' obligations and Security Council powers. In contrast to Chapter VI, which deals with situations that *may* lead to a breach or threat to international peace and security, Chapter VII deals with the existence of such threats, breaches of the peace or acts of aggression. Under this chapter, the Security Council determines the existence of a threat to or breach of international peace and security. It has the power to take or call for provisional measures in order to "prevent an aggravation of the situation," and has at its disposal various options short of armed force to use in response to a situation. Finally, and, most importantly, the Security Council has the power to use force, if necessary, to deal with international peace and security problems.

Article 39, the first under Chapter VII, is critical: "The Security Council shall determine the existence of any threat to the peace, breach of the peace, or act of aggression and shall make recommendations, or decide what measures shall be taken in accordance with Articles 41 and 42, to maintain or restore international peace and security." Note that it is not left to individual member states to determine when a situation requires a response. It is the Security Council that makes that determination on behalf of member states, thereby obliging them to act as required in the charter.[2] As evident in both Chapters VI and VII, the charter drafters opted for the use of the broad phrase "international peace and security" rather than "war" or even "use of force." This choice avoided the definitional problems, so acutely evident in the league's experience, of needing a formal declaration of war before becoming involved.[3]

There is a clear sense of a process of responses. When Chapter VI peaceful methods of dispute resolution fail or are resisted by states, the provisions of Chapter VII can be invoked. As provided for in Article 39, the Security Council determines that the situation requires action. It can then recommend provisional measures and decide what measures "not involving the use of armed force" such as "complete or partial interruption of economic relations and of rail, sea, air, postal, telegraphic, radio, and other means of communication, and the severance of diplomatic relations" (Art. 41) may be needed. If these measures prove "inadequate," the Security Council "may take such action by air, sea, or land forces as may be necessary to maintain or restore international peace and security" (Art. 42).

While a sequence of responses is evident, there is no requirement that the Security Council begin with the first step and follow with the second. If the Security Council determines that the situation immediately requires the use of force outlined in Article 42, it can invoke that provision without going through any of the previous provisions. Conversely, there is no requirement for Security Council action in any given situation if the Security Council chooses not to act.

These four articles, 39 through 42, establish the basic process of response. The remaining articles in Chapter VII deal with the mechanisms to make the responses possible. Under Article 43, member states agree to "make available to the Security Council, on its call and in accordance with a special agreement or agreements, armed forces, assistance, and facilities, . . . necessary for the purpose of maintaining international peace and security." These agreements are to be negotiated and concluded with the Security Council. Article 47 establishes the Military Staff Committee (MSC), a committee comprising the chiefs of staff of the permanent representatives of the Security Council. The MSC is to "advise and assist" the Security Council in matters relating to the Security Council's military requirements and to provide "strategic direction" of armed forces at the disposal of the Security Council.[4]

In contrast to the Covenant of the League Nations, which emphasized peaceful settlement, the UN Charter's emphasis is in its enforcement provisions, providing the "teeth" that had so clearly been lacking in the league. The Security Council's ability to intervene in disputes and potential disputes is wide-ranging and almost unlimited, and its decisions represent a binding obligation on all member states. To back up its decision making, the Security Council is to be provided with military forces. The initial idea was that the permanent members of the Security Council, as during World War II, would work together and provide the bulk of the forces for UN military action. In recognition of this commitment and responsibility, the permanent members of the Security Council were given a veto over all nonprocedural Security Council matters.[5]

THE IMPACT OF THE COLD WAR

In 1954, Julius Stone, pointing to the powers of the Security Council, described the UN Charter as an "aborted break with history."[6] He argued that these provisions were less viable than the more "primitive" provisions, such as the right to self-defense, also included in the charter, and that UN experience to that point bore this out.

History, as it were, took its own revenge. . . . A premature effort to break with the immediate past can rarely escape the compulsions of continuity. . . . The greater the power which is prematurely given to an international organisation, the more severe will be the checks which the Member States impose by way of escape from the excessive powers thus granted. . . . The very ambition of the Charter, therefore, turned it into a two-faced instrument. One face looks nobly towards the beginnings of a super-State well beyond the League of Nations; the other looks grimly backwards to the anarchic self-help of the old world, ...Which was the real face? . . . In 1953, . . . all men see it as a commonplace that two systems of uncontrolled national power confront each other, each inside and outside the United Nations. . . . These opposed power systems still operate within and under the slogans of the United Nations Charter; but it is the anarchic face, not that of world order which is now most prominent.[7]

Stone's portrayal describes the first years of the United Nations' existence. Like the creators of the league covenant, the drafters of the charter created an organization that responded to the problems that led to the world war that preceded it but failed to perceive where those problems had taken international relations. The working relationship among the five permanent members that made agreement on the UN Charter possible disintegrated soon after the United Nations came into being. The increasing level of tension between the Soviet Union and the United States colored and frustrated UN activity on international peace and security issues.

The most symbolic evidence of the degree to which East-West problems would hamper UN action occurred in the Military Staff Committee. The provision of troops, as provided for in Article 43, was the mechanism by which the United Nations would be able to use the enforcement powers it had been provided in the charter. As one of its first acts, the Security Council asked the Military Staff Committee to examine the requirements for establishing the military agreements provided for in Article 43. The MSC began meeting in February 1946 and almost instantly ground to a stalemate. After two and a half years and little progress it ceased consideration of Article 43 agreements and of anything else.[8] Almost immediately, therefore, the UN security mechanisms that were meant to set it apart from the League of Nations were rendered inoperable.

PEACEKEEPING

With the exception of the UN enforcement operation in Korea, made possible only through the absence of the Soviet Union from Security Council proceedings when North Korea invaded South Korea in June 1950,[9] UN activities in the peace and security field prior to 1956 were limited and small scale.[10]

The Suez crisis in 1956 prompted the creation of a new kind of UN operation —peacekeeping. The direct involvement of two permanent members, Britain and France, in the crisis meant that the Security Council was unable to agree on any action and the issue passed on to the General Assembly for consideration.[11] After intense debate, the General Assembly passed a resolution creating the United Nations Emergency Force (UNEF).[12] The mandate of the operation was to secure and supervise the cessation of hostilities, supervise the withdrawal of forces, and ensure compliance with other UN provisions. UNEF's key function was to interpose itself between the warring parties and act as a kind of a buffer. In so doing, it facilitated a withdrawal of forces and the initiation of negotiations on resolving the crisis.[13]

The creation of UNEF established basic criteria that became the foundation stones of all peacekeeping missions. UNEF soldiers were authorized to use force only in self-defense and were, accordingly, lightly armed.[14] The goal was simply to separate the parties in conflict to allow for negotiation and peaceful settlement between the parties. No judgement about rights or wrongs in the conflict were made. No permanent members were involved in the operation. All of these factors contributed to a sense of impartiality—the only interest of the troops involved was in carrying out the UN mandate. Finally, the operation was made possible because it had the consent of all of the parties to the conflict.[15]

Peacekeeping has no direct foundation in the provisions of the UN Charter.[16] The concept falls somewhere between the peaceful dispute-resolution methods outlined in Chapter VI and the enforcement measures of Chapter VII, prompting Secretary-General Dag Hammarskjöld to call peacekeeping operations Chapter VI and a half. The success of the UNEF operation opened the way for a resurgence of interest in using the international peace and security functions of the United Nations. The potential for action remained limited since Security Council, and, therefore, superpower agreement was necessary to authorize a mission. This meant that possible areas of action were limited to those in which the United States and the Soviet Union had limited interests and were willing to allow UN involvement. While peacekeeping was a long way from the activist United Nations envisaged by the charter drafters, it did provide an opening for some action rather than none at all. A gradual though steady stream of peacekeeping missions followed UNEF. Between 1956 and 1978, the Security Council authorized ten peacekeeping missions.[17]

THE END OF THE COLD WAR

In the late 1980s, the end of the Cold War brought a new willingness on the part of the United States and the Soviet Union to work together on international peace and security issues and to use the United Nations to that end. At the same time, the new relationship between the two superpowers meant that their interests in various regions changed and they were now willing to consider, and even encourage, UN involvement in the conflicts of those regions. These developments were self-reinforcing. U.S. and Soviet support for using the United Nations made success possible in areas such as Namibia and Central America where conflict resolution had been stuck in the stranglehold of Cold War politics for years. Those successes, in turn, encouraged a belief that the United Nations could and should be used more often and effectively. It seemed, finally, as if the United Nations had come into its own and would live up to the promise of the charter.[18]

This new interest in using the United Nations brought about two major changes in peacekeeping. The first was a new willingness to authorize missions in conflicts that were primarily internal, such as in Angola and Cambodia. The wide latitude offered in the phrase "international peace and security" and the extent to which such conflicts were indeed connected to international security issues made it possible to say that the conflicts were linked to international peace and security.[19]

Second, an expansion of the functions involved in the mandates assigned to peacekeeping missions occurred. For example, peacekeeping tasks moved beyond observation of cease-fires and separation of forces to the tasks involved in peace treaty implementation. These tasks included functions such as election monitoring, facilitating the transfer of power in government changeovers and disarmament of warring factions.[20]

Iraq's invasion and annexation of Kuwait in late 1990 prompted the United Nations' second experience with full-scale Chapter VII enforcement operations.

The UN response to the Iraqi invasion came in a series of Security Council resolutions, beginning with the imposition of sanctions and then moving to enforcement measures.[21] The Security Council, as it had done in Korea, authorized a group of countries to carry out the enforcement action on its behalf. Unlike the UN response to Korea, no UN command was established and the UN flag was not used. The operation, extensively covered by the international media, provided a very strong, very public symbol of the role of the United Nations in the post–Cold War world, giving further impetus to the post–Cold War enthusiasm for using the United Nations.

AN AGENDA FOR PEACE

Fresh from success in the Persian Gulf War and flush with the possibilities of the post–Cold War era, in January 1992 the Security Council met at the level of heads of government for the first time in its history. One of the outcomes of the meeting was a request from the Security Council that the new secretary-general prepare a report on ways "the capacity of the United Nations for preventive diplomacy, for peacemaking and for peace-keeping" could be made more effective.[22] The resulting report was *An Agenda for Peace* issued later that year.[23] *An Agenda for Peace* addressed the whole spectrum of peace and security action: preventive diplomacy, peacemaking, peacekeeping, and peacebuilding.

The secretary-general defined these terms as follows:

Preventive diplomacy is action to prevent disputes from arising between parties, to prevent existing disputes from escalating into conflicts and to limit the spread of the latter when they occur.
Peacemaking is action to bring hostile parties to agreement, essentially through such peaceful means as those foreseen in Chapter VI of the Charter of the United Nations.
Peace-keeping is the deployment of a United Nations presence in the field, hitherto with the consent of all the parties concerned, . . . Peace-keeping is a technique that expands the possibilities for both the prevention of the conflict and the making of peace. . . .
Peace-building [is] action to identify and support structures which will tend to strengthen and solidify peace in order to avoid a relapse into conflict.[24]

PEACE ENFORCEMENT

With respect to the use of force, the secretary-general returned to some of the original ideas of the charter drafters and recommended that the Security Council pursue negotiations with member states to develop Article 43 agreements.

The ready availability of armed forces on call could serve, in itself, as a means of deterring breaches of the peace since a potential aggressor would know that the Council had at its disposal a means of response. Forces under Article 43 may perhaps never be sufficiently large or well enough equipped to deal with a threat from a major army equipped with sophisticated weapons. They would be useful, however, in meeting any threat posed by a military force of a lesser order.[25]

This recommendation received little attention and the Security Council has not pursued it since. The recommendation that received the most attention was the secretary-general's proposal for peace enforcement units. The secretary-general used the example of cease-fires that have been agreed to but not complied with to propose that the Security Council consider using:

peace-enforcement units in clearly defined circumstances and with their terms of reference specified in advance. Such units from Member States would be available on call and would consist of troops that have volunteered for such service. They would have to be more heavily armed than peace-keeping forces and would need to undergo extensive preparatory training within their national forces. Deployment and operation of such forces would be under the authorization of the Security Council and would, as in the case of peace-keeping forces, be under the command of the Secretary-General. I consider such peace-enforcement units to be warranted as a provisional measure under Article 40 of the Charter.[26]

In the initial responses to the proposal, most of the attention focused on the idea of volunteer forces for the United Nations, reviving past proposals for the creation of a UN standing force or legion.[27] A few months later, the secretary-general published an article in the journal *Foreign Affairs* where he clarified the idea and drew the focus away from the idea of creating peace enforcement "units" to the idea of peace enforcement itself as a midpoint between peace-keeping and enforcement.

The purpose of peace-enforcement units (perhaps they should be called "cease-fire enforcement units") would be to enable the United Nations to deploy troops quickly to enforce a cease-fire by taking coercive action against either party, or both, if they violate it. . . . [T]he concept goes beyond peace-keeping to the extent that the operation would be deployed without the express consent of the two parties. . . . UN troops would be authorized to use force to ensure respect for the cease-fire.[28]

Further redefinition occurred in the secretary-general's report on the work of the organization issued in September 1993. In that report, the secretary-general picked up and incorporated the thread of his earlier definition of peacekeeping ("hitherto with the consent of the parties") and stated that "[t]he concept of peace enforcement . . . involves peace-keeping activities which do not necessarily involve the consent of all the parties concerned. Peace enforcement is foreseen in Chapter VII of the Charter."[29] The question of definitions remains one of ongoing debate.

In its consideration of the secretary-general's recommendations, the Security Council focused its attention on strengthening and developing the peacekeeping concept and stayed away from any direct approval of peace enforcement units or the concept of peace enforcement.[30] This apparent conservatism was in contrast to the council's enthusiasm at the Security Council summit for new and creative ways of using the United Nations. Although the Council failed to formally endorse the peace enforcement idea, its authorization of the operations in Somalia and Bosnia quickly put the general concept to a very practical test. Though not peace enforcement in the carefully defined sense proposed by the secretary-general, these operations fell into the grey area between peacekeeping and full-scale enforcement and as such they were close enough to the general idea of peace enforcement that when they were dubbed peace enforcement by the media, the name stuck.

It is this experience, the use of force to compel mandate compliance in situations that fall between peacekeeping and full-scale enforcement, that this book will now explore in examining the UN operations in the Congo, Somalia, and Bosnia.

NOTES

1. The best history of the development of the UN Charter is found in Ruth B. Russell, *A History of the United Nations Charter* (Washington D.C.: Brookings, 1958). The analysis is geared towards outlining the U.S. role in the creation of the charter but involves detailed descriptions of the negotiations and factors that led to each section of the charter. For a less U.S.–oriented analysis of the history, see Robert C. Hilderbrand, *Dumbarton Oaks: The Origins of the United Nations and the Search for Postwar Security* (Chapel Hill: University of North Carolina Press, 1990), especially chapter 6, on the Security Council. Also see Leland M. Goodrich, Edvard Hambro, and Anne P. Simons, *Charter of the United Nations Commentary and Documents* (New York: Columbia University Press, 1969), which provides an article-by-article analysis of the provisions, their negotiation, and their practice up until the mid-1960s.

2. Under Article 25, member states "agree to accept and carry out the decisions of the Security Council in accordance with the present Charter."

3. In 1931, Japan invaded Manchuria. For a long time the fact that there was no formal declaration of war was used to argue that the league had no jurisdiction in the conflict. For overviews of this episode, see Qunicy Wright, "The Manchurian Crisis," in Joel Larus, ed., *From Collective Security to Preventive Diplomacy* (New York: Wiley, 1965), 91–108; also see, Francis P. Walters, *A History of the League of Nations*, vol. 2 (London: Oxford University Press, 1952), 465–499.

4. For more on the Military Staff Committee, see Jane Boulden, *Prometheus Unborn: The History of the Military Staff Committee*, Aurora Papers 19 (Ottawa: Canadian Centre for Global Security, 1993).

5. "Decisions of the Security Council on all other matters [than procedure] shall be made by an affirmative vote of nine members including the concurring votes of the permanent members" (Art. 27 [3]). During the negotiations on the UN Charter, some states attempted to eliminate this veto provision but the permanent members would not agree to the broad security commitments of the charter without it. A good analysis of the international peace and security powers of each of the UN organs, combined with case studies, is contained in Nigel D. White, *The United Nations and the Maintenance of International Peace and Security* (Manchester: Manchester University Press, 1990). On the issue of the Security Council veto and its relationship to the international peace and security provisions of the charter, see Inis Claude, "The Blueprint," *International Conciliation*, no. 532 (March 1961): 325–355. Claude writes, "[the charter] provides for the organization of collective force to frustrate aggression whenever the great powers are unanimously disposed to support such action; but it does not purport to create an enforcement mechanism

capable of being used to control great powers or states backed by great powers" (331). Also see Inis Claude, "United Nations Use of Military Force," *Journal of Conflict Resolution* 7, no. 2 (June 1963).

6. Julius Stone, *Legal Controls of International Conflict* (London: Stevens, 1959) 279.

7. Ibid., 279–281.

8. The Military Staff Committee has continued to meet since 1947 but has not considered any issue of substance since then. Boulden, *Prometheus Unborn*.

9. The UN Commission on Korea was in the border area when hostilities broke out. This meant that the news came from a reliable source and was communicated almost immediately to the secretary-general and the Security Council. This in turn facilitated a quick emergency meeting of the Security Council. The Soviet Union, in protest over the issue of Chinese representation, was not sitting in on Security Council meetings at that time. Its absence meant that the initial resolutions providing for UN action in Korea passed without a Soviet veto. An excellent overview of the operation is provided in Rosalyn Higgins, *United Nations Peacekeeping 1946–1967, Documents and Commentary*, vol. 2, *Asia* (London: Oxford University Press, 1970), 153–312.

10. Between 1945 and 1956, the UN undertook three observer missions: the UN Special Committee on the Balkans, from 1947 to 1951; the UN Truce Supervision Organization, from 1948 to the present; and the UN Military Observer Group in India and Pakistan, from 1949 to the present. Although these operations predate peacekeeping as we know now it, they are generally included in lists of UN peacekeeping operations.

11. The issue passed to the General Assembly under the authority of the "Uniting for Peace" resolution (Resolution 377[V], 3 November 1950), which was a product of the Korean crisis.

12. General Assembly Resolution 1001, 7 November 1956.

13. For a description of the experience, see United Nations, *The Blue Helmets: A Review of United Nations Peace-keeping* (New York: United Nations, 1990), 43–78. For a comprehensive first hand view, see E.L.M. Burns, *Between Arab and Israeli* (Toronto: Clarke, Irwin, 1962). Also see Rosalyn Higgins, *United Nations Peacekeeping 1946–1967, Documents and Commentary*, vol. 1, *The Middle East* (London: Oxford University Press, 1969), 221–530.

14. For more on this issue, see Kjell Goldmann, *Peace-keeping and Self-defence*, Monograph no. 7 (Paris: International Information Center on Peace-keeping Operations, March 1968).

15. See the secretary-general's analysis of the UNEF experience and the principles developed as a result. "Summary Study of the Experience Derived from the Establishment and Operation of the Force: Report of the Secretary-General," A/3943, 9 October 1958. Also see Brian Urquhart, *Hammarskjöld*, (New York: Norton, 1994), 132–230.

16. John W. Halderman argues that the basis for these operations is clearly found in Article 1(1) of the UN charter, which provides for "collective measures" to maintain international peace and security. See John W. Halderman, "Legal Basis for United Nations Armed Forces," *American Journal of International Law* 56, (1962): 971–996.

17. See United Nations, *Blue Helmets*, for descriptions. Good overviews can be found in William J. Durch, ed., *The Evolution of UN Peacekeeping* (New York: St. Martin's, 1993). Two works from that time analyze the legal, political and military requirements and implications of UN operations. See Derek W. Bowett, *United Nations Forces* (London: Stevens, 1964); and Finn Seyersted, *United Nations Forces in the Law of Peace and War* (The Hague: A.W. Sijthoff-Leyden, 1966). Also see Indar Jit Rikhye, *The Theory and Practice of Peacekeeping* (London: C. Hurst, 1984). For an excellent reflection of the nature of international debate on the role of the UN midway through the cold war, see Alan James, *The Role of Force in International Order and United Nations Peace-*

keeping, Report of a Conference at Ditchley Park, Ditchley Park, The Ditchley Foundation, 16–19 May 1969.

18. Secretary-General Javier Pérez de Cuéllar oversaw the changes at the United Nations that came with the end of the cold war. In his final report he wrote: "New vistas are opening for States to work together in a manner they did not do before. The earlier posture of aloofness and reserve towards the Organization has been replaced by more ardent participation in its endeavours. An era of law and justice may not be around the corner but the United Nations has defined the direction. If dynamic efforts are made, obstacles in the way may no longer prove insuperable. Today there are far more solid grounds for hope than there are reasons for frustration and fear." See Javier Pérez de Cuéllar, *Anarchy or Order, Annual Reports, 1982–1991* (New York: United Nations, 1991), 362. Good analysis reflecting the mood of the time is also found in Oscar Schacter, "Authorized Uses of Force by the United Nations and Regional Organizations," in Lori Fisler Damrosch, and David J. Scheffer, *Law and Force in the New International Order* (Boulder, Col.: Westview Press, 1991).

19. A good examination of the UN involvement in internal conflicts is Lori Fisler Damrosch, ed., *Enforcing Restraint: Collective Intervention in Internal Conflicts*. (New York: Council on Foreign Relations, 1993).

20. Excellent discussions on these changes are found in: Adam Roberts, "The Crisis in UN Peacekeeping," *Survival* 36, no. 3 (Autumn 1994): 93–120; and Marrack Goulding, "The Evolution of United Nations Peace-keeping," *International Affairs* 69, no. 3, (1993): 451–464. This latter article is based on the Cyril Foster Lecture 1993, which was delivered by Marrack Goulding, UN undersecretary-general for Political Affairs, at the Examination Schools, Oxford University, on 4 March 1993. Also see Sashi Tharoor, *Peace-keeping: Principles, Problems, and Prospects*, Strategic Research Department Research Report 9-93 (Newport, Va.:Center for Naval War Studies, U.S. Naval War College, 1993).

21. Good analysis and overview is available in Ian Johnstone, *Aftermath of the Gulf War: An Assessment of UN Action*, Occasional Paper Series (New York: International Peace Academy, 1994), and in Erskine B. Childers, "Gulf Crisis Lessons for the United Nations," *Bulletin of Peace Proposals* 23, no. 2 (1992): 129–138.

22. S/23500, 31 January 1992.

23. Boutros Boutros-Ghali, *An Agenda for Peace* (New York: United Nations, 1992). Originally issued as A/47/277, 17 June 1992. For an overview and commentary of the preparation and recommendations in An Agenda for Peace, see David Cox, *Exploring An Agenda for Peace: Issues Arising from the Report of the Secretary-General* Aurora Papers 20 (Ottawa: Canadian Centre for Global Security, 1993).

24. An Agenda for Peace, 17 June 1992, para. 20. The definition of "peacekeeping" as involving "hitherto" the consent of the parties created a stir. According to James Sutterlin, who was involved in the drafting of An Agenda for Peace, the word was apparently added to take account of the preventive deployment operation in Macedonia, which occurred without the consent of local Serbs. Sutterlin is quoted in Don Daniel and Bradd Hayes, "Securing Observance of UN mandates Through the Employment of Military Force," *International Peacekeeping* 3, no. 4 (Winter 1996): 107. The word was removed from later definitions. See, for example, the secretary-general's *Supplement to An Agenda for Peace*, S/1995/1, 3 January 1995. For a collection of the various definitions of peacekeeping and peace enforcement see the glossary in *Wider Peacekeeping, Army Field Manual*, vol. 5, *Operations other Than War*, part 2 (London: Her Majesty's Stationary Office, 1995) C-1-C-5.

25. A/47/277, An Agenda for Peace, 17 June 1992, para. 43.

26. Ibid., para. 44. The placement of the proposal in the section on peacemaking (which he defines as bringing hostile parties to agreement by peaceful means) contributed to a general misunderstanding of the concept.

27. For an overview of the reaction to the proposal, see Cox, *Exploring an Agenda for Peace,* 29–36. The idea of creating a standing force or UN legion has been the subject of interest at different periods in the United Nations' existence. The first round of proposals and debate was the result of Secretary-General Trygve Lie's proposal for the creation of a UN force at the time of the Korean War and just after the assassination of Count Folke Bernadotte af Wisborg in Palestine. For the secretary-general's proposal see "A United Nations Guard—Report of the Secretary-General to the General Assembly," A/656, 28 September 1948. Also see William R. Frye, ed., *A United Nations Peace Force* (New York: Oceana Publications, 1957). Brian Urquhart's papers at the UN Archives contain a number of internal UN documents of the time discussing the legal and political factors involved. Interest resurfaced after the combined experiences of the UNEF and Congo operations. See, for example, the special issue, "International Force—A Symposium," which is the full issue of *International Organization* 27, no. 2, (Spring 1963). Secretary-General Boutros-Ghali's proposals in An Agenda for Peace contributed to another round of discussions, best represented by Urquhart's proposals in Brian Urquhart, "For a UN Volunteer Military Force," *New York Review of Books,* 10 June 1993, 3–4. For an example of the debate this generated in the international law literature, see Andrew S. Miller, "Universal Soldiers: U.N. Standing Armies and the Legal Alternatives," *Georgetown Law Journal* 81, (March 1993): 773–828.

28. Boutros Boutros-Ghali, "Empowering the UN," *Foreign Affairs* (Winter 1992–1993): 93.

29. Boutros Boutros-Ghali, *Report on the Work of the Organization from the Forty-seventh to the Forty-eighth Session of the General Assembly* (New York: United Nations, DPI/1420, September 1993), para. 278.

30. The Security Council did, however, outline a series of operational principles for peacekeeping that included a requirement for "the consent of the government and, where appropriate, the parties concerned, save for exceptional cases". See S/25859, Note by the President of the Security Council, 28 May 1993.

Chapter 3

The Congo

I. CONTEXT

The Congo gained independence from Belgium on 30 June 1960 and almost immediately descended into a state of conflict and disarray. The Congo is a vast country, covering territory about the size of western Europe and including a wide variety of distinct geographic regions. As a colonial power, Belgium undertook a strong and extensive education program, making the Congo the most literate country in Africa. However, this policy extended only to early education. The Belgian government did not encourage education beyond the primary level, creating a situation in which the most literate country in Africa had by 1960 only twelve university graduates.[1] Similarly, the Belgian government did not encourage the involvement of locals in the government and the civil service. In terms of administration, this meant that the country was exclusively run by Belgian citizens. Belgian nationals occupied all of the top administrative layers of the civil service, and the officer corps of the armed forces was entirely Belgian.

Belgium was slow to plan for Congo's independence, only beginning to consider the prospect in the late 1950s and anticipating a long and methodical process. That timeframe was dramatically encapsulated when in 1959 pressures from inside and outside the Congo forced Belgium to consider moving more quickly. The degree of decolonization in Africa by that time was beginning to have an effect in the Congo where people began to agitate for the kind of freedom from their colonizers that others in the region had achieved. In January 1959, serious antigovernment rioting took place in Leopoldville for the first time in the Congo's history. At the same time, the negative decolonization experience of European countries, such as France in Algeria, was weighing on the minds of the Belgian government.[2]

In January 1960, a four-year transitional plan was outlined by Belgian authorities and rejected by Congolese representatives who demanded immediate independence. In response, the Belgian government, apparently anticipating that its role in the country would be little changed, but also feeling pressured by mounting unrest in the Congo, announced that independence would be granted on 30 June. "This decision was regarded by close observers as an act of panic, if not of irresponsibility."[3]

It was, in retrospect, a recipe for disaster: a colonial administration unaware and unprepared for the strength and fervor of the independence movement and a colonial people unaware and unprepared for the responsibilities and implications of government.

Independence was achieved on 30 June 1960, and almost instantly the internal situation of the Congo began to seriously disintegrate. On 2 July, tribal clashes began in the Leopoldville and Luluabourg areas. On 5 July, soldiers in Leopoldville and Thysville mutinied against their Belgian officers. The resulting disorder spread to other areas and included attacks on Europeans. Belgian citizens began to panic and flee the country in large numbers. Only marginally in control of the situation, the Congo government was now also losing the core of its administrative capabilities. Over the next few days, the situation deteriorated further with panic and violence spreading throughout the country.

The Treaty of Friendship, signed by Belgium and Congo at independence, provided for Belgium to continue to station troops at two bases (Kitona and Kamina) until agreements were made to have Congo take over the bases.[4] On 9 July, Belgian military reinforcements arrived at the bases, an action considered by the Congo government to be a violation of the treaty. On 10 July, against the wishes of the Congo government, Belgium began using the troops stationed at the two bases to intervene in the Congo to restore order and protect their citizens.

On 11 July, Moise Tshombe, the head of the provincial government of Katanga, declared Katanga independent. Katanga was by far the richest and most economically developed province in the country and had the strongest ties to Belgium. Katanga accounted for 40 percent to 50 percent of the Congo's revenue and foreign trade. It provided one-third of all domestic production in the country, producing 60 percent of the world's cobalt and 8 percent of the world's copper at that time. It was also the base of Union Minière, a Belgian mining company with exclusive mining rights in Katanga as well as control over a number of other economic enterprises in the province.[5]

It was in this context that Joseph Kasavubu, the new president of the Congo, and Prime Minister Patrice Lumumba made a joint appeal to the United Nations for assistance. On 12 July 1960, the Secretary-General of the United Nations, Dag Hammarskjöld, received a cable from President Kasavubu and Prime Minister Lumumba. Citing the arrival of "metropolitan Belgian troops in violation of the treaty of friendship," the cable requested "urgent dispatch by the United Nations of military assistance." The cable then went on to: "accuse the Belgian Government of having carefully prepared the secession of the Katanga with a view to maintaining a hold on our country. . . . The essential purpose of the requested military aid is to protect the national territory of the Congo against the present external aggression which is a threat to international peace."[6]

The cable itself was not a surprise to the secretary-general but its contents were. Ralph Bunche was in the Congo in order to represent the United Nations at the independence ceremonies and to discuss what kind of technical assistance the United Nations might be able to give the new country in order to aid its transition. On 10 July, after meeting with Congolese cabinet ministers, Bunche told the secretary-general that the government would be requesting military technical assistance with a view to restoring internal order. The phrasing of the cable, however, with its emphasis on international peace and external aggression, took the request out of the realm of technical assistance and into the Security Council territory of peace and security. Other signals were also being sent: a request for help had gone from the Congo government to the United States who referred it to the United Nations; and, in a second cable to the secretary-general, the president and prime minister indicated that if help was not forthcoming from the United Nations they would be forced to turn to the Bandung Treaty powers.[7] This last message was quickly followed by a cable to the Soviet Union, asking Nikita Khrushchev to follow the situation "hour by hour."[8]

II. MANDATE

The secretary-general thus faced a government clearly desperately searching for assistance, and the possibility that outside powers might fill the resulting vacuum if the UN did not. Acting under Article 99 of the charter[9] for the first time in the organization's history, the secretary-general called for a Security Council meeting to discuss the issue. In doing so, Hammarskjöld set in motion the UN involvement in the Congo. That involvement took the form of an operation that, until the 1990s, was the largest UN peacekeeping operation on record. It was also an involvement that prompted a crisis so deep and an experience so devastating for the United Nations that once the UN operation in the Congo (ONUC) was officially over the UN did its best not only to put the experience behind it but to forget it altogether.

THE PEACEKEEPING MANDATE—RESOLUTIONS 143, 145, AND 146

The Security Council met on the evening of 13 July 1960 and debated the issue well into the night. The Security Council debate did not focus on whether or not something should be done; that appeared to be agreed. Much of the debate was about whether or not Belgium was an aggressor and should be named as such in the resolution, and whether a specific timeframe for Belgian withdrawal should be included.[10] In the end, neither of these issues was addressed in the resolution. Resolution 143 (1960), based on a text proposed by the Tunisian representative, was passed in the early morning hours of 14 July with eight votes in favor, none against, and three abstentions from Britain, China, and France.[11] The resolution called on Belgium to withdraw its troops and authorized the secretary-general to "take the necessary steps, in consultation with the Government of the Republic of Congo, to provide the Government with such military assistance as may be necessary" for an interim period until the Congo national security forces were able to manage things themselves.

By avoiding any mention of Belgium as an aggressor or as having threatened international peace and security, the Security Council avoided having to directly invoke Chapter VII of the charter. Indeed, the resolution makes no specific mention of the charter and is deliberately general in its provisions. There is no timetable for Belgian withdrawal and the UN response is couched in the very undefined form of "military assistance as may be necessary."

The general terms of the resolution aided its passage. Other factors also came into play. The proposed text came from an African state, Tunisia, thus making any negative vote a doubly strong political statement. In addition, there was general agreement that something needed to be done and that Belgian intervention was aggravating rather than stabilizing the situation. The Congo had escaped Cold War politics until that point and both the United States and the Soviet Union saw an advantage in UN intervention to stabilize the situation in the near term if only as a way of preventing the other one from getting involved or of buying time until they could get themselves involved.

An advance unit of UN troops from Tunisia was on the ground by the next day. They were followed very quickly by contributing troops from other nations, along with Major General Carl von Horn, a Swedish commander who had been serving with the UN operation in Lebanon and had been appointed by the secretary-general to head ONUC. The initial contingent of troops included battalions from Ethiopia, Ghana, Guinea, Morocco, and Tunisia for a total of four thousand. They were joined soon after by troops from Argentina, Brazil, Canada, Ceylon, Denmark, India, Ireland, Liberia, Mali, Norway, Sweden, and Yugoslavia.[12]

In spite of the speed of the UN response, events on the ground continued to deteriorate. The Belgian intervention occurred with such force and speed that many Congolese saw it as an invasion. Members of the Congo armed forces and Congolese citizens responded by harassing and in some cases raping and killing Belgian and other European citizens, which further exacerbated internal tensions and panic.[13]

Developments in the breakaway province of Katanga contributed to the deteriorating situation. Tshombe, having declared Katanga's independence, was totally opposed to any UN presence in the province, arguing that Katanga was not part of the Congo and, therefore, not subject to the UN resolution. After initially declining to support Katanga's independence, the Belgian government changed tactics and decided to provide military and administrative support to the province although they continued to refrain from giving the province formal recognition.

In addition, the very general nature of the mandate and the speed with which the operation got underway seemed to complicate the situation on the ground for the UN operation, contributing to internal disputes among those running the operation.[14] Uncertainty about the exact nature of the mandate also extended to Congolese officials. In order to deal with these problems, the secretary-general returned to the Security Council for further debate and clarification of the mandate.

On 22 July 1960, the Security Council passed a second resolution—adopted unanimously—that clarified and added to Resolution 143. The preamble to Resolution 145 (1960) cites with appreciation the work of the secretary-general and member states in getting the operation going so quickly. The resolution notes that the "complete restoration of law and order" in the Congo "would effectively contribute to the maintenance of international peace and security" and points out that the Congo had gained membership in the United Nations "as a unit." The resolution then calls upon Belgium to withdraw its troops "speedily," "authorizes the Secretary-General to take all necessary action to this effect" and "[r]equests all States to refrain from any action which might tend to impede the restoration of law and order and the exercise by the Government of the Congo of its authority and also to refrain from any action which might undermine the territorial integrity and the political independence of the Republic of the Congo."

The resolution did not change the nature of the mandate but it gave the secretary-general specific responsibility for ensuring the quick withdrawal of Belgian troops with authorization for "all necessary action." It also emphasized the restoration of law and order, linking it to the international peace and security aspect of the situation, while emphasizing the importance of considering the Congo as a unit, thereby sending a signal about Katangan secession without specifically mentioning it.

Within a short period of time much of the mandate was fulfilled. By the beginning of August 1960, only a few weeks after the arrival of the United Nations, Belgium had withdrawn its troops from everywhere except Katanga and law and order had been restored in the country. However, as problems were resolved in other areas, they grew in Katanga. Tshombe and the provincial legislature took further steps towards independence. On 4 August, the legislature approved a new constitution and three days later they elected Tshombe as president. Tshombe remained steadfast in his refusal to allow UN troops to enter Katanga and the Belgian government was unwilling to withdraw its troops from the area, arguing that its withdrawal would prompt an exodus of European nationals. A kind of catch-22 existed whereby UN troops were barred from entering Katanga and Belgian troops would not withdraw until UN troops were present.

The secretary-general himself was in the Congo at this time. He hoped to facilitate the quick entry of ONUC troops into Katanga and the consequent withdrawal of Belgian troops. To this end, he sent Bunche, now acting as the secretary-general's special representative, to Katanga to try to negotiate the UN entry into Katanga with Belgian and Katangan authorities. Bunche left for Elisabethville, the capital of Katanga, on 4 August. The secretary-general's plans were, after a go ahead from Bunche, to send ONUC troops in to Katanga on 6 August. Bunche's experience in Katanga, however, led him to report to the secretary-general that, in his view, the situation in Katanga was such that the entry of ONUC troops would be met with violence and that entry of ONUC troops would require the use of force.[15]

Throughout this period, the secretary-general was under heavy pressure from the Congo government and from other governments, especially the Soviet Union, to do just that—use force to fulfill the mandate. Hammarskjöld did not believe that the existing Security Council mandate allowed that kind of choice.[16] Faced with Bunche's determination that a peaceful ONUC entry was not possible at this time, the secretary-general returned to the Security Council for a new mandate. The secretary-general told the Security Council that the opposition within Katanga "would require military initiative from the United Nations Force to which I would not be entitled to resort short of a formal authorization of the Council."[17]

The Security Council passed Resolution 146(1960) on 9 August 1960 by a vote of nine in favor, none against, and two abstentions from France and Italy. Like Resolution 145, this resolution did not change the basic nature of the mandate. Rather, it made explicit aspects of the mandate previously thought to be implicit and thereby sent a signal of strong Security Council resolve with respect to their implementation, although it stopped short of an authorization of the use of force. In particular, the resolution called upon Belgium to "withdraw immediately" from Katanga and declared "that the entry of the United Nations force into the Province of Katanga is necessary for the full implementation of this resolution." Emphasizing the impartiality of the mission, paragraph 4 of the resolution "[r]eaffirms that the United Nations force in the Congo will not be a party to or in any way intervene in or be used to influence the outcome of any internal conflict, constitutional or otherwise."

The resolution initially had the desired effect and three days later, on 12 August, secretary-general Hammarskjöld led the first UN units into Katanga. Both Hammarskjöld and Tshombe could claim success in the arrival of the ONUC troops. Hammarskjöld had achieved the entry of ONUC troops into Katanga without the use of force. Tshombe could point to the fact that the arrival of UN troops had not affected Katanga's claim to independence. The success was relative and short-lived. Having allowed this initial step, Tshombe resisted further cooperation with the United Nations, especially any efforts to extend the authority of the government of the Congo over Katanga.

In spite of these developments and the new Security Council resolution, Prime Minister Lumumba continued to engage the secretary-general in a protracted, sometimes personal struggle over the interpretation of the Security Council mandate, in particular about the extent to which the UN force was authorized to use force to deal with Katanga. The Security Council met again on 21 August 1960 to discuss the nature of the mandate. It confirmed the secretary-general's interpretation of the mandate even though there was no new resolution.[18] Lumumba, frustrated at UN unwillingness to order ONUC troops to take control of Katanga by force, sent Congolese troops to Luluabourg and began an attack on Katanga on 26 August 1960.[19]

THE COLLAPSE OF GOVERNMENT

Shortly thereafter, on 5 September 1960 President Kasavubu dismissed Prime Minister Lumumba. Lumumba promptly announced that it was he who was dismissing the president. The resulting power struggle created a constitutional crisis and meant that the Congo was without an effective government. The resulting power vacuum opened up a wider internal power struggle in which various aspiring leaders struggled to establish enough of a power base to take control of the country.[20] The United Nations then found itself in a situation in which it was involved inside a country with no recognizable government in the midst of a civil war with a mandate that specifically prevented it from becoming involved in internal politics. It is difficult to understate the complexity of the situation this created for the United Nations. The government that had given its consent to the presence of ONUC troops was now gone with no replacement in sight. The fact that there was now tension between ONUC troops and the Congolese army made the position of the ONUC mission even more delicate. For the United Nations, making a judgment about which of the groups vying for control should be recognized as the official government would effectively amount to interference in the Congo's internal affairs. This problem extended to the question as to who should be considered the official representative of the Congo government at the United Nations.

These events prompted further Security Council meetings to discuss the mandate. By now, however, the situation on the ground in the Congo made Security Council agreement on any new resolution elusive. Since the start of the ONUC operation, Kasavubu found increasing support for his policies in the West while Lumumba leaned more and more towards policies that found support in the Soviet Union. The power struggle between the two and the resulting crisis in leadership, therefore, created a new tension between the United States and the Soviet Union at the Security Council.

These events meant that it was increasingly difficult for ONUC to maintain a position of impartiality. The collapse of the government on 5 September prompted Andrew Cordier, the special representative of the secretary-general, to order the closure of the airports and then that ONUC troops take control of the radio station. Cordier took both of these measures to avoid a descent into full-scale civil war and to maintain law and order. Lumumba's base of support was in the Stanleyville area, while Kasavubu's was primarily in and around the capital city. The closure of the airports and of the radio station, therefore, made it very difficult for Lumumba to activate and consolidate his own base of support. So while the closure of the airports and the control of the radio station by ONUC troops might very well have stopped a slide into outright civil war, supporters of Lumumba, inside and outside the Congo, perceived the actions as supporting Kasavubu's position.[21]

On 17 September 1960, having been unable to reach agreement, the Security Council passed the issue on to the General Assembly, which met in an emergency session to discuss the issue. On 20 September 1960, the General Assembly adopted Resolution 1474. The resolution supported the previous Security

Council resolutions, reaffirmed the secretary-general's approach to the mandate, and requested that the secretary-general continue "to take vigorous action" in support of those resolutions.[22] The Soviet Union, thwarted at the Security Council in its attempts to get the United Nations to take stronger action and now effectively defeated at the General Assembly, turned its fury on the secretary-general and his office, beginning a long-term campaign against the secretary-general and the ONUC operation.[23]

THE ARREST OF LUMUMBA

On 27 November 1960, Lumumba left Leopoldville for Stanleyville, apparently with the intent of trying to establish a rival regime there. Until 27 November, he had been under UN protection at his home in Leopoldville, but was free to come and go as he pleased. A few days later, on 1 December, the Congolese army fulfilled an arrest warrant issued by Kasavubu and arrested Lumumba while he was en route to Stanleyville.

Lumumba's arrest generated strong reactions at the United Nations. Many states, including, but not exclusively, those states who had been advocating a more forceful use of ONUC, believed that ONUC troops should have intervened, if not to prevent Lumumba's arrest then to retrieve him from army officials after the arrest. Responding to such calls for action, the secretary-general stated: "The UN had neither the power nor the right to liberate Mr. Lumumba from his captors. I say the UN because to my knowledge not even this Council or the General Assembly would have such a right, much less did it exist for the UN representatives in the Congo under this mandate."[24]

The sense that ONUC actions at the time of the collapse of the government on 5 September worked to Lumumba's disadvantage, preventing him from traveling or using the radio to raise supporters, was still fresh in the minds of many states.[25] If the United Nations acted then, the argument went, there was no reason for it not to act in this instance.[26] There was a growing sense that the secretary-general's policy of strict noninterference in internal affairs was de facto interference. The reaction to ONUC inaction was so strong that a number of states withdrew their national contingents from the ONUC operation, seriously weakening the operation militarily and politically. Guinea, Indonesia, Morocco, Sudan, and the United Arab Republic withdrew their contingents over the next few months.[27]

USING FORCE—RESOLUTION 161

On 17 January 1961, Lumumba was transferred to Elisabethville in Katanga. On 13 February, the Katangan government announced that Lumumba and the two who were arrested with him had been killed while trying to escape.[28] Lumumba's death changed the political equation entirely, creating a new resolve for action at the United Nations. After a lengthy and intense debate,[29] on 21 February 1961 the Security Council passed Resolution 161(1961), authorizing the use of force in order to prevent civil war.

Resolution 161 has two sections. Section A deals specifically with the civil war situation and creates a commission of inquiry into Lumumba's death. Section B deals with the recall of Congo's parliament and measures relating to the Congolese armed forces. In recognition of a growing problem associated with foreign military personnel technically not under the control of any country (mercenaries), in section A the Security Council urges the immediate withdrawal of all "Belgian and other foreign military and para-military personnel and political advisers."

In paragraph 1 of the resolution, the Security Council "[u]rges that the United Nations take immediately all appropriate measures to prevent the occurrence of civil war in the Congo, including arrangements for cease-fires, the halting of all military operations, the prevention of clashes, and the use of force, if necessary, in the last resort." This marked a very distinct change in the Security Council's attitude to mandate implementation. The use of force was, however, geared strictly towards the goal of avoiding a civil war and not towards any kind of political settlement. In the Security Council debate, the U.S. representative stated that although this was an authorization of the use of force, the authorization was restricted by the charter's prohibition of intervention in internal affairs.[30] Similarly, the British representative expressed its understanding that "force will only be used by the United Nations to prevent a clash between hostile Congolese troops. There can be no question of empowering the United Nations to use its forces to impose a political settlement."[31]

There were no further Security Council actions on the Congo until November 1961. In the meantime, events in the Congo took dramatic and unprecedented turns that shook the United Nations. During this time, ONUC troops were involved in a number of military clashes and two major military operations. On 17 September 1961, secretary-general Hammarskjöld was killed in a plane crash while en route from the Congo to Ndola, Rhodesia.

On 24 November 1961, the Security Council passed Resolution 169(1961) which contained the strongest and most detailed language to date. Previous resolutions called for the withdrawal of Belgian and other foreign military personnel. This time the Security Council specifically authorized ONUC troops to use force in apprehending and deporting foreign mercenaries. The Security Council "[a]uthorizes the Secretary-General to take vigorous action, including the use of the requisite measure of force, if necessary, for the immediate apprehension, detention pending legal action and/or deportation of all foreign military and paramilitary personnel and political advisers not under the United Nations Command, and mercenaries, as laid down in [Resolution 161]."

This was the last substantive Security Council resolution on the situation in the Congo. The operation ended in 1964.

SUMMARY

The basic objectives of the ONUC operation remained the same from the first resolution to the fifth. Each successive Security Council resolution added to or elaborated on the initial mandate but did not fundamentally change the goals of the operation. The overall purpose of UN action remained the two basic objectives outlined in the first resolution: the withdrawal of Belgian military personnel (later expanded to include mercenaries) and military assistance in order to ensure internal stability.[32] Both of these objectives were considered important for the maintenance of international peace and security: the first because the Belgian actions represented a violation of the sovereignty of an independent country, albeit a very newly independent one, by an outside state; the second because the internal instability was such that it left the country open to manipulation by other countries, especially the United States and the Soviet Union.

The methods prescribed to achieve these objectives did change, however, in response to constraints and a lack of cooperation within the Congo. Subsequent Security Council resolutions clarified or emphasized each objective and outlined the means to pursue it. For example, the first resolution simply called for Belgian withdrawal. The second emphasized the need for a "speedy" withdrawal, and the third demanded "immediate" withdrawal. The fourth resolution added other foreign military, paramilitary, and political advisers to the list of those who should be withdrawn, and the fifth resolution provided for the use of force in detaining and deporting them.

With respect to restoring internal stability, the first resolution called on the United Nations to provide necessary military assistance until the national security forces of the Congo were able to do so themselves. The second resolution linked the maintenance of law and order to international peace and security and emphasized that the Congo was to be treated as a whole in this regard. The third resolution went beyond that to specifically say that ONUC troops must enter the province of Katanga. In the fourth resolution, the Security Council authorized the use of force, as a last resort, to prevent civil war, and in its fifth resolution it called for an end to Katangan secession and "completely reject[s] the claim that Katanga is a 'sovereign independent nation.' "

In both instances where force was authorized, it was as the culmination of a series of progressively stronger provisions in the Security Council resolutions and when all other efforts had failed to achieved the resolutions' objectives.

CHARTER BASIS

Throughout UN involvement in the Congo, the Security Council and the secretary-general struggled to define the exact nature of the operation. This was an especially difficult task given that the United Nations was on new ground with respect to the charter, and given the changing nature of the political and military situation in the country. The first resolution authorizing UN action in the Congo, Resolution 143, made no mention of the charter and did not use the phrase "international peace and security." Resolution 145 contains the first mention of the phrase "international peace and security." It was not until the third resolution, Resolution 146, that specific charter articles are cited. In that resolution, the Security Council calls upon member states "in accordance with Articles 25 and 49 of the Charter" to carry out and support the Security Council resolutions.

Speaking to the Security Council before the passage of the resolution, the secretary-general mentioned those two articles[33] and then elaborated.

However, I want to go one step further and quote also Article 40 of the Charter, which speaks about actions taken by the Security Council in protection of peace and security, first of all, by certain so-called "provisional measures". . . . Please permit me here to remind you also of Article 41: "The Security Council may decide what measures not involving the use of armed force are to be employed to give effect to its decisions". . . . The resolutions of the Security Council of 14 July and 22 July were not explicitly adopted under Chapter VII, but they were passed on the basis of an initiative under Article 99. For that reason I have felt entitled to quote three articles under Chapter VII, and I repeat what I have already said in this respect: . . . the problem facing the Congo is one of peace or war— and not only in the Congo.[34]

Because it was the first time the United Nations authorized force in this way, it prompted a considerable academic and legal debate about whether ONUC, because it was based in Chapter VII, qualified as an "enforcement" operation and, therefore, should have evoked Article 42 of the charter, providing for members to take action by sea, air, and land to restore international peace and security.[35] The issue relates directly to the question of noninterference since Article 42– type enforcement overrides the protection of domestic jurisdiction provided for in Article 2(7).[36] But the Security Council resolutions clearly avoid using language or references that would invoke Article 42-type enforcement. The secretary-general was consistently and repeatedly clear that his view was that the mandates, even those including specific references to the use of force, did not involve a shift to enforcement—with an accompanying shift from noninterference to involvement in internal affairs.

III. THE USE OF FORCE

RULES OF ENGAGEMENT

When the secretary-general first brought the Congo question before the Security Council, he told Security Council members that he believed that the principles established in the UN Emergency Force (UNEF)[37] in the Suez could and should be applied to the proposed operation in the Congo.[38] Shortly after the first resolution was passed, the secretary-general reported to the Security Council, outlining these principles in detail:

- the force would be under the exclusive command of the secretary-general;
- the operation would not interfere in the internal affairs of the Congo or become involved in internal conflicts;
- the force must have freedom of movement throughout the country;
- force would only be used in self-defense, no use of force would be initiated by UN troops; and
- national units in the UN force would only take orders from the UN command, not from their governments.[39]

In his first report to the Security Council, the secretary-general quoted directly from his report on the UNEF operation, stating that the self-defense principle meant that UN soldiers

may never take the initiative in the use of armed force, but are entitled to respond with force to an attack with arms including attempts to use force to make them withdraw from positions which they occupy under orders from the commander acting under the authority of the Security Council and within the scope of its resolution. "The basic element involved is clearly the prohibition against any *initiative* in the use of armed force."[40]

Events on the ground made it apparent that defining self-defense in such a limited fashion was risking and costing lives in the field. At the end of October 1960, UN headquarters issued broader rules of engagement (ROE) for ONUC troops, although the prohibition against the initiation of force remained. The new ROE allowed for the use of force:

a. if attempts were being made to force them to withdraw from a position already held;
b. if attempts were being made to disarm them;
c. if attempts were being made to prevent them from carrying out orders given to them by their commanding officers; and
d. if attempts were being made to violate UN installations or to arrest or abduct UN personnel.[41]

Even after the February 1961 Security Council resolution authorizing the use of force as a last resort to prevent civil war, this approach was little changed. In the Security Council debate at the time of the passage of the resolution, the U.S. representative stated that his country would accept the use of force clause, but said that "[c]leary, this resolution means that force cannot be used until agreement has been sought by negotiations, conciliation and all other peaceful means."[42] The British representative expressed similar reservations noting that "the interpretation which my delegation puts upon the words . . . is that force will only be used by the United Nations to prevent a clash between hostile Congolese troops."[43]

General Indar Jit Rikhye, the military advisor to the secretary-general at the time, prepared an analysis of the implications of the February resolution for the Congo Advisory Committee.[44] He told the committee that there were two options for proceeding with mandate implementation. The first involved maintaining the current approach "in which force was used only in self-defence and as a last resort when all other means had failed."[45] The second involved using military initiative. Since the troop strength of ONUC had been severely depleted since Lumumba's arrest in December, and since it was unlikely that the amount of military support required for taking the initiative would be forthcoming, Rikhye proceeded on the assumption that the first course of action would continue to be the basis for implementation. "I presumed that all further UN military action would follow political negotiation and mediation, as the earlier statements of many of the members of the committee had envisaged."[46]

After Operation Rumpunch, when the United Nations moved to round up mercenaries in Katanga, ONUC officials proposed a further set of actions that contained the strong possibility of the use of force, raising again the question of mandate interpretation. In response, secretary-general Hammarskjöld reiterated his view of the overall guidelines for the operation in detail. These included:

1. The mandate of the UN for the protection of law and order authorized it to deploy troops to protect civilians when they were threatened by tribal war or violence.
2. Paragraph A-1 of the Security Council's resolution of February 21 also authorized preventive action by the UN to deal with incitement to or preparation of civil war.
3. The right of UN troops to use force in self-defense covered attempts to overrun or displace UN positions. It also covered attempts to injure or abduct UN personnel.
4. The act of self-defense against attack could include disarming and, if necessary, the detention of those preparing to attack UN troops.
5. Incitement to or preparation for violence, including troop movements and confirmed reports of an impending attack, would warrant protective action by UN troops, but criticism of the UN, however pungently expressed, or peaceful demonstrations against the UN, could not be held to justify protective action.
6. The maintenance of law and order or the prevention of civil war might justify, in certain circumstances, the closing of radio stations and airports if it was clear they were being used to foment civil war or for other unlawful purposes.
7. Arrest or detention of civil leaders was only justifiable if they were engaged in overt military action or were caught in flagrante delicto inciting violence.
8. Political leaders could be arrested by the UN if the UN was requested to do so by both the central government and the provincial authorities.[47]

In December 1961, after the Security Council authorized the use of force in Resolution 169 in November 1961, secretary-general U Thant issued instructions "to take the necessary action to ensure the freedom of movement of the UN troops and to restore law and order in Katanga so that the UN resolutions could be implemented."[48]

MANDATE IMPLEMENTATION

The Civil War Mandate

By 1961, ONUC was in a complicated situation. Not only were they facing the rebel Katangese forces accompanied and led by foreign mercenaries, but the Congolese national army (ANC), had also turned against the UN because of its unwillingness to take Katanga by force. Complicating the situation even further, fighting was ongoing between the ANC and Katangan forces who, in the Manono region, were also fighting with Baluba tribe members. After the Security Council authorized the use of force in Resolution 161, Katangese gendarmes and the foreign mercenaries leading them took an even more openly hostile attitude towards ONUC soldiers, resulting in several violent incidents between ONUC soldiers and Katangese gendarmes.[49] Katangese officials also stepped up their

propaganda campaign against ONUC, encouraging demonstrations and harassment of ONUC troops by civilians.[50]

At the time of Resolution 161, ONUC strength was quite low as a result of
withdrawals of troop contingents after Lumumba's arrest. It was some time before ONUC had rebuilt sufficient strength to consider taking on the kinds of
tasks envisaged in Resolution 161. In the meantime, the low level of ONUC
strength was a source of vulnerability. ANC troops took advantage of the ONUC
position to attack the UN troops and remaining Belgian and European nationals.
ONUC troops were forced simultaneously to protect civilians in danger and to
protect themselves at a time of reduced strength. A Sudanese battalion, stationed
at Matadi, a key supply point for the United Nations, was forced to withdraw
after being attacked by ANC troops on 4 March 1961, leaving UN forces temporarily without access to a critical supply point. A report from the field underlines
the seriousness of the problem for the United Nations.

The withdrawal of United Nations Forces from Matadi constitutes a serious blow to the
United Nations operation in the Congo by its psychological effects. This withdrawal also
deprives the United Nations Force of its life line to the sea. The vital importance of this
line to the outside world can be judged from the fact that in the next three weeks alone
thirty-three ships with United Nations supplies are due to berth at Matadi, not counting
troop transports . . . Without the United Nations presence at Matadi, arms ammunition
and other war material can enter unchecked into the Congo; this, obviously, can have
immeasurable consequences on the development of the civil war situation.[51]

By early April, ONUC strength had increased to eighteen thousand.[52] This
reinforcement of troop numbers enabled ONUC to take a more proactive approach to the mandate. In early April, the first evidence of a shift in the military
balance in favor of ONUC occurred in an incident involving an Ethiopian battalion, ANC troops, and Baluba fighters. The Ethiopian battalion intervened in a
clash between Katangese gendarmes and Baluba fighters. In the resulting ex-
changes of fire, including heavy fighting between Katangese and Baluba, and
aerial bombing by the Katangese, the Ethiopian contingent managed to prevent
the Katangese from taking the area.[53] This is generally considered to be the first
instance of implementation of Resolution 161.

During this same time period, leaders of the different groups involved in the
struggle for power within the country attended two conferences, the first at
Tananarive and the second at Coquilhatville, that were intended to develop some
form of political agreement on the future of the country.[54] In May 1961, during
the Coquilhatville meeting, delegates made progress towards agreement on a
new federal government structure for the Congo. President Kasavubu announced
that he would reconvene parliament in order to endorse the proposals agreed to
at the meeting. Parliament reconvened on 22 July 1961. On 2 August 1961,
Prime Minister Cyrille Adoula formed a government with the unanimous approval of both chambers of parliament. ONUC officials, while careful to avoid
direct involvement in the nature of the discussions, did everything possible to
facilitate the negotiations and the reconvening of parliament. This included providing security for delegates and for the reopening of parliament as well as

transportation for delegates. These efforts, though designed by the United Nations to ensure that ONUC was facilitating the process without interfering in it, served to confirm the views of those who believed that ONUC was working towards the establishment of a pro–Western government in the Congo.

Dealing with the Mercenaries

Over the summer, Tshombe's continued unwillingness to negotiate the details of implementing Resolution 161, combined with the ongoing harassment of ONUC troops by Katangese gendarmes and the evidence of ongoing mercenary activity,[55] contributed to pressure inside and outside the United Nations for firmer action against the mercenaries. Operation Rumpunch was launched early in the morning of 28 August 1961 in Elisabethville. Considerably aided by the advantage of complete surprise, the operation proceeded successfully and peacefully. By that afternoon eighty-one foreign military personnel had been arrested. Arrests came to an end when Conor Cruise O'Brien, the secretary-general's representative in Katanga, agreed to a request by foreign diplomatic consuls that they be allowed to complete the deportations themselves. O'Brien's well-intentioned agreement to the request backfired as the foreign consuls almost immediately reneged on their commitments.[56]

Operation Rumpunch, undertaken prior to the Security Council's authorization of the use of force, is important because of its role as a precursor to Operation Morthor. As a moment in time in the course of the ONUC mission as a whole, Operation Morthor marks an unexpected and tragic turning point. The operation is critical not only because it went badly wrong and resulted in fighting between UN and Katangese troops, but also because of its connection to the secretary-general's death. Operation Morthor, apparently initially intended to be a stepped up version of Operation Rumpunch to finish the job that was interrupted there, somehow became something quite different.

The circumstances of the planning and implementation of the operation remain mired in confusion and controversy.[57] The general sequence of events, however, can be outlined. ONUC troops began Operation Morthor in Katanga on 13 September with the objective of finishing the rounding up of mercenaries begun two weeks previously in Operation Rumpunch. In fact, the intention of the ONUC planners in the area, or perhaps their hope, was that the operation would go farther than that and result in an end to Katangan secession. The operation, which did not have the secretary-general's direct authorization, began while he was en route to the Congo.

The operation was very much along the lines of Rumpunch. As a result, once it began, the Katangese gendarmes were able to anticipate UN moves and respond quickly. In his authoritative biography of Hammarskjöld, Brian Urquhart, a UN insider at the time (and since), notes that "[t]he origins of the fighting which started in Elisabethville in the early morning of September 13 are still a matter of controversy and of some mystery."[58] Whatever the specifics, almost as soon as the operation began fighting broke out between ONUC troops and Katangese gendarmes.[59]

At a press conference later on that first day, O'Brien announced that the secession of Katanga was over. O'Brien's statement, made prematurely in every sense, was widely interpreted as an announcement that the United Nations had ended Katangan secession by force. The statement contributed to the school of thought that believes that the ONUC in-country decision makers sought to bring about this end under cover of an operation ostensibly geared towards finishing the rounding up of foreign mercenaries.[60]

Once the fighting began that morning, attacks against ONUC troops took place in a number of locations and included attacks by a Katangese fighter jet, which, in the absence of its own fighter jets or air defense, ONUC forces were unable to counter.[61] Fighting continued sporadically over the next few days, resulting in, inter alia, an Irish unit being pinned down by European-led Katangan forces in Jadotville.[62] The sequence of events raised considerable concern in Britain and the United States. Unhappy about the possibility, or even just the perception, that the UN was using force to end the secession of Katanga, and worried that the fighting might undo the political progress made to that point, the U.S. and British governments pressured the secretary-general to find a way to bring an end to the fighting.[63]

On his arrival in the Congo, the secretary-general was clearly caught off guard by the turn of events and immediately turned his attention to trying to bring an end to the fighting. In an effort to get a grip on the situation, on 16 September Hammarskjöld agreed to meet Tshombe in Ndola, just across the Rhodesian border, to discuss a cease-fire. The next day, en route to the meeting, just before arriving at the Ndola airport, the secretary-general's aircraft crashed, resulting in the deaths of all on board.[64] On 20 September, Mahmood Khiary, head of ONUC civilian operations signed a cease-fire agreement with Tshombe.[65]

The events surrounding Operation Morthor and the death of the secretary-general had far-reaching consequences. At the United Nations, the personal and institutional void created by Hammarskjöld's death was immense. U Thant was named as the new secretary-general on 3 November. As secretary-general, his approach to the Congo was to prove much different from that of Hammarskjöld. In the meantime, the political positions of key member states had changed. In the face of a sense in some African states that ONUC had pulled back from efforts to end Katangan secession under pressure from Western states, and worried about continued Soviet pressure for a troika arrangement to replace the post of secretary-general, the United States now sent signals of strong support for the United Nations generally and strengthened its support of the ONUC operation.[66]

In Katanga, the resulting cease-fire agreement was treated as a victory over the United Nations. This, in conjunction with the apparent poor communication and lack of unity of purpose among UN officials, made so clearly evident by Operation Morthor, encouraged further anti–UN political and military activities in Katanga. The problems faced by ONUC were not just in Katanga. On 11 November, thirteen Italian pilots arriving in Kindu were beaten and shot by the Congolese military. Their bodies were then cut into pieces and distributed to a watching crowd.[67] Events such as these, in combination with the death of Hammarskjöld and the political changes that followed, contributed to a new determination among member states to deal with the Congo question. This new political determination contributed to the strength and passage of Resolution 169 in November 1961.

In Katanga, Tshombe's gendarmes continued their harassment and attacks on ONUC troops. The activities of Katangese military were often flagrant violations of the cease-fire signed by Tshombe. So much so that ONUC officials issued stern warnings to them about the consequences if such actions continued. For example, Katangese military aircraft were used to bomb ANC positions. This prompted the officer-in-charge to threaten the use of force, as he reported to the secretary-general.

ONUC has the responsibility to stop such violation, first by calling on the Katangese authorities to halt such operations and secondly, if that fails, to take additional measures consistent with the basic mandate of ONUC. . . . The provincial authorities were therefore put on notice that, if all Katangese military aircraft were not at once immobilised, those positively identified as engaged in offensive military operations in Kasai would be brought down. If necessary they would be pursued into Katanga and destroyed. Finally, failure to heed this warning would justify further necessary counter-action, which could include bringing down such aircraft operating in Katanga and eventually destroying them by air to ground action.[68]

In spite of the use of force authorization in Resolution 169, in November the harassment of ONUC forces and the cease-fire violations became stronger and more flagrant with the gendarmes taking and holding the initiative. The military tempo continued to increase with Katangese sniper attacks, aerial attacks, and ground assaults, and the detention of a number of UN personnel.[69] The Katangan military was also establishing roadblocks that inhibited communication and travel between UN troops.[70] By the beginning of December 1961, Katangese activity suggested preparation for a full-scale attack against ONUC forces.[71]

The secretary-general told UN officials in Katanga to "act vigorously to establish law and order and protect life and property in Katanga."[72] General Rikhye, the military adviser to the secretary-general, provides a good account of the UN perspective.

The UN command had no choice but to remove the road-blocks to regain freedom of movement. This operation was named Unokat. Realising that more troops and ammunition were needed to deal with the deployment of the gendarmerie, who outnumbered them, the UN plan called for a defensive operation with limited efforts to reopen surface communications. . . . Once the reinforcements were in position, the UN command could press forward to remove all road-blocks. . . . The instructions from U Thant were clear and precise: to take the necessary action to ensure the freedom of movement of the UN troops and to restore law and order in Katanga so that the UN resolutions could be implemented.[73]

From 5 to 15 December, therefore, ONUC military activity focused on holding on to its existing positions while awaiting reinforcements.[74] As fighting between ONUC troops and Katanga fighters increased, the secretary-general, responding to allegations from Belgium about UN actions, outlined the principles guiding ONUC military action.

the purpose of the present military operations is to regain and assure our freedom of movement, to restore law and order, and to ensure that for the future the United Nations forces and officials in Katanga are not subjected to such attacks; and meanwhile to react vigorously in self-defence to every assault on our present positions, by all the means available to us. The military operations will be pursued up to such time, and only up to such time, that these objectives are achieved, either by military or by other means, and we have satisfactory guarantees in this regard for the future, not only in Elisabethville but over the whole of Katanga.[75]

The United States, who through this period was also becoming more determined about bringing an end to the ongoing problems associated with Katanga, was a key supplier of the military reinforcements that made Operation Unokat possible.[76] The reinforcements were in place by 15 December, allowing ONUC forces to begin taking direct action to deal with the roadblocks and reestablish their freedom of movement.[77] These actions had the desired effect and as the operation was getting underway Tshombe finally agreed to meet with Prime Minister Adoula to discuss the status of Katanga. The meeting took place on 20 December and the secretary-general announced that the United Nations would cease offensive activities while the meeting was occurring.

On 21 December 1961, Tshombe, under heavy pressure from the United Nations and the United States,[78] signed a declaration, known as the Kitona Declaration, formally recognizing the authority of the Congo government over all of the Congo territory. The declaration comprised eight points, including Tshombe's acceptance of Kasavubu as the head of state, his acceptance of the authority of the Congo government over all of the territory of the Congo, including Katanga, and his agreement that the Katangan gendarmes would be placed under the authority of the president of the Congo. In a covering letter to Bunche, who was representing the secretary-general at the negotiations, Tshombe stated that decision needed to be authorized by the Katangan government. Bunche then communicated the Kitona Declaration to Prime Minister Adoula but did not include Tshombe's covering letter. This format—of a unilateral declaration and a separate covering letter—was the key to success since Adoula would not agree to a declaration that included Tshombe's reservation and his insistence that the Katangan government must be consulted. The agreement appeared to be a major breakthrough that signaled the end to Katanga's aspirations for independence. It soon became apparent, however, that Tshombe's agreement was simply a tactic to buy time rather than a commitment to give up Katangan secession.

During the following year, Tshombe consistently stalled and backtracked on the commitments he made in the Kitona Declaration, and there was increasing evidence that he was using the time to prepare for a new push for independence. In the months that followed the declaration, the question of Katangese secession became, once again, a critical one for ONUC. In October 1962, intelligence information demonstrated that Katangese gendarmes and the mercenaries leading them were preparing themselves for a conflict. In General Rikhye's words "[t]hey were spoiling for a fight."[79] In response, the United Nations began its own preparations.[80]

As in the previous year, over time harassment of UN personnel began to escalate, involving the abduction of ONUC personnel and direct attacks on ONUC troops, such as the shooting down of an ONUC helicopter.[81] When, during December 1962, a full year after the Kitona Declaration, Katangese officials demonstrated a complete unwillingness to pursue the reconciliation plans for reintegrating Katanga into the Congo put forward by the secretary-general,[82] the United Nations changed its strategy.

After consultations with the Congo Advisory Committee, U Thant switched from his policy of persuasion in dealing with Tshombe to pressure, just short of resorting to force. Two methods were decided. First, measures to implement decisions relating to integration were introduced, whether or not Tshombe agreed. . . . The second series of actions were to be taken by the UN troops for their own security. They had withstood harassment and provocative road-blocks, and now they would assume a vigorous posture to remove them to regain their freedom of movement. Our men were not to use force except in self-defence, if fired upon first.[83]

The Katangan military eliminated the need for the United Nations to take the military initiative by beginning an offensive against UN troops. An attack on Ethiopian troops by Katangese gendarmes, on 24 December, marked the beginning of four days of military activity directed against ONUC positions. ONUC troops responded either not at all or only to the extent required for self-defense.[84] The extent and type of military actions undertaken by the Katangese gendarmes in combination with formal statements from Katangese authorities,[85] made it evident that the gendarmes were intending to take ONUC forces on militarily. In response, the secretary-general ordered a new military operation.[86]

Operation Grandslam began on 28 December 1962. Its purpose was to "restore the security of ONUC troops in the Elisabethville area and their freedom of movement by clearing the gendarmerie road-blocks from which fire had been directed at United Nations troops."[87] The operation had two phases. The first focused on Elisabethville and was intended to eliminate the roadblocks there and the positions being used to attack ONUC forces. The second involved an expansion of UN control in the province to Kipushi and Jadotville. The first phase of the operation was successfully completed by 30 December. In speaking to the Security Council on 31 December, secretary-general U Thant stated:

Some may say loosely that there was a "third round" in Katanga. That was not the case. There would have been no fighting at all if the Katangese gendarmerie had not made it unavoidable by indulging in senseless firing for several days. In view of the results of the ONUC operation, there may be some who would be inclined to refer to a United Nations "military victory." I would not like this to be said. The United Nations is not waging war against anyone in that province.[88]

On the basis of that initial success, ONUC troops expanded outwards as far as possible based on their strength. Their success in Elisabethville and environs was mirrored by quick success as they expanded outwards into the province.

The ease of the expanded operation was so unexpected that an Indian battalion moved very quickly to and then across the Lufira River, exceeding their initial orders. They then proceeded to Jadotville securing the area without incident. This advance, though unopposed, generated considerable controversy because the commander clearly exceeded his orders. A UN report notes, "the exact timing and speed of the move came as a surprise to United Nations Headquarters."[89] During the following week, Bunche, the undersecretary for Special Political Affairs, investigated the "serious breakdown in effective communication and coordination between United Nations headquarters and the Leopoldville office."[90] Bunche's report remains a relevant description of the problems associated with communication in UN military operations that are time sensitive. He concluded that: "the underlying cause of the difficulties . . . was that the United Nations troops and the ONUC organization suddenly encountered far less resistance and far more local encouragement than they had anticipated . . . and that this happened more quickly than they could digest it. . . . I have found beyond doubt that it is our machinery that is at fault, far more than individuals."[91]

In early January, Tshombe alternately expressed a willingness to concede defeat and threatened a scorched earth policy. ONUC troops continued to consolidate their freedom of movement and to secure major towns and industrial locations through the first weeks of January. Eventually, and with some prompting from Belgium, Tshombe met with ONUC officials on 17 January 1963 and agreed to facilitate ONUC entry into Kolwezi, an area containing significant mining and electrical power installations and the only remaining area in Katanga under his control.[92] "By January 1963, the United Nations Force had under control all important centres hitherto held by the Katangese and was quickly restoring law and order at all places. The Katangese gendarmerie had ceased to exist as an organized fighting force. The military actions begun on 28 December 1962 had thus ended."[93]

IV. ISSUES

OPERATIONAL ISSUES

Troop Numbers

The ONUC operation had little difficulty generating troop contributions when the mission first began. And even once the Security Council authorized the use of force, troop contributions remained strong. In any operation where force may be used, there is a risk that states will disagree with the degree of force used, the extent to which their troops are put at risk, or the way the operation is being handled in general, and pull out of the operation. This is what happened after Lumumba's arrest, although in this case the troop withdrawals were prompted by the lack of UN action rather than because the United Nations had taken action that was considered too strong. This is in contrast to the UN Protection Force (UNPROFOR) in the former Yugoslavia and the second UN Operation in Somalia (UNOSOM II) where the pressure from troop-contributing states was related to fears about too forceful an approach being taken. Although a lack of troops posed problems for the operation at certain times, reinforcements were forthcoming and did then make it possible for ONUC forces to take stronger action.

Command and Control

The willingness to use force in the Congo was a first for the United Nations and it came in the early days of UN experience with peacekeeping. Some of the logistical and communication problems associated with the operation, therefore, can be attributed to a general lack of experience and procedures. Command and control problems, for example, such as those associated with the final unexpected push into Jadotville that surprised UN headquarters, fall into this category. It remains possible, though, that the Jadotville example, like the murky background to Operation Morthor, is an example of a disconnect between decision making in the field and decision making at UN headquarters, either deliberately or because of the pressure of events. And, in that sense, both examples demonstrate the difficulties inherent in running an operation where force might and is being used, while using a peacekeeping decision making structure. In both situations, commanders in the field made decisions that contravened directives from the secretary-general. The speed of the resultant events and their unexpected nature posed difficult political problems for the secretary-general and, in the case of Operation Morthor, undermined the credibility and the impartiality of the operation.

MANDATE ISSUES

Consent and Governmental Collapse

Congo's period of constitutional crisis meant that the government that had requested the ONUC presence no longer existed. Until the constitutional crisis was resolved, in August 1961, this created a kind of political vacuum where there was no political entity to give consent to the continued presence of the ONUC mission or to ask for its withdrawal. This created an interesting dilemma for the UN mission. What happens in such a vacuum? Is the absence of the government that originally gave consent to the operation equivalent to a request for withdrawal of the force? Do the parameters of the operation change in the absence of a consenting entity? There were and still are no clear answers to these questions.

For some, the collapse of the Congo government provided a window of opportunity for ONUC troops to take firmer more proactive action in the country to bring about the objectives established in the mandate. Hammarskjöld believed

that the ONUC mandate remained the same even after the collapse of the government and, therefore, that especially in the absence of the government, any
more forceful action by ONUC would constitute interference in the internal affairs of the country. He chose to put the ONUC mission in a kind of holding pattern, maintaining mandate implementation to the greatest extent possible, and
awaiting and facilitating a political solution. The collapse of the government and
Hammarskjöld's decision to keep the ONUC mission in place with the same
mandate made the fine line of impartiality razor sharp. Without a government in
place, in the context of a number of rival groups competing for power and with
Katanga continuing to assert its independence, almost any action ONUC took,
even facilitating any kind of political reconciliation process, could be interpreted
as favoring one group or the other. In fact for some member states even the decision to maintain impartiality was seen as a decision that favored certain actors
over others.

Impartiality and Noninterference

Hammarskjöld faced the difficult task of being the first secretary-general to
deal with a peace enforcement operation, and to do so at a time when the general
UN experience in running military operations was limited and cold war politics
were strong. The only experience on which Hammarskjöld could draw was the
UNEF peacekeeping operation. This peacekeeping background may have contributed to his focus on noninterference and impartiality in an operation where
typical peacekeeping conditions soon disappeared. His determination that
ONUC would not interfere in the situation in the Congo was a persistent, even
overwhelming concern in his approach to the crisis. As outlined in the introduction, in choosing to become involved in a situation the Security Council effectively makes a decision to "interfere," at least in the sense of becoming a participant with a political agenda. Implementation of a mandate to end civil war
and to detain and expel foreign military personnel, by definition, was not going
to be seen as noninterference by anyone supporting or believing in Katanga's
independence. Equally, the decision not to use force with respect to Katanga was
seen by Congolese government officials as favoring the Katangese and
prompted their decision to use military force themselves, further complicating
the situation for the United Nations. In these respects, for those on the receiving
end, ONUC was interfering. That did not mean, however, that the United Nations was not acting impartially with respect to the nature and implementation of
the operation. Again, as outlined earlier, the Security Council's political agenda
(the mandate), can itself be impartial (without prejudice to the positions of the
parties in the sense of Article 40 of the charter) as can the implementation of the
mandate. In that sense, therefore, Hammarskjöld's concern about noninterference was a concern about the maintenance of impartiality in the implementation of the mission.

This may explain Hammarskjöld's sense that the use of force was almost in
and of itself the equivalent to interference in internal affairs because of a concern that it was likely to affect the positions of the parties and would, therefore,

not be impartial. It is interesting, in this respect, that under U Thant ONUC found success in returning to the very basic objective of restoring security and freedom of movement rather than by focusing on the broader civil war and mercenary objectives.

Means and Ends

In balancing means versus ends, Hammarskjöld always weighed in on the side of noninterference as an end. This meant a very cautious approach to mandate implementation. Hammarskjöld was also scrupulous about maintaining the integrity of the mandate established by the Security Council, returning to the Security Council for clarification when issues of interpretation arose. For those who advocated that ONUC troops take a stronger role early on in the operation this aspect of his approach was the most frustrating. They believed that the mandate was sufficiently broadly defined to allow for interpretation without clarification from the Security Council, and that returning to the Security Council took time and did not always generate a result. By contrast, Thant was far less concerned with the means used than with mandate implementation, giving direction about desired outcomes and leaving the choice of means to the operation decision makers.

An argument could be made that Thant did not need to be as concerned with definitional issues relating to the use of force because of the changes in the mandate that had already been made by the Security Council. In addition, events on the ground meant that Thant was dealing with different military and political contexts than those faced by Hammarskjöld. There is no way of determining, therefore, whether or to what extent a different approach by Hammarskjöld, for example, would have altered the outcome. The use of force by ONUC troops under Thant, however, was initiated and carried out for the purposes of ensuring troop security and restoring ONUC freedom of movement. These objectives paved the way for moving fully into Katanga and for bringing an end to the mercenary problem. The end of the civil war and the mercenary problem came, therefore, not by using the Security Council's authorization of force to achieve those ends, but by pursuing basic operational goals whose authorization was available to ONUC from the beginning.

NOTES

1. Colin Legum, *Congo Disaster* (London: Penguin, 1961), 44. The actual number of university graduates at that time varies from source to source and range from zero to twenty. The Belgian policy was that local Congolese students were not allowed to go overseas to university, yet there were no local universities until 1954.

2. For a good in-depth discussion of the factors contributing to Congo's drive for independence and the reasons for the crisis, see Legum, *Congo Disaster*.

3. Ernest W. Lefever, *Crisis in the Congo: A United Nations Force in Action* (Washington D.C.: Brookings, 1965), 8.

4. Treaty of Friendship between Belgium and the Congo, reprinted in Lefever, *Crisis in the Congo*, 199–200.

5. For details of Union Minière's financial interests as well as those of other foreign companies, see Catherine Hoskyns, *The Congo since Independence, January 1960 to December 1961* (London: Oxford University Press, 1965), 14–19. Also see Lefever, *Crisis in the Congo*, 13.

6. "Cable dated 12 July 1960 from the President of the Republic of the Congo and Supreme Commander of the National Army and the Prime Minister and Minister of National Defense addressed to the Secretary-General of the United Nations," S/4382, 13 July 1960.

7. Ibid. The Bandung Treaty powers comprised twenty-nine Asian and African states. They originally came together at a meeting in April 1955, held in Bandung, Indonesia. The membership included Communist China, who had not yet been recognized by the United States. Many of the members were newly decolonized states and they shared a general belief in the importance of decolonization. In addition, Hammarskjöld placed great importance on making the United Nations a viable forum for dealing with the concerns of newly independent African and Asian states and, therefore, was anxious that this crisis be dealt with within the United Nations.

8. Quoted in Hoskyns, *Congo since Independence*, 127.

9. Under Article 99, the secretary-general "may bring to the attention of the Security Council any matter which in his opinion may threaten the maintenance of international peace and security."

10. S/PV.873, 13 July 1960.

11. The three abstentions all related to issues in the first paragraph of the resolution rather than its overall intent. The first paragraph called "upon the Government of Belgium to withdraw its troops from the territory of the Republic of Congo." See Security Council Resolution 143, 14 July 1960. The Security Council meeting ended at 3:25 a.m.

12. A total of thirty countries contributed to the ONUC mission at one time or another through the duration of its mandate. The mission's maximum strength was 19,828 in July 1961. Statistics from United Nations, *The Blue Helmets: A Review of United Nations Peace-keeping* (New York: United Nations, 1990) 221–222, 435–436.

13. See Hoskyns, *Congo since Independence*, especially 122–124. Also see "Interview with Sture Linner," UN Oral History Collection, Yale University Library. (Linner was the UN chief of civilian operations.)

14. See, for example, Major-General Carl von Horn, *Soldiering for Peace* (London: Cassel, 1966) especially 157–160; and Lefever, *Crisis in the Congo*, 35.

15. For the secretary-general's public comments about his plans, his instructions to Ralph Bunche, and Bunche's reasons for delay, see the report by the secretary-general: S/4417, 6 August 1960. General Horn reports: "I do not know what transpired in Elizabethville, but on 5 August Ralph returned a shaken man." See Horn, *Soldiering for Peace*, 171. Also see Brian Urquhart, *Hammarskjöld* (New York: W.W. Norton & Co., 1994), 418–419.

16. See Urquhart, *Hammarskjöld*, 418–422.

17. S/PV.884, 8 August 1960, para. 12. Also see the exchange between the Soviet representative and the secretary-general later the same day: S/PV.885, 8 August 1960, especially para. 128. The secretary-general's written report to the Security Council contains a fuller explanation of the issue as he saw it. See S/4417, 6 August 1960, 10–12.

18. S/PV.887-889, 21–22 August 1960.

19. This situation became even more complicated when, in the process of moving to attack Katanga, the Congolese troops massacred members of the local Baluba tribe.

20. See Lefever, *Crisis in the Congo*, and Hoskyns, *Congo since Independence*, for descriptions of the machinations of the struggle, especially the involvement of Joseph Mobutu, then the chief of staff of the military, who became president in 1965, and Antoine Gizenga, who tried to establish his own regionally based regime.

21. General Horn notes that it may be the case that ONUC actions constrained Lumumba more than Kasavubu, but "never for a moment had there been any political bias in [Cordier's] decision; it had been motivated solely by the urgent need to prevent civil war and safeguard our own operations." Horn reports that ONUC officials were also concerned that the Soviet Union might begin an airlift in support of Lumumba. With respect to the closure of the radio station, Kasavubu's supporters began broadcasting from across the border, a fact that encouraged the view that ONUC actions were weighted against Lumumba. Horn, *Soldiering for Peace*, 194.

22. General Assembly Resolution 1474 (ES-IV), 20 September 1960. The resolution was sponsored by a combination of African, Middle Eastern, and Asian states and passed by a vote of seventy to zero with eleven abstentions. The eleven abstentions included the Soviet Union and most of its Eastern European allies, as well as France and South Africa.

23. This was the beginning of the famous Soviet campaign to replace the secretary-general's office with a "troika" arrangement, which would include a representative from the West, one from the East, and one from the nonaligned.

24. SG/1008, 3.

25. For descriptions of these events, see Lefever, *Crisis in the Congo*, 46–47; and Hoskyns, *Congo since Independence*, 201–204.

26. For the debate see S/PV.912 through S/PV.920, December 1960. Also see the General Assembly debates of the same time period.

27. These withdrawals resulted in a total decrease of 5,985 troops from the ONUC operation (although they were later replaced) as well as reducing the number of African nations involved in the operation. At its highest level of contributions (July 1961), the operation involved nineteen thousand eight hundred and twenty-five personnel. See Rosalyn Higgins, *United Nations Peacekeeping 1946–1967, Documents and Commentary*, vol. 3, *Africa* (Oxford: Oxford University Press, 1980), 95.

28. For an examination of the events prior to and including Lumumba's death, see the report of the Commission of Inquiry established by the UN: S/4964, 11 November 1961.

29. S/PV.941 and S/PV. 942, 20 February 1961.

30. S/PV.941, 20 February 1961, para. 83.

31. S/PV.942, 20 February 1961, para. 21.

32. Other authors separate the internal stability objective from the issue of Katangan secession. See Higgins, *United Nations Peacekeeping,* and R. Simmonds, *Legal Problems Arising from the United Nations Military Operations in the Congo* (The Hague: Martinus Nijhoff, 1968).

33. Article 25 requires members of the United Nations to "accept and carry out the decisions of the Security Council in accordance with the present Charter." Article 49 requires members to "join in affording mutual assistance in carrying out the measures decided upon by the Security Council."

34. S/PV.884, 8 August 1960, 4–5.

35. See, for example, Higgins, *United Nations Peacekeeping,* 57; Simmonds, *Legal Problems*, 63–64; and Finn Seyersted, *United Nations Forces in the Law of Peace and War* (The Hague: A.W. Sijthoff-Leyden, 1966), 137. The Soviet Union took the issue of financing the Congo operation to the International Court of Justice (ICJ). They argued that military force could only be used by the United Nations under Article 43 of the

charter and, therefore, only Security Council members should be required to finance the operation. The ICJ ruled against the Soviet argument. In the process, the court found that "It cannot be said that the Charter has left the Security Council impotent in the face of an emergency situation when agreements under Article 43 have not been concluded. Articles of Chapter VII of the Charter speak of 'situations' as well as disputes, and it must lie within the power of the Security Council to police a situation even though it does not resort to enforcement action against a State." See International Court of Justice, *Certain Expenses of the United Nations*, 20 July 1962, 20.

36. Article 2(7) states that nothing in the charter "shall authorize the United Nations to intervene in matters which are essentially within the domestic jurisdiction of any state . . . but this principle shall not prejudice the application of enforcement measures under Chapter VII."

37. The secretary-general submitted a major report on UNEF to the Security Council in 1958 describing the principles and practices of the operation. This constitutes the first outline of the basic principles of peacekeeping. See A/3943, 9 October 1958, especially para. 13–17.

38. S/PV.873, 13 July 1960, para. 28.

39. *Security Council Official Records*, 15th Year, Supplement July, August, September 1960, S/4389, 18 July 1960.

40. S/4389, 18 July 1960, 5.

41. Outlined by Hoskyns, *Congo since Independence*, 294–295, based on an unofficial summary given to her at UN headquarters.

42. S/PV.941, 20 February 1961, 17.

43. S/PV.942, 20 February 1961, 6.

44. Indar Jit Rikhye, *Military Adviser to the Secretary-General* (London: Hurst, 1993), 200–201.

45. Ibid., 201.

46. Ibid.

47. Quoted by Urquhart, *Hammarskjöld*, 561–562. No document reference is given. However, General Rikhye outlines the same guidelines.

48. Rikhye, *Military Adviser*, 295.

49. For an overview, see S/4791, Report of the Special Representative to the Secretary-General, 15 April 1961.

50. This resulted in some crowd scenes reminiscent of the problems encountered many years later in Somalia. For example, on 4 April, after a speech by Tshombe, a crowd estimated to consist of ten thousand to fifteen thousand people went to the Elisabethville airport and destroyed airport and UN equipment. Later, a crowd attacked a convoy of four ONUC cars, wounding five ONUC personnel. See S/4791, 15 April 1961.

51. S/4761, Report of the Special Representative to the Secretary-General, 8 March 1961, para. 29–30. In the same report, a vivid account of the Matadi incident is given by a Canadian, Captain Bélanger, who was part of a Canadian signals detachment located with the Sudanese contingent, and who hid in a nearby ravine during the fighting.

52. United Nations, *Blue Helmets*, 233.

53. S/4791, 15 April 1961, para. 17–23.

54. The Tananarive Conference took place in March 1961. A second conference was held in Coquilhatville in late April 1961. Two key regional leaders, Gizenga and Tshombe, did not attend either meeting. Tshombe came to the Coquilhatville meeting and then left when his attempt to have the meeting endorse the proposals made at the first conference was rejected.

55. For example, the activities of the Ethiopian battalion at Kabalo (see earlier description in the text) in April included the capture of thirty foreign mercenaries, none of them

from Belgium. Incidents such as these demonstrated the degree of mercenary involvement and proved that the foreign mercenary situation was not solely connected to Belgium. This brought about a change in attitude in countries such as Great Britain. (Eight of the thirty soldiers captured by the Ethiopians were British citizens.)

56. For O'Brien's own version of events, see Conor Cruise O'Brien, *To Katanga and Back* (London: Hutchinson, 1962), 195–225. Also see Urquhart, *Hammarskjöld*, 556–557; and S/4940, Add. 1, 14 September 1961.

57. The sequence of events set in motion by Operation Morthor remains among the most contested and controversial in UN history. A number of different overviews and theories are available. For his account, see O'Brien, *To Katanga and Back*. Note that O'Brien's account in the book differs from an initial account he gave in articles in *The Observer*, in December 1961, immediately after resigning from the United Nations. For another personal, though more deliberately distanced point of view see Urquhart, *Hammarskjöld*, 581–597. Other good accounts include Hoskyns, *Congo since Independence*, 428–435; and Rikhye, *Military Adviser*, 267–285.

58. Urquhart, *Hammarskjöld*, 566.

59. Urquhart also states that the operation suffered from bad military planning and preparation: "the military preparations to carry out, even at their minimum interpretation, the instructions which Khiary gave O'Brien were totally inadequate and were based upon an entirely unrealistic estimate of the opposition likely to be encountered. . . . The September 13 operation, . . . was poorly planned and abysmally executed." See Urquhart, *Hammarskjöld*, 567–568.

60. Many people have speculated that UN officials hoped to present the secretary-general with a *fait accompli* on his arrival in the Congo. O'Brien's comments that Katangan secession had been ended tend to support the idea that he and other UN officials in the Congo intended that the operation, ostensibly to complete the round up of mercenaries, would force Tshombe to capitulate on secession.

61. United Nations, *Blue Helmets*, 245.

62. For a description of the attacks on UN troops, see S/4940, 14 September 1961. Good examples of the initial confusion and chaos of events can be found by reading the news reports of the time. See, for example, Thomas J. Hamilton, "U.N. Endorsed Use of Force in Congo," *New York Times*, 14 September 1961, 3; and Henry Tanner, "Katanga Key to Unity in Congo," *New York Times*, 17 September 1961, E5.

63. Madeleine G. Kalb, *Congo Cables* (New York: Macmillan, 1982), 296–297.

64. The report from the UN Commission of Inquiry into the airplane accident is: A/5069, 24 April 1962.

65. S/4940, 14 September 1961.

66. Since the beginning of the operation, the United States had provided logistics and airlift support to the ONUC operation. Whereas prior to Operation Morthor and Hammarskjöld's death the US had been reluctant to provide additional physical support to ONUC, the United States now provided more transport planes as well as privately agreeing to supply eight fighter jets to provide protection for transport aircraft. See Kalb, *Congo Cables*, 302–303.

67. For the UN report on this incident, see S/4940/Add. 13, 15 November 1961.

68. "Report on Action Taken in Implementation of the Protocol of Agreement Between the Katanga Authorities and ONUC Subsequent to the Cease-fire and on Other Matters," S/4940/Add. 12, 2 November 1961, para. 8, 10.

69. For a description of the events and detentions of UN personnel, see S/4940/Add.10–19, 6 December 1961. This includes a description of the events of 28–29 November 1961 when Ivan Smith, the acting secretary-general's representative in

Katanga, and Brian Urquhart, also representing the UN, were taken at gunpoint from a reception at the U.S. consulate.

70. Hoskyns, *Congo since Independence*, 451. Also see Henry Tanner, "U.S. Planes Halt Katanga Flights after One is Hit," *New York Times*, 8 December 1961, 1, 3, which describes the location and strategy of the fighting within the city.

71. The UN report to the secretary-general notes: "There were other indications that the Katanga plan for a general assault was more advanced and comprehensive than had been suspected." See S/4940/Add. 16, para. 28.

72. Kenneth Love, "Thant Threatens Force to Restore Peace in Katanga," *New York Times*, 4 December 1961, 1, 3.

73. Rikhye, *Military Adviser*, 293–295.

74. The reports from the officer-in-charge to the secretary-general provide a quite detailed description of ONUC's military activities in the area during the period between 5–15 December. See S/4940/Add. 17, 9 December 1961.

75. "Telegram Dated 15 December 1961 from the Secretary-General to the Minister for Foreign Affairs of Belgium B.III," S/5025, 15 December 1961.

76. Kalb, *Congo Cables*, 314. The US provided planes to transport troops within the Congo as well as antiaircraft guns and armored cars.

77. For a detailed description, see S/4940/Add. 18, 20 December 1961; and S/4940/Add. 19, 22 December 1961.

78. The U.S. Ambassador to the Congo, Edmund Guillon, played a major role in saving the talks beween Adoula and Tshombe from collapse. He, along with Bunche, who had been appointed by the secretary-general as one of his representatives at the talks, were instrumental in getting Tshombe to agree to the declaration.

79. Rikhye, *Military Adviser*, 301.

80. A. Cordier and M. Harrelson, eds., "Remarks to the Advisory Committee on the Congo," in *Public Papers of the Secretaries-General of the United Nations*, Vol. 6, *U Thant, 1961–1964* (New York: Columbia University Press, 1976), 272–274.

81. For a description, see "Report to the Secretary-General from the Officer-in-Charge of the United Nations Operation in the Congo," Section B, S/5053/Add. 14, 11 January 1963.

82. "It was becoming ever more obvious that the reintegration of Katanga, under the Secretary-General's plan or otherwise, was far removed from the minds of the secessionist leaders." Ibid., para. 27. For the reconciliation plan, see, S/5053/Add. 13, Annex 1, 29 November 1962. For the exchange of letters between the UN and Tshombe, in which Tshombe claims not to know about the national reconciliation plan, see S/5053/Add. 14, Annex 25 and 26, 11 January 1963.

83. Rikhye, *Military Adviser*, 303.

84. S/5053/Add. 14, 11 January 1963, para. 30–45.

85. See, for example, the statement calling on all Katangese to resist the UN by any means possible. See S/5053/Add. 14, Annex 28, 11 January 1963.

86. In his memoirs Thant says "[a]t last . . . I authorized the ONUC military actions." See U Thant, *A View from the UN* (New York: Doubleday, 1978), 142. For his description of the personal issues he faced in making the decision to use force, see 144–145.

87. S/5053/Add. 14, 11 January 1963, para. 14.

88. A. Cordier and M. Harrelson, eds., "Statement with Regard to Recent Events in the Elisabethville Area," in *Public Papers of the Secretaries-General of the United Nations*, Vol. 6, *U Thant, 1961–1964* (New York: Columbia University Press, 1976), 276.

89. S/5053/Add. 14, 11 January 1963, para. 72. The situation was made more complicated by the fact that the secretary-general had promised the Belgian ambassador to the United Nations that UN troops would not cross the Lufira River to Jadotville. See

"Interview with Jonathon Dean," UN Oral History Collection, Yale University Library, 11. For the secretary-general's version of events see Thant, *View from the UN*, 142–144.

90. "Special Report Dated 10 January 1963, Addressed to the Secretary-General by Mr. Ralph J. Bunche, Under-Secretary for Special Political Affairs, on the Subject of Communication and Co-ordination between United Nations and ONUC Headquarters, with Specific Reference to the Jadotville Operation," S/5053/Add. 14, Annex 34, 11 January 1963, para. 1.

91. Ibid., para. 9. In spite of Bunche's conclusions, the questions of the authorization of the operation remains open. First-hand accounts continue to suggest that local UN officials deliberately used the slow communications system to sit on the orders not to proceed to Jadotville until it was too late for the troops to turn back. See, for example, the interviews with George Sherry, General G. McMahon, and Sture Linner, UN Oral History Collection, Yale University Library. Officially, ONUC communications went through the Congo post office. Unofficially, ONUC officials used the U.S. embassy to communicate to New York, although they always kept up the routine of going to the post office so as "not to give the impression that we were relying on other forms of communication." See Linner, UN Oral History, 13.

92. The text of the agreement is reprinted in S/5053/Add. 15, Annex 9, 30 January 1963.

93. S/5053/Add. 15, 30 January 1963, para. 37.

Chapter 4

Somalia

I. CONTEXT

In the late 1800s, the territory now known as Somalia was colonized by Britain, France, Italy, Egypt, and Ethiopia. By the turn of the century, the political map had settled somewhat, with Britain holding the northern portion of what is now Somalia and Italy governing most of the area bordering on the Indian Ocean.[1] The border between British and Italian Somaliland ran through the area inhabited by the Ogaden clan, arbitrarily separating the clan and setting in place a division that was to become a long-standing problem. After conquering Ethiopia in 1935, Italy went on to conquer British Somaliland (thus reunifying the Ogaden). Britain counterattacked in 1941 and laid claim to the entire area. In retaking the area, Britain also drove the Italians out of Ethiopia and reinstated Emperor Haile Selassie.

After the war, a commission made up of the victorious allied powers was established to determine the future of Somalia. Britain wanted to administer the entire area of Somalia in a trusteeship arrangement until it became independent. The other allied powers, accusing Britain of imperialist motives, would not agree to this. In the meantime, in an effort to appease Emperor Selassie, the United States and the Soviet Union pressured Britain to hand over part of the Ogaden area to Ethiopia. In spite of strong Somali opposition to the idea, Britain gave in to this request in 1948, reestablishing a separation of the clan based in that area. In the end, the commission was unable to agree on Somalia's future and turned the issue over to the United Nations. In November 1949, the UN General Assembly made southern Somalia a trust territory under Italian control, stipulating that the country was to be made independent by 1960. Britain continued to hold its area as a protectorate. The British and Italian sectors both gained independence in 1960 and merged to form one country. At this point, the country entered into a period of parliamentary democracy.[2]

The democratic experiment was short-lived. In 1969, President Abdirashid Ali Shirmarke was assassinated. Taking advantage of a sense of frustration and dissatisfaction with the corruption associated with the democratic government, the army, in cooperation with the police, seized power. From the army group, Mohammed Siad Barre emerged as the leader and was installed as president and head of the Supreme Revolutionary Council (SRC). SRC leaders suspended the constitution, dissolved the National Assembly, disbanded political parties, and arrested most of the civilian politicians.

In the mid-1970s, the Selassie regime in Ethiopia collapsed when military officers overthrew the emperor. A war then ensued among the groups that had taken part in the overthrow, who were joined by rebel groups from various parts of the country. Barre saw the unrest in Ethiopia as an opportunity to regain the Ogaden area and in late 1977 he sent Somali troops across the Ethiopian border. Somalia lost the war the following year, after the Soviet Union chose to end its support of Somalia and side with Ethiopia. The Soviet Union's decision to abandon Somalia meant the end of almost ten years of Soviet aid and military support. The obvious alternative was for Somalia to turn to the United States to fill the vacuum. The United States, however, did not begin to support Somalia until 1980, and even then only on a limited scale.[3]

Somalia's defeat in the war put in motion the internal discontent and clan-based insurgency that would lead to Barre's overthrow as leader of Somalia. Members of the Isaak clan, in exile in London, formed the Somali National Movement (SNM) in 1981. The SNM established a base in Ethiopia from which they began guerrilla activity. By the mid- to late-1980s, other clans formed their own movements. The Ogaden clan formed the core of the Somali Patriotic Movement (SPM) and the Hawiye clan formed the United Somali Congress (USC).[4] Barre's response to these movements was to send the military to the regions where the clans were based and launch vicious and lethal attacks on the civilian population and their agricultural base, generating new support for the rebel movements.

SNM forces made significant inroads into the northern Somalia countryside through the mid-1980s. In May 1988, it launched a major military offensive and occupied the cities of Hargeysa and Burao. Somali armed forces responded with aerial bombardment of the cities in conjunction with ground attacks. The result was the devastating physical destruction of the cities, thousands of civilian deaths, and the creation of thousands of refugees as people fled the cities. The troops also destroyed and poisoned water supplies and massacred livestock.[5] These events, which took the conflict to a whole new level, were a watershed point for the internal struggle in Somalia. The events gave impetus to other opposition groups. The government now clearly faced a strengthening civil war and soon the battle shifted to the capital city, Mogadishu. In 1989, Barre launched a campaign against USC forces based in Mogadishu. The campaign resulted in considerable destruction to the city and also destroyed any existing loyalty to the Barre regime within Mogadishu.

By the end of January 1991, fighting in and around Mogadishu forced the collapse of the now barely functioning government and Barre fled to his home area in the south, near the Kenyan border. Rather than banding together in victory, the final collapse of the government brought disunity to the various rebel groups. Without consulting any of the other clans or USC clan factions, the USC executive named Ali Mahdi Mohammad as interim president. The other groups rejected this choice, as did Mohammad Farah Aidid, who believed that as the military leader of the victory in the battle for Mogadishu he deserved to be named leader. Aidid created a split within the USC by forming his own USC faction. This split, in combination with the inability to get agreement from the other rebel groups on the formation of a government, led to a year of uncertainty and turmoil in Somalia.

From January 1991, therefore, Somalia was a state without a government in the midst of a civil war. Throughout the year, various unsuccessful attempts were made by regional actors as well as clan elders to find a resolution to the crisis. The SNM, in large measure the key player in bringing about the collapse of the Barre regime and certainly the longest serving of the rebel groups, once again faced the prospect of a national government dominated by the south. In May 1991, in order to distance themselves from the infighting of the other clans, and trying to hedge off the possibility of domination by stronger southern groups, SNM officials declared the independence of the Republic of Somaliland in the north. In August, meetings in Djibouti resulted in agreement on the Djibouti Accords, the essence of which was to accept Mahdi as interim president on the condition that he take steps to end the conflict, develop a basic civil infrastructure, and reconstitute a national army. The accords were never adhered to, and the situation continued to deteriorate.

In the absence of any clear political settlement and with the widespread availability of arms and ammunition, the conflict continued at a low level.[6] In September 1991, the two USC factions in Mogadishu fought for three days until the intervention of a subclan brought an end to the flare-up. The fighting resulted in three hundred to four hundred deaths and seven hundred to fifteen hundred wounded. In spite of several further efforts to resolve the crisis, the split between the Mahdi and Aidid USC factions could not be overcome. In mid-November, the fighting between these two groups began again in Mogadishu with both sides intending to solve the problem militarily.

During this year of anarchy and fighting, conditions throughout the country deteriorated dramatically. A drought exacerbated the food situation, which had been thrown into crisis by the effects of the war, particularly by the destruction of livestock and water supplies carried out by Barre's forces. The war also generated massive population dislocations in all parts of the country, further exacerbating the food shortage. As the food crisis worsened, people were again on the move, now heading towards major cities in search of food. In Mogadishu, the influx of refugees in the context of the fighting there only served to make a very bad situation much worse.[7]

II. MANDATE

The UN response to the Somalia crisis ran the gamut from the extreme of total disregard to total involvement then back to total disregard. During the first year of anarchy, the situation within the country became so dangerous that most non-governmental organizations (NGOs) and UN humanitarian agencies left the country. With the exception of the UN agencies, most organizations moved their headquarters to Nairobi and continued to try to run aid and assistance programs in Somalia.[8] A small staff from UN agencies returned to Mogadishu, Berbera, and Borama in August 1991, but left Mogadishu again in November when the conflict escalated.

Formal UN involvement in the conflict did not begin until a full year after the fall of the Barre government. In December 1991, the then outgoing UN secretary-general Javier Pérez de Cuéllar wrote to the Security Council to apprise them of the situation and to inform them that he was sending James Jonah, his undersecretary-general for political affairs with responsibility for Africa, to Somalia. He also asked that the Security Council consider the situation in Somalia with a view to encouraging a peaceful resolution to the conflict, as had been requested by the prime minister of Somalia and the secretary-general of the Organization of African Unity (OAU).[9] Jonah went to Mogadishu for three days from 3–5 January 1992.[10]

ARMS EMBARGO AND PEACEKEEPING

The Security Council included Somalia on its agenda for the first time on 23 January 1992, after being prompted by a request from the Prime Minister of Somalia and the representative of Somalia at the United Nations.[11] That same day, the Security Council unanimously passed Resolution 733. The resolution called on all states to "immediately implement a general and complete embargo on all deliveries of weapons and military equipment to Somalia until the Security Council decides otherwise." The resolution also called for a cease-fire and action on a political settlement, and called on all parties to facilitate the delivery of humanitarian assistance. An arms embargo was a traditional and, given the Somalia situation, understandable first response to the conflict. It was also clearly a step without any hope of implementation and as such it represented a very minimal response.

In mid-February, Jonah supervised three days of talks in New York under the auspices of the United Nations, the Organization of African Unity, the Arab League, and the Islamic Conference. Aidid and Mahdi never met face-to-face during these talks but they did agree to a cease-fire. Jonah returned to Mogadishu at the end of February, and Aidid and Mahdi signed the formal cease-fire document on 3 March 1992.[12]

The cease-fire agreement included provisions for a UN role in monitoring the cease-fire arrangements. On 17 March 1992, the Security Council unanimously passed Resolution 746. The resolution approves the secretary-general's proposal to send a "technical team" to Somalia to develop a plan for a UN monitoring mechanism and for the unimpeded delivery of humanitarian aid. In spite of the cease-fire agreement and the arms embargo, the delivery of humanitarian aid was becoming ever more difficult as deliveries were increasingly hijacked by armed gangs.

On 24 April 1992, the Security Council authorized an initial peacekeeping mission to Somalia known as the UN Operation in Somalia (UNOSOM). Resolution 751 called for the immediate deployment of fifty military observers to Somalia to monitor the cease-fire. The Security Council also agreed "in principle" to the secretary-general's proposal that a "security force" of five hundred military personnel be established under the direction of the secretary-general's special representative to provide security for UN personnel, equipment, and supplies at the port and the airport in Mogadishu, and in escorting humanitarian aid deliveries from there to distribution centers.[13] While the parties to the conflict had agreed in principle to the deployment of the fifty observers, the actual deployment of the security force awaited further consultations with the parties to the conflict.[14]

Over the next few months, the situation in Somalia continued to deteriorate. In spite of the initial agreement by Aidid and Mahdi to the deployment of military observers, Aidid was reluctant to give final agreement for their deployment. He finally agreed to the deployment of the observers (though not yet the security force), on 25 June 1992. Deployment of the observers began in mid-July—more than two months after the initial authorization.[15] In two reports to the Security Council, one in July and a second in August,[16] secretary-general Boutros Boutros-Ghali proposed new measures to deal with the situation. In particular, the secretary-general pushed for a broadening of UN action beyond its focus on the south to take in the whole country by establishing four operational zones in which a "consolidated" UN operation would carry out the basic activities of establishing a secure environment, ensuring humanitarian aid delivery, and monitoring the cease-fire. He suggested that this would involve deploying a maximum of thirty-five hundred troops (including the original five hundred) as part of the UNOSOM operation. In arguing for this expansion, the secretary-general stated:

The complexity of the situation and the inherent dangers of working in Somalia, combined with the almost total absence of central, regional or local government, pose enormous operational difficulties for the United Nations in establishing a large-scale effective presence. None the less, the threat of mass starvation facing large segments of the population and the potential renewal of hostilities which could affect peace and stability throughout the Horn of Africa region require an immediate and comprehensive response from the United Nations and the international community.[17]

The Security Council approved the secretary-general's proposals in Resolution 767 on 27 July 1992 and in Resolution 775 on 28 August 1992. Resolution 767 also called for a massive humanitarian aid effort, requesting that the secretary-general "make full use of all available means and arrangements, including the mounting of an urgent airlift operation, . . . in accelerating the provision of humanitarian assistance to the affected population." This last provision reflected increased concern about the depth of the humanitarian crisis in the country, which was simultaneously expanding in its seriousness and becoming a focus of international media attention.

At the end of August 1992, the secretary-general reported that:

Present estimates, which may be conservative, indicate that as many as 4.5 million Somalis [sixty-five percent of the population] are in desperate need of food and other assistance. . . . The United Nations and its partners are ready and have the capacity to provide substantially increased assistance but they have been prevented from doing so by the lawlessness and lack of security that prevail throughout Somalia, often including Mogadishu itself. Heavily armed gangs overrun delivery and distribution points and loot supplies directly from docked ships as well as from airports and airstrips. . . . [O]n 16 August, while the technical team was in Somalia, armed gangs looted the first large-scale [World Food Program] shipment to Kismayu, as well as the entire consignment of diesel oil, which is essential for the transport of food to distribution centres. Current security conditions do not permit the assured delivery of humanitarian assistance by overland transport and are thus the main cause of the current food crisis in Somalia.[18]

Implementation of the measures approved by the Security Council continued to be a problem. It was only now, in August, that General Aidid, who held out on giving consent to the deployment of UN troops, agreed to the deployment of the five-hundred-strong security force approved by the Security Council in April, and only after difficult negotiations with the secretary-general's special representative, Mohammed Sahnoun.[19] Even then, the troops did not arrive until the beginning of October, and once on the ground Aidid blocked their deployment within the city. The Pakistani peacekeeping troops managed to take control of the airport by 10 November 1992, thus enabling the secure arrival of aid deliveries by plane, but they were unable to extend their control beyond the airport itself and came under attack a few days after securing the area.[20] The UNOSOM mission, though limited, was effectively done for as soon as the cooperation and consent of Aidid disappeared. According to Sahnoun, the delay in deploying the UN troops in conjunction with the arrival of a Russian aircraft, with UN markings even though at that point it was not operating for the UN, that was delivering support to Mahdi's factions contributed to Aidid's shift to an anti–UN stance and, therefore, his unwillingness to allow the Pakistani troops to move once they arrived.[21] Vastly outnumbered and outarmed, and limited to using force only in self-defense, the Pakistan contingent very quickly found itself almost entirely focused on maintaining its own security with mandate implementation a secondary consideration.

A further significant setback came with Sahnoun's resignation at the end of October. He submitted his resignation in protest over the lack of support from the United Nations for the Somali operation and the unacceptable length of time taken to implement approved measures.[22] Sahnoun was well regarded and widely considered to have won the confidence of the various factions in Somalia, to understand the Somali way of doing things, and consequently to be extremely well placed to further the UN operation. His resignation, accepted by the secretary-general, created a serious gap in the UN operation at a critical juncture.[23] Ismat Kittani, the secretary-general's new representative, replaced Sah-noun on 8 November.

By the end of November, the humanitarian and security situation had deteriorated so significantly[24] that the secretary-general wrote to the Security Council about the possibility of changing the parameters of the UNOSOM operation.

[I]n the absence of a government or governing authority capable of maintaining law and order, Somali "authorities" at all levels of society compete for anything of value in the country. Armed threats and killings often decide the outcome. Looting and banditry are rife. Amidst this chaos, the international aid provided by the United Nations and voluntary agencies has become a major (and in some areas the only) source of income and as such is the target of all the "authorities" . . . In essence, humanitarian supplies have become the basis of an otherwise non-existent Somali economy. . . . The net result is that, while massive amounts of relief supplies have been readied in the pipeline for the implementation of the 100-day action programme, the humanitarian assistance that reaches its intended beneficiaries is often barely more than a trickle. . . . I am giving urgent consideration to this state of affairs and do not exclude the possibility that it may become necessary to review the basic premises and principles of the United Nations effort in Somalia.[25]

THE DECISION TO USE FORCE

The Security Council informally discussed the secretary-general's letter on 25 November, and the need for reevaluation of the operation was generally supported. Council members requested that the secretary-general prepare a series of options for new ways forward. On the same day, Lawrence Eagleburger, the acting secretary of state for the outgoing George Bush administration, informed the secretary-general that, "if the Security Council were to decide to authorize Member States to use forceful means to ensure the delivery of relief supplies to the people of Somalia, the United States would be ready to take the lead in organizing and commanding such an operation in which a number of other Member States would also participate."[26]

The U.S. offer was, in large measure, a response to the extensive press coverage within the United States of the deteriorating humanitarian situation. On 29 November, the secretary-general provided the Security Council with five options to consider. The first was to continue to pursue the efforts to deploy UNOSOM as originally authorized, as a peacekeeping operation and therefore dependent on the consent and cooperation of the parties to the conflict. The second was to give up pursuing any kind of military-related operation, leaving NGO and humanitarian agencies to deal with the situation as best they could. The secretary-general found both of these options inadequate as a response to the extent of the humanitarian crisis. "While acknowledging that the expectations that I had of UNOSOM have not been fulfilled, I am more than ever convinced of the need for international military personnel to be deployed in Somalia. The current difficulties are due not to their presence but to the fact that not enough of them are there and that they do not have the right mandate."[27]

The remaining three options all involved varying degrees of the use of force. The third involved using UNOSOM to "undertake a show of force" in Mogadishu as a way of creating the conditions for humanitarian aid delivery and achieving local cooperation for the deliveries. The secretary-general expressed his opinion that the situation was such as to require a country-wide rather than just a Mogadishu-based response. The fourth option, therefore, was "a country-wide enforcement operation undertaken by a group of Member States authorized to do so by the Security Council."[28] This option was directly connected to the U.S. offer delivered by Eagleburger. The final option, the one the secretary-general himself preferred, was a country-wide enforcement operation carried out under UN command and control.[29]

All Necessary Means

Four days later, the Security Council opted for the fourth option and unanimously approved Resolution 794 on 3 December 1992. In the resolution, the Security Council states that, "the magnitude of the human tragedy caused by the conflict in Somalia, further exacerbated by the obstacles being created to the distribution of humanitarian assistance, constitutes a threat to international peace and security." The Security Council then, *inter alia*, acting under Chapter VII, authorizes "the Secretary-General and Member States cooperating to implement the offer [from an unnamed member state] to use all necessary means to establish as soon as possible a secure environment for humanitarian relief operations in Somalia." The resolution also emphasizes the Security Council's determination to "restore peace, stability and law and order with a view to facilitating the process of political settlement." But the driving force behind the Security Council actions and the operation it authorized was the humanitarian crisis.

In passing the resolution, many Security Council members spoke of the "unique" situation in Somalia that resulted from the absence of government and the inability to deliver humanitarian aid. The representative of the United Kingdom stated that, "food and security have thus become inextricably linked."[30] As a result of these circumstances, Security Council members agreed with the secretary-general's conclusion that "the Security Council had no alternative but to decide to adopt more forceful measures to secure the humanitarian operations in Somalia."[31] The U.S. representative stated that:

our point should be clear: our mission is essentially a peaceful one, and we will endorse the use of force only if and when we decide it is necessary to accomplish our objective. . . . By acting today to provide a secure environment for the delivery of humanitarian relief to the people of Somalia, the Council has once again taken an essential step to restore international peace and security. . . . But in the case of Somalia, and in other cases we are sure to face in the future, it is important that we send this unambiguous message: the international community has the intent and will to act decisively regarding peace-keeping problems that threaten international stability.[32]

The specific mandate, as outlined in Resolution 794, was to take "action under Chapter VII of the Charter of the United Nations . . . in order to establish a secure environment for humanitarian relief operations in Somalia as soon as possible." The mission, titled Unified Task Force (UNITAF), established a unified command under U.S. leadership, but did not operate under the UN flag or use the traditional peacekeepers' blue helmets. The Security Council resolution established an ad hoc commission of Security Council members to monitor the implementation of the resolution on behalf of the Security Council and invited the secretary-general to attach a "small Operational liaison staff" to the field headquarters of the unified command. Because the operation was under the command of the United States, not the secretary-general, on behalf of the Security Council, technically this operation does not qualify as a peace enforcement operation as the term is used in this book.

The U.S. Central Command (CENTCOM) was assigned command of the UNITAF operation. The text of the mission statement issued by CENTCOM, reads:

When directed by the National Command Authority, USCINCCENT will conduct joint/combined military operations in Somalia, to secure major air and sea ports, to provide open and free passage of relief supplies, to provide security for relief convoys and relief organizations, and to assist the United Nations/nongovernmental organizations in providing humanitarian relief under UN auspices.[33]

Although in many ways this resolution represented a logical extension of the previous resolutions passed by the Security Council, it was by no means an expected outcome. The US had not previously expressed a willingness to lead or participate in such an operation in Somalia. In fact, during the debate on the Security Council resolutions earlier in the year, the US had sought to downplay the possibility of UN military involvement in Somalia because of concern about congressional unwillingness to accept the escalating costs of U.S. involvement in peacekeeping. But by autumn, several factors came together to bring about a change in the attitudes of the Bush administration: increasing press coverage, especially of the famine, which generated increasing public pressure;[34] a resolution calling for UN peacekeepers to be deployed even without Somali consent, put forward by two key U.S. senators, one from each party, was passed by both houses of Congress;[35] and President Bush himself became convinced of the need for action, and even though he had lost the election, or perhaps because of it, he became determined that the United States had a moral obligation to respond in some way to the humanitarian crisis.[36] The Security Council resolution was made possible not only because of the impetus for action from the United States, but also because of a newfound post–Cold War atmosphere of enthusiasm in the Security Council for the possibilities of significant and important Security Council action. The unanimous approval of Resolution 794 by the Security Council reflected this enthusiasm.

PEACE ENFORCEMENT—UNOSOM II

The U.S. and UN intention was that UNITAF would be an interim measure that would provide the intensive response required by the crisis. Once the situation was stabilized, UNOSOM or some version thereof would resume control.

By March 1993, though the situation was improved the secretary-general did not believe that it was sufficiently stable to recommend that the planned shift to a peacekeeping operation occur. Instead, he argued that the next phase of the operation should continue to be under Chapter VII.

It is clear to me that the effort undertaken by UNITAF to establish a secure environment in Somalia is far from complete and in any case has not attempted to address the situation throughout all of Somalia. Moreover, there have been, especially recently, some disheartening reverses. Accordingly, the threat to international peace and security. . . is still in existence. Consequently UNOSOM II will not be able to implement [its] mandate unless it is endowed with enforcement powers under Chapter VII of the Charter.[37]

The secretary-general proposed that the new UN operation—UNOSOM II—be given a wide-ranging mandate and that it apply to the entire country.

The mandate of UNOSOM II, as conceived in the present report, would confer authority for appropriate action, including enforcement action as necessary to establish throughout Somalia a secure environment for humanitarian assistance. To that end, UNOSOM II would seek to complete, through disarmament and reconciliation, the task begun by UNITAF for the restoration of peace, stability, law and order. The mandate would also empower UNOSOM II to provide assistance to the Somali people in rebuilding their shattered economy and social and political life, re-establishing the country's institutional structure, achieving national political reconciliation, recreating a Somali State based on democratic governance and rehabilitating the country's economy and infrastructure.[38]

In a historic move, the Security Council adopted virtually all of the secretary-general's recommendations for UNOSOM II's mandate, establishing, for the first time, a combined peacebuilding, peace enforcement mission under the direction of the secretary-general in order to deal with a situation that "continues to threaten peace and security in the region." Speaking before the resolution was put to a vote, the U.S. representative at the Security Council, Madeleine Albright, stated:

The United States does not want to understate the tasks ahead; as great as the challenges in Somalia have been, those before us are even greater. . . . It is now time for the United Nations to complete the work begun by the Unified Task Force. By adopting this draft resolution, we will embark on an unprecedented enterprise aimed at nothing less than the restoration of an entire country as a proud, functioning and viable member of the community of nations . . . .At the same time, we are soberly conscious of the fact that this draft resolution engages the world community to provide the most comprehensive assistance ever given to any country, but to do so with few lessons and no models to guide our path.[39]

Resolution 814, passed unanimously on 26 March 1993, has three sections. The first section deals with humanitarian and political rehabilitation measures, asking the secretary-general, through his special representative, to undertake a variety of "assistance" tasks. The tasks included providing assistance in: economic rehabilitation, the repatriation of refugees, political reconciliation, the reestablishment of a Somali police force, and the development of a demining program.

In the second section of the resolution, the Security Council "acting under Chapter VII" authorizes a long series of military tasks including:

- the prevention of the resumption of violence;
- control of heavy weapons;
- the seizure of small arms of "all unauthorized armed elements";
- the maintenance of security of ports, airports, and lines of communication for humanitarian aid deliveries;
- the protection "as required" of UN, International Committee of the Red Cross (ICRC), and NGO personnel, installations and equipment;
- mine clearing;
- assistance in refugee repatriation; and,
- "other functions as may be authorized by the Security Council."

The disarmament provisions were based on an undertaking made by the faction leaders at a meeting in Addis Ababa in early January.[40] The provision for the protection of UN and NGO personnel contains the added specific authorization for the use of "such forceful action as may be required to neutralize armed elements that attack, or threaten to attack, such facilities and personnel, pending the establishment of a new Somali police force which can assume this responsibility."[41] The third section deals exclusively with financial and administration issues.

The day after the passage of the resolution, fifteen faction leaders reached agreement on the broad outlines of a national reconciliation process.[42] The United Nations embraced the Addis Ababa Accords, named for the location of their signing, as the basis for moving ahead. Three days later, the factions signed another agreement that addressed how members of a transnational council (TNC) would be chosen. The procedures agreed to in this arrangement differ from those agreed to in the Addis Ababa Accords. The United Nations, however, stuck to its support of the initial accords without acknowledging those signed on 30 March even though the same group of faction leaders had reached the second agreement and the procedures agreed represented a completely different approach to the TNC set-up. This, in conjunction with the passage of Resolution 814 in advance of an agreement among the factions, encouraged the view that the United Nations was seeking to impose its own political solution on the Somalis.

THE ARREST MANDATE

The situation within Somalia did not improve after the UNITAF–UNOSOM II transition in May 1993. There was trouble with virtually every aspect of the mandate. The issue of a secure environment was the most problematic. After the handover to UNOSOM II the security situation deteriorated and there were an increasing number of incidents between UN troops and Somali gunmen. On 5

June 1993, after the first ever arms inspection carried out by UNOSOM II troops, Pakistani troops were attacked in two different locations in Mogadishu, resulting in the death of twenty-four soldiers.[43]

In response to this incident, the next day the Security Council unanimously approved a resolution that in strongly condemning "the unprovoked armed attacks," reaffirmed:

that the secretary-general is authorized under resolution 814 [establishing UNOSOM II] to take all necessary measures against all those responsible for the armed attacks . . . including those responsible for publicly inciting such attacks, to establish the effective authority of UNOSOM II throughout Somalia, including to secure the investigation of their actions and their arrest and detention for prosecution, trial and punishment.[44]

The tracking down and arrest of "those responsible" was, therefore, added as another task to the UNOSOM II mandate. The resolution asked the secretary-general to "urgently inquire into the incident, with particular emphasis on the role of those factional leaders involved." The Security Council also reemphasized the importance of disarmament and "of neutralizing radio broadcasting systems" contributing to the violence and attacks on UN troops. In view of the attacks, the Security Council also urged states to contribute "on an emergency basis" military equipment and support, especially in the form of tanks and attack helicopters in order to give UNOSOM II troops a better capability to "confront and deter" armed attacks. The resolution brought about a major shift in the UNOSOM II operation and its implementation brought about a new emphasis on the use of force.

The Security Council did not make any further changes to the mandate for the rest of the year. The situation within Somalia did not improve during that time period and international commitment quickly began to wear thin. UNOSOM II troops had difficulty implementing their mandate and attacks against them by various Somalia militias persisted and strengthened. In October, a raid by U.S. troops, who were not under UN command but were in Somalia to pursue the mandate to arrest Aidid, resulted in a vicious firefight. Eighteen U.S. soldiers were killed, seventy-three were wounded, and one was detained by Somali fighters. Under the glare of television cameras, one of the dead soldiers was dragged through the streets in victory by groups of Somalis. The overall effect was to bring an effective, though not immediate, end to the U.S. commitment to the UNOSOM II effort. With the U.S. withdrawal from the mission on the cards, other states also announced their intention to withdraw.

In this context, in January 1994 the secretary-general reviewed the UNOSOM II mission. Noting that "there are unmistakable signs of fatigue among the international community,"[45] he advocated a scaling back of the UNOSOM mandate to bring it into line with the likely military support available from member states. The mandate remained multifaceted and included the basic elements initially authorized. The provision for the use of force was not eliminated. However, the secretary-general suggested that UNOSOM II would "not use coercive methods but would rely on the cooperation of the Somali parties" except in protecting itself. The Security Council approved the secretary-general's scaled down approach in Resolution 897. UNOSOM II would still act under Chapter VII,[46] but the use of forceful means would no longer be used in relation to disarmament and would be primarily reserved for force protection.

Through the rest of the year, the UNOSOM II mandate was maintained in a holding pattern that awaited the inevitable winding down of the mission.[47] On 4 November 1994, the Security Council, "[r]ecognizing that the lack of progress in the Somali peace process and in national reconciliation, in particular the lack of sufficient cooperation from the Somali parties over security issues, has fundamentally undermined the United Nations objectives in Somalia and, in these circumstances, continuation of UNOSOM II beyond March 1995 cannot be justified,"[48] extended the UNOSOM II mandate one more time, until 31 March 1995, maintaining the Chapter VII provision and calling for a "secure and orderly" withdrawal. UNOSOM II forces were specifically authorized "to take those actions necessary to protect the UNOSOM II mission and the withdrawal of UNOSOM II personnel and assets, and to the extent that the Force Commander deems it practicable and consistent, in the context of withdrawal, to protect personnel of relief organizations."[49]

CHARTER BASIS

Unlike the Security Council and secretary-general approach in the Congo, but like the mandate for Bosnia, the Security Council and the secretary-general did not cite any specific charter articles in relation to the mandate and its development. Clearly, the initial determination that a threat to international peace and security existed related to Article 39 and provided the basis for the use of Chapter VII. In authorizing the UNITAF mission, the Security Council found that the crisis in Somalia was of such a magnitude that the situation constituted a threat to international peace and security. Along with the sheer scale of the humanitarian problem, the particular combination of a lack of a viable government, the level of violence, and the double frustration of thwarted peacekeeping efforts and humanitarian aid deliveries contributed to the determination that a threat to international peace and security existed. In transitioning to UNOSOM II, the Security Council accepted the secretary-general's argument that the situation required a continuation of Chapter VII authorization, and there was relatively little debate about whether or not the Chapter VII authorization was necessary.

But the creation of UNITAF was due, in the first instance, to the offer of the United States to undertake a military operation. A Chapter VII authorization was needed to make such an operation possible under the auspices of the United Nations. Although there was widespread acceptance of the Security Council view that the situation had become "intolerable,"[50] the exact link to international peace and security is somewhat controversial. Under the terms of the charter, the criterion for deciding when a situation threatens international peace and security is simply a decision by the Security Council that such a threat exists. The Security Council's decision that Somalia represented a threat to international peace and security reveals the power inherent in Chapter VII. If the Security Council says that a situation is a threat to international peace and security, then the international peace and security mechanisms of the charter can be brought to bear on that situation regardless of the specific nature of the situation.

III. THE USE OF FORCE

RULES OF ENGAGEMENT

The rules of engagement (ROE) for the UNITAF operation reflected the Chapter VII environment and the primary goal of establishing a secure environment. They applied to all of the countries participating in UNITAF. The ROE were established by CENTCOM officials, the U.S. command in charge of the operation, using CENTCOM peacetime ROE as a base. These were modified to take into account the abundance of weapons in the control of unstable persons or groups in Somalia and the need to create a secure environment.[51]

Crew served weapons are considered a threat to UNITAF forces and the relief effort whether or not the crew demonstrates hostile intent. Commanders are authorized to use all necessary force to confiscate and demilitarize crew served weapons in their areas of operations. If an armed individual or weapons crew demonstrates hostile intentions, they may be engaged with deadly force. . . . Within areas under the control of UNITAF Forces, armed individuals may be considered a threat to UNITAF and the relief effort whether or not the individual demonstrates hostile intent. Commanders are authorized to use all necessary force to disarm individuals in areas under the control of UNITAF. Absent a hostile or criminal act, individuals and associated vehicles will be released after any weapons are removed/demilitarized.[52]

With respect to weaponry, therefore, the basic ROE policy amounted to implementing four "nos"—no technicals (trucks with mounted weapons), no banditry, no roadblocks, and no visible weapons[53]—an approach that created security by eliminating weapons from open display. Beyond self-defense, a minimum and proportionate use of force could be used in responding to attacks or threat of attacks. The ROE card given to all soldiers stressed that "the United States is not at war," all persons were to be treated with dignity and respect, minimum force should be used in carrying out the mission, and that soldiers "always be prepared to act in self-defense."[54]

In the outcome, a minimum of force was used. UNITAF officials made a determined effort to get the ground rules publicized and to ensure that they were well understood by the faction leaders.[55] Soldiers generally approached individuals and crew-served vehicles without using force and disarmed them with little trouble. Within a short period of time, weapons and technical vehicles were not carried or operated openly in the streets of Mogadishu.

These same ROE were maintained by UNOSOM II when it took over in May 1993. Almost as soon as the transition occurred, however, the security situation in Mogadishu began to deteriorate. This prompted Lieutenant General Çevik Bir, the UNOSOM II commander, to issue Fragmentary Order 39. This order amended the ROE to allow for the use of force on a much broader basis. Specifically, "organized, armed militias, technicals and other crew-served weapons are considered a threat to UNOSOM Forces and may be engaged without provocation." This marked a change from the previous ROE where "deadly force" was authorized against crew-served weapons only when they demonstrated hostile intent. In addition, the fragmentary order allowed for air attacks on "'armed Somalis in vehicles moving from known militia areas' at night, after obtaining approval from the Quick Reaction Force Commander."[56]

MANDATE IMPLEMENTATION—UNITAF

On 9 December 1992, UNITAF troops made a successful, unopposed landing on the beaches at Mogadishu. The operation plan had four phases: establishing a base in Mogadishu, including gaining control of the ports and airport; moving inland, and securing areas there; further expansion, especially to Kismayo; and finally, handing over the operation to the follow-on operation. The unopposed landing characterized the general reception for the mission. There were relatively few instances where force was used as UNITAF troops sought to establish themselves in Mogadishu. By 28 December, ahead of schedule, the first two phases of the operation were complete. By mid-January UNITAF officials reported to the Security Council that it was time to begin preparation for the transition back to UNOSOM.[57]

Disagreeing about Disarmament

Almost from the moment the UNITAF mandate was passed, the United States and the secretary-general disagreed about whether or not the disarmament of armed Somali factions was a mandate task. The secretary-general felt that disarmament was a fundamental aspect of the mandate, represented by the call for a secure environment and the establishment of a cease-fire. The U.S. attitude was that disarmament was a secondary, operational decision to be made by the field commander rather than a fundamental part of the mandate. A number of accounts exist as to what happened during the initial discussions between the secretary-general and U.S. representatives about the mandate for the mission but none of them provide any clear indication as to the source of the problem.[58] Regardless of what was said or even agreed to, it is evident that there was never a clear understanding between the two parties as to the whether or not disarming the factions was part of the mandate.

The UNITAF policy of no visible weapons provided a kind of de facto disarmament but only by putting the weapons out of sight.[59] This was not what the secretary-general had in mind. In his initial letter to the Security Council outlining the possible options for action, the secretary-general stated that one of the objectives of an operation using force should be to ensure "that the current violence against the international relief effort was brought to an end. To achieve this, it would be necessary for at least the heavy weapons of the organized factions to be neutralized and brought under international control and for the irregular forces and gangs to be disarmed."[60]

This became a consistent theme with the secretary-general. Nonetheless, UNITAF command and U.S. policymakers remained steadfast in refusing to undertake such a broad and definitive approach to the issue, arguing that in any case the equipment and personnel requirements for such a mission exceeded their capabilities. For example, Brigadier General Anthony Zinni, the UNITAF deputy for operations, stated that a broader disarmament policy would be costly. "You would take a lot of casualties, and you would kill a lot of Somalis, and you would be in a running gun battle continuously, especially in places like Mogadishu." [61] In the end, the U.S. position was the one that won out, not because the U.S. argument convinced the secretary-general but because the bottom line was that the United States, not the secretary-general, was in charge of the operation.

There is considerable debate about whether or not a serious disarmament effort would have made a difference to the situation in Somalia in the long term. In retrospect, there is certainly agreement that the UNITAF operation provided the only window of opportunity for disarmament to be carried out.

A Secure Environment

The dispute over disarmament was at the heart of problems associated with the transition between UNITAF and UNOSOM II. The United States, from the very beginning of the operation, was clear about its belief that UNITAF should be short term—dealing with the worst elements of the humanitarian crisis and then handing the operation back to the United Nations.[62] The secretary-general argued that a transition to UNOSOM II could not be considered until the secure environment aspect of the mandate was fulfilled and that that required the kind of disarmament he had always understood to be part of the mandate. In addition, the secretary-general wanted the operation to deal with all of Somalia rather than just the southern portion of the country dealt with by UNITAF troops. In his March 1993 report outlining a possible mandate for the UNOSOM II mission the secretary-general wrote that "[i]t is clear to me that the effort undertaken by UNITAF to establish a secure environment in Somalia is far from complete."[63]

The United States, however, was determined to end the UNITAF mission. In part, this was a function of the ingrained U.S. desire to avoid any situation that might turn into a Vietnam-like quagmire for U.S. troops. In part, it was driven by the Bush administration's commitment to the incoming William Clinton administration that U.S. troops would be in and out quickly, thereby not saddling the new administration with a long-term military commitment it did not make. The combination of U.S.–UNITAF determination to keep the mission short and the secretary-general's belief that it was too soon to consider a transition meant that the UN was ill-prepared to take on the UNOSOM II mandate when the time came, especially one as broadly based as authorized in Resolution 814.

UNOSOM II—Force and Disarmament

The formal transition from UNITAF to UNOSOM II occurred on 4 May 1993. Although the formal transition was anticipated, the full departure of the final elements of the UNITAF force was not.[64] The speed of the transition, when it occurred, and the lack of extensive prior planning meant that UNOSOM II began the mission scrambling to find its feet and waiting for resources, including troop contributions, with only a basic plan for mandate implementation. Even before UNITAF drew to a close, the security situation in Somalia had become more tenuous with increasing clashes between militia and UNITAF troops. Because of a lack of sufficient military support when UNOSOM II began, activities such as patrols in Mogadishu were scaled back. The local militias responded accordingly, taking advantage of the situation.[65]

Most of those involved in the operation fully expected that the local militias would very quickly try to test the strength and resolve of the UNOSOM II mission. That test was not long in coming. On 6 May, Colonel Omar Jess, an ally of Aidid, tried to retake Kismayo and was pushed back by UNOSOM II troops.[66] The conflict and the loss by Colonel Jess entrenched an already strong anti–UN attitude in Aidid and his followers. This anti–UN feeling was reinforced by the UNOSOM II political approach.[67]

During this time, broadcasts by Radio Mogadishu, controlled by Aidid, became more virulent and more directed to inciting violence against UN troops. UNOSOM II officials seriously considered the possibility of closing down Radio Mogadishu, something that became generally known outside of UNOSOM II circles. At the same time, by the end of May, planning was in motion for UNOSOM II troops to begin implementing the disarmament aspects of the mandate. On 4 June, UNOSOM II personnel delivered an inspection notice to representatives of the Somali National Alliance (SNA). The inspections were to be of authorized weapons storage sites associated with Radio Mogadishu property. There are different versions of the circumstances relating to the delivery of the notice. Two commissions of enquiry, established later, determined some basic facts.[68] The notice was delivered on the Islamic day of rest and was received by a SNA member, who responded that the SNA would need time to respond and if the inspection went ahead as planned it would mean war. This response was not communicated back to the Pakistani forces planning on carrying out the inspection.[69]

The inspection began early on the morning of 5 June and was carried out successfully. On returning from the inspection site (which was also the site of Radio Mogadishu), the Pakistani troops were ambushed. Reinforcements coming from UNOSOM II headquarters were also attacked. At about the same time, other Pakistani troops manning a feeding point were attacked. Troops sent to their aid were attacked en route. In an initial attempt to assist, Italian troops in attack helicopters mistakenly shot and wounded three Pakistani soldiers. The battles ended early that afternoon leaving twenty-four Pakistani soldiers dead, and fifty-seven wounded; one Italian and three U.S. soldiers were also wounded.

The battles were a major turning point for the UNOSOM II operation. The next day, the Security Council passed Resolution 837 calling for the arrest of those responsible. General Aidid was not directly named in the resolution, pending a determination as to who was involved, although this was for all intents and purposes treated as a formality, at least by the media. On 17 June, Admiral Jonathon Howe, special representative of the secretary-general publicly named Aidid as responsible and issued an arrest warrant.[70]

The Summer Military Campaign

The events of 6 June and the decisions made in response marked the beginning of a more determined proactive use of force by UNOSOM II troops.[71] Within UNOSOM II circles, the attack on the Pakistanis created a strong sense that such actions could not go unpunished and generated a new determination to carry out the disarmament measures authorized in Resolution 814 as a way of preventing further such actions. Technically, the military campaign initiated by UNOSOM II was oriented to the disarmament aspects of the mandate with the arrest of Aidid as a secondary objective.[72] In practice, however, these two different objectives were hard to keep separate, especially in the media, which reported on the hunt for Aidid very closely.

UNOSOM II military action began on 12 June with a combined air and ground attack against three weapons sites, and sites associated with Radio Mogadishu.[73] In response, the next day two Somali demonstrations against UNOSOM II took place. The demonstrations degenerated into violence when Pakistani troops fired into the Somali crowd.[74] Further air and ground attacks against weapons targets continued over the next couple of days with the primary objective of initiating the disarmament process and neutralizing all heavy weapons.[75] On 17 June, the day that Admiral Howe announced that UNOSOM II was formally seeking to apprehend Aidid, Moroccan, Pakistani, Italian and American UNOSOM II troops undertook a well-rehearsed (and, therefore, well-observed) cordon and search operation in an SNA enclave. The Moroccan troops came under attack during the operation by Somalis who used women and children as human shields. The resulting battles lasted several hours. Five Moroccan soldiers were killed, including the battalion commander, and forty were wounded.[76] This first week of attack and counterattack set the tone for the rest of the summer. Aidid remained elusive and the stepped-up UN military activities contributed to resentment of the United Nations among Mogadishu residents rather than generating support for the actions taken against Aidid.

Command and Control

Serious command and control issues further complicated the UN military efforts. As part of the U.S. commitment to UNOSOM II (in addition to the naming of Admiral Howe as special representative of the secretary-general), the deputy force commander of UNOSOM II was Major General Thomas Montgomery of the United States. Along with his UN duties, General Montgomery also acted as commander of the U.S. Quick Reaction Force (QRF). Comprising eleven hundred and fifty troops, the QRF was available to support UNOSOM II activities but remained solely under U.S., not UN, command and was, therefore, not responsible to General Bir, the overall commander of the UNOSOM II operation.[77] Three thousand U.S. logistics personnel also supported the UNOSOM II mission and operated under the UNOSOM II command.[78]

The UNOSOM II command was also beset by more than the usual problems associated with a multinational command.[79] In spite of the Chapter VII authorization of the operation, some national contingents participated in the operation only on the basis of being involved in implementing the assistance tasks—those where force would not be used. In addition, a number of contingents would not carry out orders from General Bir before checking them through their own national commands at home. This had a negative effect on the "unity of effort" aspect of the operation and also created serious time constraint problems in situations where decisions had to be made quickly. In particular, the Italian contingent's disagreement with the forceful approach of UNOSOM II policy led to a deliberate refusal to carry out orders it received from General Bir and created a serious internal controversy for the operation, prompting the UN command to ask that the Italian commander be sent home. The problem was eventually resolved without sending the Italian commander home, but it revealed some serious internal strains in the operation and the controversy was widely covered in the press.[80]

Turning Points

On 12 July, QRF troops attacked Abdi House, considered a SNA command and control center, where it was believed a number of militia leaders were meeting. The raid was carried out without prior consultation with UNOSOM II headquarters and other UNOSOM II troop contributors and, in contrast to previous military activities, without prior warnings to the local population. UNOSOM II estimates are that twenty adult Somali males were killed, while ICRC estimates put the number at fifty-four.[81] Four journalists reporting on the raid were killed by Somalis when they arrived at the scene.

Prior to the raid, the heavy UN emphasis on military tactics had been generating criticism from inside and outside the operation, not just because of the use of force but also because the military raids required large numbers of personnel so that fewer were available for humanitarian and other tasks.[82] In addition, the distinction between activities carried out by the United Nations as opposed to those carried out by the United States was often obscured in press coverage and there was a sense that if UNOSOM II was not, in fact, being run by the United States it was certainly being dominated by it. The 12 July raid brought some of these brewing tensions to the surface, threatening an already tenuous sense of unity within the operation at precisely the time when the UNOSOM II operation was experiencing its highest level of military activity.[83]

After the 12 July raid, the impetus for action switched to the SNA militias who engaged in a variety of attacks against UN and U.S. forces. The 12 July raid

pushed the SNA militias from a general anti–UN-U.S. posture to a very determined one. Attitudes among the general Somali population also changed. "The
change in the atmosphere was evident; the effect of the raid irrevocable. Any
question of SNA accommodation with the United States or United Nations was
overtaken by the impact of the carefully planned attack, which affected Somali
attitudes as much as the attack on the Pakistanis had influenced attitudes within
UNOSOM."[84]

In response to this change in the environment, the posture and activities of the
UNOSOM II operation became defensive in their orientation; humanitarian
tasks took second place, and many NGOs left the city because of the high tension and anticipation of more violence. Nonetheless, the secretary-general remained determined about the objectives of UNOSOM II. Writing shortly after
the QRF raid on Abdi House, the secretary-general stated:

The ambushing of UNOSOM personnel by such elements on 5 June and on subsequent
occasions left UNOSOM no choice but to take forceful action to effect the disarming
required. . . . The exploitation of such actions to provoke hostilities towards UNOSOM . .
. has led to loss of life for which the responsibility rests squarely with the faction leaders,
in particular Mohammed Farah Aidid. I am conscious of the feeling in some quarters that
UNOSOM is deviating from its primary task of ensuring the safe distribution of humanitarian assistance, rehabilitation and reconstruction of Somalia, and is concentrating dis-
proportionate efforts and resources in military operations. I know that some of this criticism is well motivated by good intentions. However, the international community has
known from the beginning that effective disarmament of all the factions and warlords is
conditio sine qua non for other aspects of UNOSOM's mandate, be they political, civil,
humanitarian, rehabilitation or reconstruction.[85]

Discontent about the nature of the mission was also brewing within the United
States, especially in the U.S. Congress.[86] When the mandate for the arrest of
"those responsible" was originally authorized in June, Admiral Howe and General Montgomery sent a request to the Pentagon asking for special forces, helicopters, and tanks to assist in the added military tasks. The United States did
send some attack helicopters, but the Clinton administration denied the rest of
the request and continued to deny pleas from the field throughout the summer.[87]
The main reason for the denial was the fear that sending more military assets to
Somalia, especially tanks, would look like the United States was becoming more
deeply involved in Somalia and resurrect fears that Somalia would become a
quagmire for U.S. forces.[88]

During August, two remote-controlled mine detonations used against U.S.
troops brought about a change in U.S. policy.[89] After the second attack, on 22
August, President Clinton ordered that Howe and Montgomery's request for
special forces be fulfilled. The addition of Delta Force commandos and U.S.
Army Rangers, together named Task Force Ranger, added new complications to
the already difficult command and control arrangements. The task force was
under a separate chain of command that extended through the commander of
U.S. special operations to CENTCOM.[90] Task Force Ranger's main objective
was the arrest of Aidid and other top SNA leaders.

The arrival of the special forces had a twofold effect, simultaneously reinforcing the focus on the arrest of Aidid and the perception that the UNOSOM II operation was essentially being run by the US. At the same time, SNA militias stepped up their attacks on U.S. and UNOSOM II forces. There were now daily attacks of one kind or another against UNOSOM II troops who were, of necessity, very much in a defensive posture.[91]

The Olympia Hotel Raid

The pivotal event for UNOSOM II occurred on 3 October 1993 when Task Force Ranger conducted a raid on the Olympia Hotel believing that a meeting of top Aidid advisors was taking place there. The raid on the hotel began at 3:45 that afternoon. Twenty-four people were detained. As the operation was drawing to a close a Black Hawk helicopter was shot down. U.S. troops, by helicopter and by ground, attempted to rescue those in the downed helicopter and came under heavy fire themselves.[92] The resulting battle between Somalia militia and U.S. and then UN troops lasted through the night. Since no prior notification had been given of the raid, no reinforcements had been readied in advance. Reinforcements from UNOSOM II troops, therefore, took some time to arrive and were ill prepared for the scale of fighting that they had to face.[93]

In total, eighteen U.S. soldiers and one Malaysian soldier were killed, and seventy-three U.S. soldiers were wounded. Estimates of the number of Somali dead and injured vary widely from three hundred to five hundred killed, and seven hundred wounded. Triumphant crowds dragged the body of one U.S. soldier through the streets of Mogadishu. Television crews captured the event on film and the film footage was broadcast widely by the international media. One U.S. soldier was taken hostage and pictures of him in captivity became a feature of international media attention in the days that followed.

The battle had a profound effect on the UNOSOM II mission. The most immediate impact was President Clinton's announcement, a few days later, that he would be augmenting U.S. forces in Somalia but that all U.S. forces would be withdrawn from Somalia within six months, by 31 March 1994. [94] Clinton also instructed U.S. forces to end the hunt for Aidid, bringing an end to that aspect of the mission, although there was no formal UN revocation of that aspect of the Security Council mandate. [95] The U.S. announcement meant the end of a number of other troop-contributors' commitments whose involvement was directly linked to the involvement of the United States, leaving UNOSOM II looking at a future of dramatically reduced troop contributions.[96] The announcement was also a major psychological blow for those involved in the operation. For them it seemed that the effective end of the operation was coming just at a point when they felt they were on the verge of turning things around.[97] Later, UNOSOM II officials changed their policy on Aidid, seeking once again to deal with him, as a local leader rather than a criminal, as a way of ensuring a safe and smooth withdrawal and in order try to put some form of political reconciliation process back in motion.[98]

As it became clear that the proactive use of force by UNOSOM II troops was over, SNA and other Somali militias began to react accordingly. Soon the streets of Mogadishu began to look as they had prior to UNITAF involvement—full of arms and technicals. This reinforced the UNOSOM II focus on protective self-defense. In terms of the use of force, the overriding objective became force protection rather than mandate implementation. Snipers from the Thirteenth Marine were sent to Somalia as part of the beefing up of the U.S. commitment in anticipation of withdrawal. They became a key element in ensuring UNOSOM II security until the U.S. departure, especially around UNOSOM II compounds.

By the end of October 1993 major parts of the city were off limits to U.S. forces, and no patrolling was conducted due to the increased threat. UNOSOM forces, as well as their U.S. protectors were essentially confined to their strong points and compounds, where periodic fire into the compounds, including occasional mortar rounds, was a real threat. Marine snipers . . . were placed at key intersections and in overwatch positions above the UNOSOM/U.S. Forces compounds. Snipers began to engage targets, whether or not they demonstrated a hostile act or showed hostile intent.[99]

The Security Council's authorization of a change in mandate, to an emphasis on the humanitarian aspects of the mandate, in February 1994 was simply an authorization of what had become UNOSOM II policy since October. The mandate remained a Chapter VII one but this was primarily to allow for a strong self-defense capability. UNOSOM II continued to implement various aspects of its mandate to the greatest extent possible. When UNOSOM II left Somalia on 31 March 1995, the original mandate was far from fulfilled. Somalia had no effective government and a bitter conflict continued between the Mogadishu factions. Considerable progress had been made, however, in dealing with the humanitarian situation,[100] although, as the secretary-general pointed out, without a functioning government Somalia would continue to be vulnerable to even minor emergencies.[101]

Aidid died, apparently of a heart attack, on 1 August 1996. Leadership of his faction has been taken over by his son, Hussein Aidid, a former U.S. soldier. As of November 2000, there is still no effective government in Somalia. Peace initiatives during the year led to an agreement to establish a new parliament for the first time in a decade. A number of key rebel groups, however, have remained outside of this process.

IV. ISSUES

OPERATIONAL ISSUES

Command and Control

The complicated and convoluted command and control arrangements established UNOSOM II and then added to as the mission changed provide a good example of how not to design an efficient and useful command arrangement, especially in a peace enforcement operation. The traditional problems associated with running a multinational operation were exacerbated by the separation of certain U.S. forces. This became a critical problem in situations where force was being used, as in the raid on the Olympia Hotel. Because U.S. forces gave no prior notification of their plans to UNOSOM II officials, there was no prior preparation for possible support and reinforcement from other troops.

After it was all over, the United States used the United Nations as a scapegoat. President Clinton and other key policymakers did not make it clear that the ranger operation was solely an American one, thereby insinuating that the United Nations was somehow to blame for putting U.S. soldiers in harm's way. While it may have been politically expedient to do so at the time, administration officials reinforced an already deep-seated mistrust of the United Nations within the U.S. Congress, with considerable long-range implications for future UN operations.[102]

Overdependence on the United States

These problems are related to the fact that the United Nations is heavily dependent on the United States for political and physical resources. One of the effects of the end of the cold war has been that the United States has taken on the role as a leading major power in the Security Council. In simple resource terms, this is a fact of life for the United Nations. It has had the effect, however, of creating a kind of overdependence on the United States when the United Nations is considering major operations. This was the case with respect to the UN operations in Somalia.

A heavy reliance on a country that has taken on the bulk of the operation creates two tracks of thinking and decision making when it comes to planning and implementation. The United Nations tends to give in, or at least not to insist on alternative options, on issues such as command and control, or decisions such as the timing of the UNITAF–UNOSOM II transition, because of an overwhelming need to keep the United States in the picture. With respect to the use of force, this means that U.S. issues become UN issues. As evidenced by the events surrounding the Olympia Hotel raid, the UN thus becomes subject to the vicissitudes of U.S. politics about the involvement of U.S. troops overseas.

The decision to subcontract the UNITAF operation to the United States, and then to accept heavy U.S. involvement in and control of the UNOSOM II operation in order to keep U.S. resources involved also created other problems. For example, because of UN resistance to the end of the UNITAF operation and the U.S. insistence on leaving, the planning for the transition from UNITAF to UNOSOM II lagged far behind what was needed. The sudden, and to some surprising withdrawal of the remaining UNITAF forces on 4 May 1993 left the UNOSOM II command scrambling. A formal transfer of command had not been organized and only a small proportion of the personnel and equipment required for the mission had arrived. The mission began, therefore, in something of a state of disarray at precisely the time that it most needed to present a united coherent front.

MANDATE ISSUES

The Mixing of Political and Military Goals

The military and political goals of the UNITAF mission were clear—the need to deal with the massive humanitarian crisis and the use of force to create a secure environment in which that was possible. Under the UNOSOM II mandate, the specific political goals were less clear. As a result of the nature of the situation, the political objectives of the mission were of a very general nature. Unlike other operations, such as Cambodia and Central America, there was no formal agreement or understanding that the UN mission was seeking to implement. The UNOSOM II mandate was tied to the agreements made by faction leaders at Addis Ababa, but only loosely. The fact that the Security Council authorized Resolution 814 only just prior to the signing of new accords at Addis Ababa and that it did not recognize the agreements made three days later, after the end of the UN–sponsored part of the meeting, is symbolic of the looseness of that connection.

The absence of a clear set of political goals for the United Nations and the parties to the conflict contributed to an intertwining of the political and military aspects of the mission, making it possible for the military to supersede the political. In principle, the military objectives of the mission are driven by the mandate of the mission with the former serving the latter. In practice, however, this distinction was difficult to implement in the context of a broad assistance mandate aimed at facilitating political reconciliation and nation-building. Initially, in UNOSOM II, the use of force, if necessary, was directed to the disarmament, protection, and refugee resettlement aspects of the mandate. Ideally, the disarmament provisions would be carried out voluntarily. Given the ongoing conflict and lack of political progress, this proved to be very much an ideal. For those on the receiving end, therefore, it was the same entity coercively enforcing weapons inspections and seizures, and later arresting people, on the one hand, and facilitating political reconciliation on the other. This encouraged a perception within Somalia that the United Nations was working to enforce a political solution on the country. Indeed, what was happening was a shift towards using military methods to bring about political results. The secretary-general's insistence, for example, that disarmament, voluntary or otherwise, would lead to the creation of conditions "of peace, stability, law and order"[103] gives an indication of how UN thinking was drifting this way.

Impartiality

A consequence of this mixing of military and political goals was the creation of problems with impartiality. Impartiality is critical to a peace enforcement operation. Even before the 5 June attacks the impartiality of the UNOSOM II mission vis à vis Aidid and the SNA was already in question.[104] But any remaining sense of UNOSOM II impartiality, for those on the ground, ended when the Security Council passed the mandate to arrest "those responsible" and when

UNOSOM II officials named Aidid as the target. The commission that investigated the attacks against UNOSOM II troops said that the arrest mandate "resulted in a virtual war situation between UNOSOM II and the SNA."[105] After the beginning of July, when the SNA began to take the military initiative, UNOSOM II orders referred to "enemy forces," a change from the previous term of "hostile forces."[106] The arrest mandate added another coercive element to the mix. Military efforts to arrest Aidid coincided with disarmament efforts, which often involved the use of force, contributing to perceptions that UNOSOM II was using force to bring about its own desired outcome to the conflict. With the loss of the perception of impartiality UNOSOM II also lost its ability to play a credible role in the political process. The sequence of armed clashes that followed and the resulting retreat to defense-oriented activities at the expense of mandate objectives were a result of and evidence of that change.

NOTES

1. For descriptions of the different colonial experiences, see Robert L. Hess, *Italian Colonialism in Somalia* (Chicago: University of Chicago Press, 1996); E. Sylvia Parkhurst, *Ex-Italian Somaliland* (New York: Greenwood, 1951); E. A. Bayne, *Four Ways of Politics* (New York: American Universities Field Staff, 1965); and United Kingdom Ministry of Information, *The First to be Freed: The Record of British Military Administration in Eritrea and Somalia, 1941–1943* (London: His Majesty's Stationery Office, 1944).

2. For overviews of this time period, see especially Helen Chapin Metz, ed., *Somalia: A Country Study*, (Washington D.C.: Federal Research Division, Library of Congress, 1993); and Ian M. Lewis, *A Pastoral Democracy* (London: Oxford University Press, 1982); also see Rakiya Omaar, "Somalia: At War with Itself," *Current History* (May 1992): 230–234; Said Y. Abdi, "Decolonization in the Horn and the Outcome of Somali Aspirations for self-determination," in *The Decolonization of Africa: Southern Africa and the Horn of Africa* (Paris: United Nations Educational, Scientific, and Cultural Organization, 1981).

3. Mohammed Ayoob, *The Horn of Africa: Regional Conflict and Super Power Involvement*, Canberra Papers on Strategy and Defence, no. 18 (Canberra: Australian National University, 1978); and Marina Ottaway, *Soviet and American Influence in the Horn of Africa* (New York: Praeger, 1982).

4. For descriptions of the formation of the various rebel groups see Andre Tulumello, "Rethinking Somalia's Clanism," *Harvard Human Rights Journal* 6 (Spring 1993): 230–234; Omaar, "Somalia,"; and John Markakis, *National and Class Conflict in the Horn of Africa* (Cambridge: Cambridge University Press, 1987). Also see UNIDIR, *Managing Arms in Peace Processes: Somalia* (Geneva: United Nations, 1995, UNIDIR 95/30) especially table 1.2, 10–11.

5. See Said Samatar, "Somalia: A Nation in Turmoil," *A Minority Rights Group Report* (August 1991): 19–20. Also see Africa Watch, *A Government at War with its Own People: Testimonies about the Killings and the Conflict in the North* (New York: Africa Watch, 1990); and Metz, *Somalia*, 50–52.

6. The level of arms within Somalia was massive and had been for years. The Horn of Africa region itself was also full of arms and Somalia's border was extremely porous and

completely unmonitored, as was its coastline. For an overview of the arms situation, see the section "Foreign Military Assistance" in Metz, *Somalia*, 208–214.

7. There are a number of accounts of this time period. For the famine-refugee problem, see Jeffrey Clark, *Famine in Somalia and the International Response: Collective Failure*, Issue Paper (Washington D.C.: U.S. Committee for Refugees, November 1992); and Steve Hansch et al. *Lives Lost, Lives Saved: Excess Mortality and the Impact of Health Interventions in the Somalia Emergency* (Washington D.C.: Refugee Policy Group, November 1994).

8. For a good description of the NGO experience during this time, see John G. Sommer, *Hope Restored? Humanitarian Aid in Somalia 1990–1994*, (Washington D.C.: Refugee Policy Group, November 1994). The absence of UN agencies is a particular source of criticism in the debate about what went wrong in the early stages of the crisis. In particular, the deliberate decision of the United Nations Development Program (UNDP) to stay out of Somalia on the grounds that it was not a situation that offered much prospect for "development" has generated considerable criticism. UNDP is traditionally the lead UN agency in these situations and would have provided the mechanism for sending warning signals about the extent of the problem and activating stronger international involvement. Instead, ICRC and other NGOs found themselves having to develop a strategy to try to draw international attention to the crisis. Their success in that regard exceeded their expectations to such an extent that some of those involved later became the chief critics of the nature and extent of the international response.

9. Letter dated 27 December 1991 from the Secretary-General to the President of the Security Council.

10. This visit has been criticized as too long in coming, coming only as a result of pressure from ICRC and other organizations, and when it did occur Jonah was said to have been poorly prepared for what he faced. See Omaar, *"Somalia,"* 233; and Jonathan Stevenson, "Hope Restored in Somalia?" *Foreign Policy* no. 91 (Summer 1993): 144.

11. S/23445, 20 January 1992.

12. The cease-fire agreement is reprinted in S/23693, Annex 3, 11 March 1992.

13. S/23829, 21 April 1992, para. 27–29.

14. "Letter of 27 March 1992 from General Mohammed Farah Aidid, Chairman of the United Somali Congress, to the United Nations," and "Letter of 28 March 1992 from Ali Mahdi Mohamed, Interim President of Somalia, to the United Nations," S/23829, Annex 1, 21 April 1992.

15. S/24179, 25 June 1992.

16. S/24343, 22 July 1992; and S/24480, 24 August 1992.

17. S/24343, 22 July 1992, para. 55.

18. S/24480, 24 August 1992, para. 11–12.

19. S/24451, 12 August 1992.

20. Jane Perlez, "Food Piling up in Somali Port As Many Starve," *New York Times*, 2 November 1992, 1, A8; and S/24859, 27 November 1992, 3. Also see the UN concept of operations, Document FA000323, Commission of Inquiry into the Deployment of Canadian Forces to Somalia, *Information Legacy, A Compendium of Source Material from the Commission of Inquiry into the Deployment of Canadian Forces to Somalia*, (Ottawa: Government of Canada, 1997) [hereafter cited as *Information Legacy*].

21. Mohamed M. Sahnoun, "Prevention in Conflict Resolution: The Case of Somalia," *Irish Studies in International Affairs* 5 (1994): 11.

22. In particular, the secretary-general's recommendation to deploy a further three thousand troops was approved by the Security Council on 28 August 1992, just after Sahnoun managed to get Aidid's agreement to the initial five hundred. This apparently occurred without any prior consultation or even notification to the UNOSOM staff in Somalia. Mohamed Sahnoun, *Somalia: The Missed Opportunities* (Washington D.C.:

United States Institute for Peace, 1994), especially 37–41. Also see Sahnoun, "Prevention in Conflict Resolution."

23. Jane Perlez, "Top UN Relief Official in Somalia Quits over Dispute," *New York Times*, 28 October 1992, A6. "UN Envoy to Somalia Says His Ouster is Official," *New York Times*, 30 October 1992, A7; and "Aide's Departure another Blow to UN in Somalia," *New York Times*, 31 October 1992, 2. For a discussion of Sahnoun's accomplishments, see Stevenson, "Hope Restored in Somalia?" Also see John L. Hirsch, and Robert B. Oakley, *Somalia and Operation Restore Hope* (Washington D.C.: United States Institute for Peace, 1995), 29–31.

24. An October 1992 assessment of the situation found that "[a]lmost one million Somalis are on the brink of death by starvation and disease, and millions more may die if urgent assistance is not forthcoming. Furthermore, hundreds of thousands of Somalis may be forced to join the one million Somali refugees who have already fled. . . . Over the past months conditions in many parts of Somalia have continued to deteriorate exponentially. Against this grim backdrop of urgent needs and an escalating death rate from starvation and disease, relief efforts continue to be impeded by looting and diversion of relief supplies. The onset of the rains in many places has further exacerbated a desperate situation. Unless humanitarian assistance programmes are accelerated as many as 250,000 Somalis may die before the end of this year." "100-Day Action Programme for Accelerated Humanitarian Assistance for Somalia," 6 October 1992, reprinted in United Nations, *the United Nations and Somalia, 1992–1996*. The United Nations Blue Book Series vol. 8 (New York: United Nations, 1996), 194–196.

25. "Letter Dated 24 November 1992 from the Secretary-General Addressed to the President of the Security Council," S/24859, 27 November 1992.

26. S/24868, 30 November 1992. For more on the U.S. decision to make the offer, see John R. Bolton, "Wrong Turn in Somalia," *Foreign Affairs* 73, no. 1 (January/February 1994): 56–66; Hirsch and Oakley, *Somalia and Operation Restore Hope*, 35–47; *A "Seamless" Transition: United States and United Nations Operations in Somalia— 1992–1993*, Parts A and B, CO9-96-1324.0, CO9-96-1325.0, Case Program, John F. Kennedy School of Government, Harvard University, 1996 [hereafter cited as *A "Seamless" Transition*].

27. S/24868, 30 November 1992.

28. Ibid.

29. Although this was the secretary-general's preferred option, it was a choice that would have required considerable effort on the part of the Secretariat. The secretary-general stated: "The Secretariat, already overstretched in managing greatly enlarged peacekeeping commitments, does not at present have the capability to command and control an enforcement operation of the size and urgency required by the present crisis in Somalia. It would therefore be necessary for the Member States contributing troops for such an operation to provide personnel not only for the headquarters in the field but also in New York, where considerable additional staff would be required." Ibid.

30. S/PV.3145, 3 December 1992, 34.

31. S/24868, 30 November 1992.

32. S/PV.3145, 3 December 1992, 36–38.

33. As quoted by F. M. Lorenz in "Law and Anarchy in Somalia," *Parameters* 23, no. 4 (Winter 1993–1994): 40 fn. 2.

34. For an example of the tone of the coverage, see "Shoot to Feed Somalia," *New York Times*, 19 November 1992; and Anthony Lewis, "Action or Death," *New York Times*, 20 November 1992.

35. An overview of the congressional response is provided by Harry Johnston and Ted Dagne, "Congress and the Somali Crisis," in Walter Clarke and Jeffrey Herbst, eds., *Learning From Somalia* (Boulder, Colo.: Westview Press, 1997), 191–204.

36. The U.S. Ambassador to Kenya, Smith Hempstone Jr., visited Somalia in the summer and wrote a now famous cable about the visit titled "A Day in Hell." The cable is said to have had a significant impact on President Bush. A U.S. relief operation, Operation Provide Relief, launched that summer, provided the United States with first-hand evidence of the scale of the problem. For a good overview of the internal U.S. decision making see *A "Seamless" Transition*, 8–12. Most top U.S. decision makers believed that President Bush would not authorize such a mission even though considerable preparatory work occurred before he agreed to the idea.

37. S/25354, 3 March 1993, para. 58.

38. Ibid., para. 91.

39. S/PV.3188, 26 March 1993, 19.

40. "Agreement on implementing the cease-fire and on modalities of disarmament," Supplement to the General Agreement signed in Addis Ababa on 8 January 1993. Reprinted in S/25168, Annex 3, 26 January 1993. The parties agreed, inter alia: to maintain control of the heavy weapons of the organized factions that will have been brought under international control pending their eventual destruction or transfer to a newly constituted national army; to the disarmament of armed elements including bandits; and to the encampment of the militias of all political movements and their eventual disarmament.

41. Ibid., para. 57 (f). Approved by Security Council Resolution 814, 26 March 1993, Section B, para. 5.

42. Addis Ababa Agreement, 27 March 1993. The document is reprinted in United Nations, *The United Nations and Somalia, 1992–1996* (New York: United Nations, 1996), 264–265.

43. "UN Demands Arrests in Ambush," *Globe and Mail*, 7 June 1993, A1; and "New Fighting Erupts in Somali Capital," *Globe and Mail*, 8 June 1993, A10. For the UN description of events, see S/26022, 1 July 1993, para. 5–12.

44. Security Council Resolution 837, 6 June 1993.

45. S/1994/12, 6 January 1994, para. 46.

46. Security Council Resolution 897, 4 February 1994.

47. Security Council Resolution 923, 31 May 1994; and Security Council Resolution 946, 30 September 1994; and Security Council Resolution 953, 31 October 1994.

48. Security Council Resolution 954, 4 November 1994.

49. Ibid.

50. In his letter to the Security Council, the secretary-general says that, in informal discussion, Security Council members "expressed the view that the situation . . . was intolerable." See S/24868, 30 November 1992.

51. The ROE were also developed within the context of the basic principles of international humanitarian law and the laws of war. See Lorenz, "Law and Anarchy in Somalia," 30.

52. *Rules of Engagement for Operation Restore Hope*, para. (10) (U), (11)(U). The ROE are widely reprinted. The full version can be found in: United States Department of the Army, *Peace Operations*, FM 100-23, 30 December 1994.

53. Kenneth Allard, *Somalia Operations: Lessons Learned* (Washington D.C.: National Defense University Press, 1995), 36.

54. The ROE card is reprinted in United States Joint Warfighting Center, *Joint Task Force Commander's Handbook for Peace Operations*, 28 February 1995, 76.

55. U.S. special envoy Robert Oakley established a Joint Security Committee that included top faction leaders and that met on an ongoing basis to discuss these types of issues. The UNITAF operation also included a strong public awareness/psyops component. The few incidents that did occur also helped drive home the point. See, for example, *A "Seamless" Transition*, 22.

56. The fragmentary order is reprinted in Col. F. M. Lorenz, "Rules of Engagement in Somalia: Were They Effective?" Staff Judge Advocate, I Marine Expeditionary Force, Camp Pendleton, California, no date. Also see, Col. F. M. Lorenz, "Forging Rules of Engagement: Lessons Learned in Operation United Shield," *Military Review* (November–December 1995): 17–25; and Allard, *Somalia Operations*, 37–38.

57. S/25126, 19 January 1993. For good detailed descriptions of the situation from a military point of view, see the situation reports of the time from the Canadian contingent in Somalia reprinted in *Information Legacy*.

58. There is some sense that disarmament was dropped from the mandate by the U.S. military. Even so, it is unclear that disarmament was ever included in the initial discussions between the US and the secretary-general. See, for example, *A "Seamless" Transition*, 14–15; and Jarat Chopra, Åge Eknes, and Toralv Norbø, *Fighting For Hope in Somalia*, Peacekeeping and Multinational Operations, no. 6 (Oslo: Norwegian Institute of International Affairs, 1995), 44–45.

59. Eventually, some weapons cantonment sites were established as a way of assisting in keeping the weapons off the street. But there was no requirement to do so and the weapons remained under the control of the factions. In Mogadishu, Mahdi's faction kept some of their heavy weapons in a cantonment site while Aidid's weapons simply disappeared. Outside Mogadishu, the situation varied depending on the location. In Baidoa, for example, UNITAF troops and community representatives agreed to measures that brought about the disarmament of local bandits associated with the Somali National Alliance. See Hirsch and Oakley, *Somalia and Operation Restore Hope*, 70. The no visible weapons policy had repercussions for NGOs and UN relief agencies who relied on security guards for protection. The weapons of these security guards were often confiscated, adding unease to an already uncertain relationship between the relief and military communities. Eventually, a registration system was established that helped but did not solve the problem.

60. S/24868, 30 November 1992.

61. Quoted in *A "Seamless" Transition*, 23.

62. Note the statement of the U.S. representative when Resolution 794 was passed: "In offering to contribute to the effort authorized by this resolution, the United States has no other objective. Once deployed, our military forces will remain in Somalia no longer than is necessary. We look forward to the early transition to an effective United Nations peace-keeping force." See S/PV.3145, 3 December 1992, 37. Also see "CDS Discussion with General Powell," document no. 810800 in *Information Legacy*.

63. S/25354, 3 March 1993, para. 58. The secretary-general was apparently profoundly strengthened in this view by his visit to Mogadishu at the beginning of January. His visit was cut short when angry demonstrations stopped a UN motorcade that included undersecretary, James Jonah. Boutros-Ghali went straight back to the airport after his first stop in Mogadishu and waited several hours before the rest of the delegation joined him. According to Elizabeth Lindenmayer, then the UN Secretariat official in charge of the Somalia operation, the visit was a "pivotal event" for the secretary-general. See, *A "Seamless" Transition*, 25. Also see Hirsch and Oakley, *Somalia and Operation Restore Hope*, 101–102.

64. The final withdrawal of troops on this day came as a complete surprise to the UN Secretariat and to many in Washington. See Hirsch and Oakley, *Somalia and Operation Restore Hope*, 112; and *A "Seamless" Transition*, 37. Elizabeth Lindenmayer recounts that on receiving the information by phone that the US troops had left Secretariat officials responded: "What do you mean the Marines have gone? How can 2,000 Marines leave just like that?"

65. See, for example, Hirsch and Oakley, *Somalia and Operation Restore Hope*, 116–117.

66. In February, UNITAF troops became involved in a struggle between Colonel Jess's forces and forces loyal to General Morgan (pro-Siad Barre). "Ultimatum Issued to Somali Warlord," *Globe and Mail*, 24 February 1993, A13. See Hirsch and Oakley, *Somalia and Operation Restore Hope*, 76–77, for an outline of events that differs from the version given by press reports at the time.

67. In particular, UNOSOM II officials' handling of a peace conference for central Somalia made Aidid feel that the UN was shutting him out of the process. See S/1994/653, 1 June 1994, para. 74–80.

68. A number of accounts of these events exist. Two "independent" analyses done for the UN provide good overviews of the sequence of events. See the report by Professor Tom Farer: S/26351, 24 August 1993; and the report of the independent commission established under Security Council Resolution 885: S/1994/653, 1 June 1994.

69. S/1994/653, 1 June 1994, para. 96–103. Also see Chopra, Eknes, and Nordbø, *Fighting for Hope in Somalia*, 95–96; and Hirsch and Oakley, *Somalia and Operation Restore Hope*, 117. Hirsch and Oakley say that a plan was, in fact, in the works for taking over the radio station.

70. Howe received considerable criticism for not authorizing the immediate arrest of Aidid, when he could have easily been picked up, and then also for actually naming Aidid and thus bringing a formal end to UNOSOM II impartiality. See *A "Seamless" Transition*, Part B, 6–8. Howe says that the public naming of Aidid was "almost inevitable."

71. Admiral Howe was virtually alone in his resistance to the military option but eventually gave in during a marathon meeting among UNOSOM II leadership. See Chopra, Eknes, and Nordbø, *Fighting for Hope in Somalia*, 97–98; Donatella Lorch, "Tension Growing in Somali Capital," *New York Times*, 9 June 1993, A13; and Douglas Jehl, "US is Sending Planes to Bolster UN in Somalia," *New York Times*, 10 June 1993, 1, A12.

72. In fact, military activities associated with attempts to arrest Aidid and other SNA leaders occurred far less than disarmament-oriented missions. See S/1994/653, Annex 4, 1 June 1994, for a good summary of the military activities.

73. See S/26022, 1 July 1993, para. 19; and S/1994/653, 1 June 1994, para. 137. For President Clinton's response, in which he names Aidid's forces as the attackers see "The President's Radio Address," *Weekly Compilation of Presidential Documents* 29, (June 12, 1993): 1070. Also see the Canadian situation reports of the time in *Information Legacy*.

74. Accounts differ as to the sequence of events, but it appears that Somalis fired into a crowd of women and children to incite a response and attempted to create a situation in which UNOSOM II would be blamed for firing at civilians. See S/1994/653, 1 June 1994, para. 138, and summary. Also see "Pakistani Soldiers Open Fire on Protesters, Kill 20," *Globe and Mail*, 14 June 1993, A1, A2; and "Bloody Sunday in Somalia," *New York Times*, 15 June 1993, A26.

75. S/26022, 1 July 1993, para. 22; Donatella Lorch, "US Aircraft Again Attack Somali Faction's Arms Sites," *New York Times*, 15 June 1993, A12; Michael R. Gordon, "US Intensifies Attack to Oust a Somali Clan," *New York Times*, 17 June 1993, A14; and "Somali Targets Hit by New Air Strikes," *Globe and Mail*, 15 June 1993, A8.

76. S/26022, 1 July 1993, para. 25–27; S/1994/653, p. 74; and "UN Hopes to Resume Somali Relief Work," *Globe and Mail*, 19 June 1993, A10.

77. For command and control charts and discussion, see Chopra, Eknes, and Nordbø, *Fighting for Hope in Somalia*, 86; William J. Durch, "Introduction to Anarchy: Intervention in Somalia," in William J. Durch, ed., *UN Peacekeeping, American Policy, and the Uncivil Wars of the 1990s* (New York: St. Martin's, 1996), 337; and Allard, *Somalia Operations*, 56–61.

78. The head of the UNOSOM II logistics unit was also American.

79. For a good overview of the operational issues facing a U.S. commander in both UNITAF and UNOSOM II see Joseph P. Hoar, "A CINC's Perspective," *Joint Forces Quarterly* (Autumn 1993): 56–63.

80. S/26317, 17 August 1993. The Italian contingent, originally based in Mogadishu, was moved outside of the city. For press coverage see, for example, "Italy Seeks Halt to Peacekeepers' Fighting," *Globe and Mail*, 13 July 1993, A1, A2; and A. Cowell, "Italy, in UN Rift, Threatens Recall of Somalia Troops," *New York Times*, 16 July 1993, A1, A2. Some contingents made private deals with local faction leaders in order to facilitate mandate implementation and to ensure their own security. The Italian contingent, whose presence was itself controversial because of its colonial past, made arrangements with the local SNA militia. When it came time to rotate the contingents, the Nigerian contingent taking over from the Italians was attacked by the local SNA militia, resulting in seven Nigerian deaths, because the local SNA wanted to continue its arrangement with the Italians. See Keith Richburg, "7 Peace Keepers Killed in Somalia, Nigerians Ambushed at U.N. Position" *Washington Post*, 6 September 1993, A1, A30, A31.

81. S/1994/ 653, Annex 5.

82. Geoffrey York, "Somali 'Success' Nearing Disaster," *Globe and Mail*, 16 June 1993, A1; Donatella Lorch, "In An Edgy Mogadishu, Relief Efforts Are in Jeopardy," *New York Times*, 23 June 1993, A3; and "Food Rots as UN Troops Focus on Military Action," *Globe and Mail*, 12 July 1993, A1, A2.

83. "UN Raids Somali Clan's Base; A Mob Then Kills 2 Journalists," *New York Times*, 13 July 1993, 1, A8; Donatella Lorch, "UN Finds Peace Elusive with Somali Leader at Large," *New York Times*, 15 July 1993, A10; "Angry Somalis Attack UN Sites," *Globe and Mail*, 15 July 1993, A6; and Geoffrey York, "What Went so Wrong in Somalia," *Globe and Mail*, 15 July 1993, 1, A6.

84. Hirsch and Oakley, *Somalia and Operation Restore Hope*, 121.

85. S/26317, 17 August 1993, para. 72–73.

86. For example, in late July the U.S. National Security Council sent a task force to Somalia on a fact-finding mission and to carry out a re-evaluation of the UNOSOM II and U.S. mission. See *A "Seamless" Transition*, Part B, 11.

87. U.S. Congress, *Current Military Operations*, Hearings, 103-440, 6 August, 4, 7, 12, 13 October 1993. See especially the testimonies of Lieutenant General John Sheehan and Rear Admiral Michael Cramer, 39–104.

88. Ibid. Also see U.S. Congress, *U.S. Military Operations in Somalia*, Hearings, 103-846, 12 May, 21 July 1994. The denial of the request for special forces and tanks has been a particular focus in the US in light of the events that followed. The controversy eventually contributed to the resignation of Secretary of Defense Les Aspin.

89. Karen de Witt, "Four U.S. Soldiers Are Killed by Mine in Somali Capital," *New York Times*, 9 August 1993, 1, A6; Michael R. Gordon, "In a Shift, U.S. Sees Wider Somali Role to Stop Clan Leader," *New York Times*, 10 August 1993, 1, A6; and Madeline Albright, "Yes, There Is a Reason to Be in Somalia," *Backgrounder*, 93-25, U.S. Embassy, Ottawa, Canada, 11 August 1993.

90. According to Allard, Task Force Ranger's chain of command "extended directly back to CENTCOM without going through either U.S. or U.N. channels." See Allard, *Somalia Operations*, 57.

91. For a chronology and description of the attacks see S/1994/653, Annex 4, 1 June 1994.

92. The members of the Rangers take an oath to never leave a fallen comrade behind.

93. S/1994/653, 1 June 1994, 86–89. For very detailed coverage, see the four part series "Mission to Somalia" by Patrick J. Sloyan in *Newsday*, 5–8 December 1993. Also see Mark Bowden, "Blackhawk Down," *Philadelphia Inquirer*, 16 November 1997. The web site associated with this series includes audio and video tapes of the raid from the

Pentagon   as   well   as   audio   interviews   with   surviving   soldiers: http://www.philly.com/packages/somalia/nov16/default16.asp. (Last visited on 22 November 2000.)

94. "Address to the Nation on Somalia," *Weekly Compilation of Presidential Documents* 29, (October 7 1993): 2022–2025. Clinton held on for this option in spite of pressure for an immediate withdrawal. For a sense of the U.S. mood of the time, see Thomas L. Friedman, "Clinton Sending More Troops to Somalia," *New York Times*, 7 October 1993, A1, A10; and Douglas Jehl, "Clinton Doubling U.S. Force in Somalia, Vowing Troops Will Come Home in 6 Months," *New York Times*, 8 October 1993, A1, A14. President Clinton had apparently already made a decision to ease off on the military emphasis, especially the arrest of Aidid, after a discussion with former president Jimmy Carter. See Ken Menkhaus, "Getting out vs. Getting through: U.S. and U.N. Policies in Somalia," *Middle East Policy* 3, no. 1 (1994): 146–162; and Patrick J. Sloyan, "Hunting Down Aidid: Why Clinton Changed His Mind," *Newsday*, 6 December 1993.

95. Douglas Jehl, "For Rangers in Somalia, the Armed Chase Gives Way to Boredom," *New York Times*, 21 October 1993, A8. Also note the absence of the arrest of Aidid in the list of tasks outlined by President Clinton in his speech to the nation: "Address to the Nation on Somalia"; and in his message to Congress outlining his decisions about U.S. troops: "Message to the Congress Transmitting a Report on Somalia," *Weekly Compilation of Presidential Documents* 29, (October 13, 1993): 2065–2066.

96. "Frustration and Anxiety at UN as US Puts Somalia Operation on 6-month Notice," *International Documents Review* 4, no. 35, (1993): 1–2.

97. *A "Seamless" Transition*, Part B, 15–16.

98. This shift of attitude towards Aidid, predictably, was the source of considerable criticism. See, for example, Menkhaus, "Getting out vs. Getting through," 158.

99. Lorenz, "Rules of Engagement," 5. Also see John H. Cushman, "How Powerful U.S. Units Will Work," *New York Times*, 8 October 1993, A14.

100. For a description, see the secretary-general's final report, S/1995/231, 28 March 1995.

101. Ibid., para. 38.

102. For example, the USS Harlan Cleveland withdrew from the Port-au-Prince harbor in Haiti on 11 October 1993 rather than confront an angry crowd on the dock. And the experience in Somalia fed a general unwillingness on the part of the U.S. government to use U.S. soldiers on the ground in Bosnia.

103. S/26738, 12 November 1993, para. 59. The secretary-general makes these kinds of statements in a number of his reports.

104. For a description of the series of political decisions during the UNOSOM II operation that seemed to marginalize Aidid see Menkhaus, "Getting out vs. Getting through," 155–156. Menkhaus was a political officer in the UNOSOM II operation.

105. S/1994/653, para. 125.

106. Surprisingly, it is apparent that those involved in the decision making did not fully appreciate the magnitude of the change they had brought about in the UNOSOM II mandate. Hirsch and Oakley note "From conversations with both senior and midlevel officials directly involved with Somalia, it is evident that there was no real appreciation of how much of a change of policy and mission this was for UNOSOM II and the United States forces associated with it. Nor was there a realistic appreciation of just how tough it would be to successfully take action called for by the Security Council against the SNA in the back alleys of south Mogadishu." See Hirsch and Oakley, *Somalia and Operation Restore Hope*, 118. The secretary-general's report of 1 July, three weeks after the arrest mandate, notes that UNOSOM II officials intended "to continue to work with all the factions, in an effort to foster conditions for the implementation of the United Nations mandate." See S/26022, 1 July 1993, para. 41.

Chapter 5

Bosnia

I. CONTEXT

Between World War II and 1991, Yugoslavia existed as a federation of six republics and after 1963 two autonomous provinces, Kosovo and Vojvodina. The republics were Bosnia-Herzegovina, Croatia, Macedonia, Montenegro, Serbia, and Slovenia. Marshal Tito, who successfully led the partisans against the Germans during the World War II, was head of the Yugoslav state until his death in May 1980. After his death, a Collective State Presidency was formed. Each republic and province had a member in the collective presidency and the posts of president and vice president rotated annually.

The seeds of the end of the federation, sown with Tito's death, began to grow a few years later with the end of the cold war. The end of Soviet control in Eastern Europe, the internal disarray in the Soviet Union, and the popular uprisings against communism in other Eastern European countries created a climate of unprecedented and unpredicted uncertainty and change in the region. The internal context of the country was also one of change. Tito's death left a tremendous political vacuum that remained unfilled by the collective presidency. The national economy suffered setbacks and began to decline, facing, as were many other countries, a serious debt crisis in a time of recession.[1]

THE LEAD-UP TO THE BREAKDOWN

During 1989, relations among the republics of Slovenia and Croatia and Serbia became increasingly contentious and nationalist movements began to take hold. Tensions in Kosovo prompted Serbia to crack down on protests in the country and to amend the Serbian constitution to take greater control over Kosovo's internal affairs. In January 1990, the Fourteenth Congress of the Communist Party of Yugoslavia collapsed when the Slovenian delegation walked out, followed later by the Croatian delegation. During 1990 the crisis deepened. Unrest continued in Kosovo. By the autumn, Serbs resident in Croatia had become organized and vocal, declaring a Serbian Autonomous Region of Krajina on 1 October. On 23 December Slovenia held a referendum on secession. The result was 94.5 percent in favor of secession with 93.5 percent of the eligible voters participating.[2]

Events then began to accelerate. On 25 January 1991, the Macedonian Assembly adopted a declaration of sovereignty, which included a right to secede from Yugoslavia. On 20 February, the Slovenian Assembly adopted a resolution calling for secession and beginning a series of steps in that direction. The next day, 21 February, the Croatian Assembly passed similar resolutions asserting the primacy of the Croatian constitution and Croatian laws over those of Yugoslavia. A week later, the Serbs living in the Krajina announced that they were unilaterally separating from Croatia. Within the next couple of days, clashes between Croatians and Serbs in Pakrac prompted the Yugoslav National Army (JNA) to step in and re-establish order. On 19 May, Croatia held a referendum on independence. The Serb population of Croatia boycotted the vote and in the weeks prior to the referendum there were violent clashes between Serbs and Croatians in the Krajina area. The referendum vote was 93.2 percent in favor of independence.[3]

Slovenia and Croatia declared independence on 25 June 1991. The collective presidency was itself in a crisis[4] but JNA leaders, having previously warned that they could not stand by while the country disintegrated,[5] reacted quickly by bombing the airport at Ljubljana and attempting, but failing, to retake control of Slovenian border crossings. Yugoslavia was in the midst of a civil war.

On 7 July 1991, the European Community (EC) troika[6] brokered an agreement between Slovenia, Croatia, and the Yugoslav government. The agreement resolved some of the border issues, put some constraints on the movements of JNA troops, provided for EC observers, and required Croatia and Slovenia to suspend the implementation of their declarations of independence.[7] In asking that the implementation of the declarations be suspended, the Yugoslav government and the European Community were effectively accepting the legitimacy of those declarations. The agreement

struck a serious blow against the authority of the faction within the army leadership that was fighting to hold Yugoslavia together and of those who still hoped to play a mediating, pacifying role in the nationalist quarrels . . . . Forced to choose between loyalty to Yugoslavia or to the new national armies, army leaders at the highest levels began to rethink their role in this political quarrel, and the balance of opinion began to shift toward those who could only see a military solution to border conflicts.[8]

The agreement brought an end to any significant military action by JNA forces in Slovenia, but it was only the beginning for Croatia. During August, fighting within Croatia between JNA troops and those loyal to an independent Croatia intensified. By mid-August, the two were in the midst of a full-scale conflict.[9] In what was to become an unhappy and familiar pattern, a cease-fire was agreed on 17 September but broke down within hours.[10]

II. MANDATE

When the Yugoslav crisis began to unfold in 1990, various European institutions became involved. The international community had only just emerged from the Persian Gulf War. Having Europe take the lead suited most of the major international actors, especially the United States. The EC's approach had a two-fold goal of preventing further fighting and maintaining a unified Yugoslavia in some form.[11] By the autumn of 1991, however, the difficulties inherent in finding an agreed European approach, combined with the momentum and seriousness of events within Yugoslavia stalemated EC efforts.[12] At the initiative of Belgium, France, and the United Kingdom, the matter came before the UN Security Council in late September 1991.[13]

Resolution 713, the first UN action on the conflict, noted that the Security Council was "concerned that the continuation of this situation constitutes a threat to international peace and security." The resolution took note of the declaration of the Conference on Security and Cooperation in Europe (CSCE), which stated that "no territorial gains or changes within Yugoslavia brought about by violence are acceptable" and urged all parties to abide by cease-fire agreements. The Security Council asked Secretary-General Javier Pérez de Cuéllar to offer his assistance to the peace efforts and then, acting under Chapter VII, imposed an immediate "general and complete embargo on all deliveries of weapons and military equipment to Yugoslavia until the Security Council decides otherwise."

No further Security Council action occurred for another two months. In the meantime, the secretary-general appointed Cyrus Vance as his personal envoy to the negotiations.[14] Events within Yugoslavia continued to escalate. Fighting between Croatian and JNA forces was most intense around Vukovar, in the area of western Slavonia, and Dubrovnik on the Croatian coast.[15] In spite of and because of the deteriorating situation in the country, European states were having difficulty establishing a common position. At an Extraordinary Ministerial Meeting in Rome on 8 November, the European Community did manage to agree to some further economic restrictions on Yugoslavia.[16] The Security Council was also reluctant to take action and, in any case, unable to develop agreement on a next step.[17] Both groups waited and hoped for a positive outcome to the ongoing peace negotiations.

UNPROFOR IN CROATIA

By November, though the situation was little improved, the idea of a peacekeeping force began to be floated at the United Nations.[18] A formal request from the Yugoslav government for a peacekeeping force was made in a letter to the Security Council on 26 November 1991.[19] On 27 November, the Security Council passed its second resolution on the crisis. Resolution 721 agreed with the general idea of a peacekeeping force but emphasized that deployment of a force could not be envisaged until the cease-fire agreement signed by the parties on 23 November was implemented.

Thereafter, on 15 December 1991 the Security Council approved a "small mission" to make initial preparations for a possible peacekeeping mission.[20] On 8 January 1992, it approved sending fifty liaison officers "to promote maintenance of the cease-fire,"[21] and then on 7 February 1992 it approved an increase in the number of liaison officers to seventy-five.[22] In each case, the Security Council reiterated its concern that the conditions for peacekeeping did not exist and that the cease-fire was not being maintained.

This was still the case when Boutros Boutros-Ghali, the new secretary-general, reported to the Security Council on 15 February 1992.[23] He pointed out that: "there remain a number of unanswered questions about the extent to which the Force will in practice receive the necessary cooperation."[24] Nonetheless, the secretary-general went on to make a remarkable recommendation.

[A]fter careful deliberation I have come to the conclusion that the danger that a United Nations peace-keeping operation will fail because of lack of cooperation from the parties is less grievous than the danger that delay in its dispatch will lead to a breakdown of the cease-fire and to a new conflagration in Yugoslavia. In reaching this conclusion I have made the assumption, which I recognize could also be questioned, that the Yugoslav parties are ready to engage seriously in the difficult task of negotiating an overall settlement. . . . the United Nations Force would remain in Yugoslavia until a negotiated settlement was achieved.[25]

The Security Council approved the secretary-general's recommendation in Resolution 743 on 21 February 1992, establishing the UN Protection Force (UNPROFOR) in Croatia for a period of twelve months. The idea was that the UNPROFOR operation would be an interim arrangement to buy time for negotiations and a permanent overall settlement. The primary purpose of the operation was to deploy peacekeepers in particularly contentious areas within Croatia. These areas, named UN Protected Areas (UNPAs), would be demilitarized and then remain so under the protection of the peacekeepers.[26]

THE SHIFT TO BOSNIA

During the autumn of 1991, while international negotiations to end the fighting were ongoing, European countries, especially Germany, began to discuss the possibility of recognizing Slovenia and Croatia as independent states. International recognition of the two republics raised two critical issues. First, recognition in advance of a negotiated political settlement prejudged some of the issues that were being considered at the negotiations, such as the status of areas with large minority populations. Second, there was considerable concern that recognition of the two republics would lead to fighting in other areas of the country such as Bosnia-Herzegovina and Macedonia. Lord Peter Carrington, head of the negotiations, expressed this concern most succinctly, warning "[t]his might be the spark that sets Bosnia-Herzegovina alight."[27]

The issue sparked an intense and unusual exchange of letters between the secretary-general and Hans-Dietrich Genscher, the foreign minister of Germany.[28] In spite of these concerns, Germany, with the European Community trailing somewhat reluctantly behind it for the sake of unity, announced on 23 December 1991[29] that Croatia and Slovenia had met the conditions for recognition established earlier that month by the European Community. Formal recognition was given on 15 January 1992.

Once Croatia had recognition, Yugoslavia and Croatia then turned their attention to the status of their "people" and their land in Bosnia. Many argue that "premature" recognition set the stage for the war in Bosnia. Whether true or not, after the recognition of Slovenia and Croatia the situation in Bosnia-Herzegovina deteriorated quickly. A referendum on independence on 29 February 1992 received a 99.4 percent vote in favor of independence, with 62.7 percent[30] of the eligible voters participating. On 2 March 1992, President Alija Itezbegovic declared Bosnia-Herzegovina independent. The United States and the European Community, hoping that recognition might act as a stabilizing factor, recognized Bosnia's independence on 7 April 1992. A Security Council resolution that same day, dealing primarily with the deployment of UNPROFOR troops in Croatia, appealed to the parties in Bosnia-Herzegovina to "cooperate with the efforts of the European Community to bring about a cease-fire and a negotiated political solution."[31]

Fighting continued to intensify within the region, particularly in areas close to borders with Croatia and Serbia and in the capital city, Sarajevo. Aside from the casualties and deaths resulting from the conflicts, the fighting also generated massive population movements. In a report to the Security Council on 12 May 1992, the Secretary-General spoke of the "grim" situation and the "intense hostilities."

All international observers agree that what is happening is a concerted effort by the Serbs of Bosnia-Herzegovina, with the acquiescence of, and at least some support from, JNA, to create "ethnically pure" regions. . . . The conclusion of a partial cease-fire agreement between Croat and Serb leaders on 6 May 1992 has revived suspicions of a Croat-Serb carve up of Bosnia-Herzegovina, leaving minimal territory to the Muslim community, which accounts for a plurality (44 per cent) of the population.[32]

When establishing the UNPROFOR operation in Croatia, the United Nations decided to locate the headquarters for the UNPROFOR operation in Sarajevo in an effort to establish a stabilizing presence there even though, at that point, the operation was entirely based in Croatia. This decision was intended to send a stabilizing signal to the parties in the area. Whatever the signal, the regular problems associated with locating a headquarters some distance from the operations in the field quickly became further complicated by the additional problems associated with being in what was now a combat area. This, together with the fighting itself and the massive population movements, was quickly creating a humanitarian emergency and a very difficult and tenuous situation for the Sarajevo-based UNPROFOR contingent.

THE RESPONSE TO BOSNIA

In the course of four weeks, the Security Council passed three resolutions dealing with Bosnia-Herzegovina. On 15 May 1992, Resolution 752 demanded an end to the fighting in Bosnia-Herzegovina, an end to all forms of "interference" from outside Bosnia-Herzegovina, the withdrawal of JNA and Croatian army units within Bosnia-Herzegovina, and the disbanding and disarming of all "irregular" forces in Bosnia-Herzegovina. The resolution also requested that the secretary-general review the feasibility of protecting humanitarian relief and the possibility of a peacekeeping operation in Bosnia-Herzegovina.

Two weeks later, in Resolution 757, the Security Council deplored the fact that their demands in Resolution 752 had not been met and declared that the situation in Bosnia-Herzegovina and other parts of the former Yugoslavia was a threat to international peace and security. The Security Council then imposed economic and diplomatic sanctions on Yugoslavia and demanded that all parties provide for the unimpeded delivery of humanitarian supplies and establish a security zone around Sarajevo and its airport. Ten days later, on 8 June 1992, the Security Council passed Resolution 758. This resolution approved the secretary-general's proposal that the UNPROFOR mandate be extended to include the "operational responsibility for the functioning and security of the Sarajevo airport."[33] Through July and the first part of August, the Security Council authorized two further increases in troop strength for UNPROFOR but took no other action aside from continuing to call for cease-fire compliance and unimpeded humanitarian aid.[34]

To this point then, the Security Council response was to call on the parties to end the conflict and negotiate a solution and to concentrate on the issue of delivery of humanitarian aid with a main focus on the Sarajevo airport area. The Council showed little interest in taking action with respect to the conflict itself, even though it deemed the conflict to be a threat to international peace and security, fighting was continuing and negotiations held little hope of success.

Indeed, the peace negotiations suffered a major setback with the failure of the Lisbon Accord in the spring of 1992,[35] and thereafter faltered and stalled through the summer. When Britain took over the EC presidency in June, the negotiations entered a new phase, breaking from the past failed EC efforts and developing a more formal partnership and coordination between EC and UN efforts. The EC and the UN, therefore, beginning with a major meeting in London at the beginning of September, undertook joint sponsorship of a second peace process that became the International Conference on the Former Yugoslavia (ICFY).[36]

DELIVERING HUMANITARIAN AID—RESOLUTION 770 AND CHAPTER VII

During the summer, the delays in moving towards the new jointly run peace process reflected an uncertainty of purpose and lack of commitment among the major international and European powers. All the while, the conflict worsened, allegations of ethnic cleansing strengthened, and humanitarian aid shipments were consistently blocked. These developments prompted the international community, under pressure from the public to do something but unwilling to deal with the conflict in other ways, to discuss the possibility of using force to ensure the delivery of humanitarian aid.[37]

The secretary-general had already raised this issue in his reports to the Security Council. In May 1992, the difficulties being encountered by UNPROFOR in Sarajevo, the deteriorating situation in Bosnia as a whole, and a request from the president of Bosnia and leaders of the other parties involved in the fighting prompted the secretary-general to examine the various options for UN action and to conclude that the conflict was not "susceptible to the United Nations peace-keeping treatment."[38] The secretary-general considered and dismissed the possibility of using a UN "intervention" force without the consent of all the parties involved, concluding that the numbers of troops required for such an operation eliminated the proposal as "a practicable proposition"[39]— code words for an acknowledgement that UN member states would be unwilling to contribute the necessary forces and equipment to the operation whether or not they might support the idea itself. The secretary-general also raised the possibility of using UN forces to protect humanitarian aid deliveries. He concluded, however, that the prospect of needing to use force for a Bosnian operation would jeopardize the consent required for the ongoing peacekeeping operation in Croatia.[40] Nonetheless, the ongoing fighting, with its overtones of ethnic cleansing, continued to be the focus of the international media, and therefore, western countries. With peace negotiations stalled, public pressure for intervention of some sort continued through the summer.

On 13 August 1992, in Resolution 770 the Security Council authorized the use of force to ensure the delivery of humanitarian aid. The Council specifically linked the delivery of humanitarian aid to international peace and security, noting that: "humanitarian assistance in Bosnia and Herzegovina is an important element in the Council's effort to restore international peace and security in that area." Acting under Chapter VII, the Security Council required states "to take nationally or through regional agencies or arrangements all measures necessary to facilitate in coordination with the United Nations the delivery by relevant United Nations humanitarian organizations and others of humanitarian assistance to Sarajevo and wherever needed in other parts of Bosnia and Herzegovina."[41]

This was a significant step for the Security Council. The invocation of Chapter VII and the approval of the use of force, through the phrase "all measures necessary," marked an important shift in the seriousness of the Security Council's response to the conflict, at least on paper. In practice, there was little change to the situation on the ground. The major European powers and the United States remained reluctant to provide the additional troops needed to make the operation truly effective. The resolution was passed without any articulated military or political plan for its implementation. This represented a break from usual Security Council practice. Usually, approval of a new operation comes after a secretary-general report, which outlines options or proposals based on military and political advice. An initial estimate by NATO military planners as to the troop requirements for ensuring humanitarian aid delivery recommended a deployment of a stunning one hundred thousand troops,[42] prompting NATO authorities to ask for other options.

In addition, the major powers' interpretation of the "all measures necessary" provision was very narrow. On the day the resolution was passed, the representative for Great Britain on the Security Council stated that the resolution "does not prescribe the use of force. That is as it should be. The use of force is not desirable, but it may be necessary."[43]

Implementation of the resolution awaited the development of a coordinated plan. The secretary-general presented his proposals for implementing the resolution in a report to the Security Council a month later.[44] The secretary-general's proposal outlined a much narrower mission than might have been anticipated from the wording of Resolution 770, scaling down the possibility of the actual use of force. The secretary-general suggested that UNPROFOR "support" the UN High Commission for Refugees' (UNHCR) delivery efforts, as the lead humanitarian agency, by providing protection "at UNHCR's request, where and when UNHCR considered such protection necessary."[45] In carrying out this "protective support" mission, UNPROFOR troops would "follow normal peace-keeping rules of engagement. They would thus be authorized to use force in self-defence. It is to be noted that, in this context, self-defence is deemed to include situations in which armed persons attempt by force to prevent United Nations troops from carrying out their mandate."[46]

The secretary-general estimated that fulfillment of the mission would require an increase in the number of UNPROFOR personnel in Bosnia-Herzegovina by "a factor of four or five." The operation would be under the overall command and control of the UNPROFOR commander but a new Bosnia-Herzegovina command would be established. The Security Council approved the secretary-general's plan on 14 September 1992 in Resolution 776. This resolution made reference to Resolution 770, but made no specific reference to Chapter VII and, therefore, effectively downgraded the enforcement aspect of Resolution 770.

THE ESTABLISHMENT OF A NO-FLY ZONE

Soon after the Security Council signalled its commitment (at least on paper) to ensuring humanitarian aid delivery, on 4 September 1992 an Italian airplane carrying aid between Split and Sarajevo was shot down by a missile. The four Italians on board were killed. At around the same time, reports began to surface that Bosnian Serb aircraft were following relief flights and using them as a cover in order to launch military attacks.[47] This prompted France to propose a ban on military flights over Bosnia. On 9 October 1992, the Security Council passed Resolution 781 which, in order to ensure the safety of humanitarian aid deliveries, established a ban on military flights over Bosnia-Herzegovina airspace. Although the resolution did not name the party or parties responsible for the overflights the ban was effectively directed against the Bosnian Serbs who were the only party to the conflict with significant access to military aircraft. The resolution asked UNPROFOR to monitor the ban, placing observers at airfields where necessary.

There were no provisions for any kind of enforcement of the ban beyond a Security Council commitment to consider enforcement measures if the ban was violated. This was the result of a compromise between the United States, which was in favor of immediate enforcement, and Britain and France, who feared the consequences to their troops on the ground if the ban was enforced. This difference in approach between the United States on the one hand and Britain and France—major UNPROFOR troop contributors—on the other became a major factor in Security Council decision making on the conflict. In spite of an initial undertaking by the Bosnian Serbs to put their planes under UN supervision,[48] the flight ban was almost completely ignored.

In the face of consistent and ongoing violations, the Security Council passed Resolution 786 on 10 November 1992. The resolution approved the secretary-general's recommendation that UNPROFOR be augmented by seventy-five military observers in order to help monitor the ban but made no further effort to provide for enforcement.

The ban was consistently and continually violated through the following months. The bombing of two villages near Srebrenica in mid-March, apparently by Serbian aircraft, finally pushed the Security Council to action.[49] On 31 March 1993, acting under Chapter VII of the charter, the Security Council extended the flight ban to include all fixed-wing and rotary-wing aircraft and authorized member states "acting nationally or through regional organizations or arrangements, to take . . . all necessary measures in the airspace of the Republic of Bosnia and Herzegovina, in the event of further violations, to ensure compliance with the ban."[50] The Security Council had previously considered a resolution requiring enforcement of the ban in December 1992. No resolution was passed at that time, not only because of troop-contributing countries' concerns that enforcement would lead to repercussions on their troops, but also because of apparent progress in the peace negotiations.[51] Having offered to take on the job of enforcing the flight ban in December, NATO now undertook the enforcement operation and began Operation Deny Flight on 12 April 1993.[52]

MISSION SECURITY AND FREEDOM OF MOVEMENT

A combination of events on the ground and at the peace negotiations prompted two interim extensions of the UNPROFOR mandate in early 1993. The first extension came in Resolution 807 on 19 February 1993. This resolution extended the mandate until 31 March. On 30 March, the Security Council extended the mandate again, this time until 30 June 1993. At this time, there were significant compliance problems with respect to the protected areas in Croatia, and in both Croatia and Bosnia UNPROFOR troops encountered significant freedom of movement problems that hindered their ability to fulfill their mandate. Resolution 807 expressed the Security Council's determination "to ensure the security of UNPROFOR" and Resolution 815 added "freedom of movement" to the same phrase. Both resolutions then "to these ends" invoked Chapter VII. Resolution

807 also demanded that "the parties and others concerned respect fully UN-PROFOR's unimpeded freedom of movement" and asked the secretary-general to study ways of strengthening troop security, "in particular providing it with the necessary defensive means."

During the late summer and early autumn of 1993, Security Council resolutions again invoked Chapter VII in this context. Resolution 871, passed on 4 October 1993, specifically gave UNPROFOR the power, when operating in Croatia, "acting in self-defence, to take the necessary measures, including the use of force to ensure its security and its freedom of movement." Over time, Security Council resolutions on Bosnia consistently, indeed almost automatically, called for UNPROFOR freedom of movement, citing Chapter VII in this regard. The Security Council's increasing focus on safe areas meant that the freedom of movement issue, even though it was a fundamental problem in all aspects of UNPROFOR operations in Bosnia, became linked to the safe area concept.

SAFE AREAS

Srebrenica

In mid-March 1993, Bosnian Serb forces began a general campaign in the area of eastern Bosnia involving a number of cities.[53] Srebrenica became a focal point for the struggle in the area. Initial attention focused on the city when the UNPROFOR commander in Bosnia-Herzegovina, General Philippe Morillon, planted himself there and announced that he intended to stay in Srebrenica until the Bosnian Serb siege of the city ended. General Morillon's determination received mixed reviews within the UN hierarchy but it did draw considerable media attention to the area.[54] Morillon's success in terms of the town itself was short-lived. After initial aid deliveries got through and Morillon left, the Bosnian Serbs resumed the siege, though now under the glare of significant international media attention. The pressure to get aid to the town or evacuate its citizens continued, especially as the Bosnian Serb assault intensified.[55]

Initial attempts to bring an end to the Serb actions focused on the possibility of imposing further sanctions on Yugoslavia. The proposal was postponed, however, in deference to Russian president Boris Yeltsin, who was in the midst of an internal power struggle and who feared that strong actions against the Serbs might have a negative impact on his chances of success.[56]

Instead, on 16 April 1993 the Security Council passed Resolution 819 by a unanimous vote. In the resolution, the Security Council strongly condemns Bosnian Serb paramilitary units for their attacks against UNPROFOR, their unwillingness to grant UN troops freedom of movement, their creation of "a tragic humanitarian emergency" in Srebrenica, and their "deliberate actions . . . to force the evacuation of the civilian population" in Srebrenica and other areas of Bosnia-Herzegovina. In that context, the resolution then demands that all parties to the conflict treat Srebrenica "and its surroundings" as a "safe area."[57] As a safe area, Srebrenica was to be free from armed attack and Bosnian Serb paramilitary units were required to withdraw. Yugoslavia was required to stop supplying arms and services to Bosnian Serb units in Bosnia-Herzegovina. The Security Council also requested that the secretary-general increase UNPROFOR's presence in Srebrenica and decided to send a Security Council mission to Bosnia-Herzegovina "to ascertain the situation." The resolution cites Chapter VII, but only in the context of Resolution 815, and, therefore, only in relation to freedom of movement.

Though strongly worded, the resolution did not represent a great deal in terms of direct UN action. No further troops or resources were authorized for UNPROFOR in spite of the Security Council's call for an increased UNPROFOR presence, and no specific enforcement measures were outlined. The success of the resolution and the safe area concept depended entirely on the willingness of the parties involved to comply voluntarily with the Security Council resolution—precisely the kind of compliance whose absence had contributed to the ongoing conflict and the creation of the Srebrenica situation in the first place. Indeed, the Secretariat told the UNPROFOR commander that the resolution "created no military obligations for UNPROFOR to establish or protect such a safe area."[58] Predictably then, the Security Council resolution had little overall impact beyond putting a temporary stop to the shelling as the Serbs shifted their focus elsewhere.[59]

The Security Council mission visited Bosnia-Herzegovina in late April. In its report, mission members described Srebrenica as "the equivalent of an open jail in which its people can wander around but are controlled and terrorized by the increasing presence of Serb tanks and other heavy weapons in its immediate surroundings."[60] Outside of the town, the mission saw evidence of further entrenchment of Serb soldiers around the town. "Evidently the Serb paramilitary forces not only are not withdrawing as demanded . . . but are increasing their pressure on the town."[61] Nonetheless, the Security Council mission went on to recommend that "the designation of certain towns/enclaves as Security Council safe areas deserves serious consideration as an act of Security Council preventive diplomacy."[62] The mission's recommendation was very clearly conditioned, however.

The Mission recognizes that such a decision would require a larger UNPROFOR presence, a revised mandate to encompass cease-fire/safe area monitoring and different rules of engagement; but it would be a step that stops short of the sort of military strike enforcement measures that are now being so openly debated. It would not rule out eventual consideration of such measures—but at a next stage, if the Serbs simply ignored the integrity of Security Council safe areas; nor would it, on the other hand, automatically predetermine a move to military strikes. . . . The Mission reckons with the fact that these actions would represent a significant strengthening of the UNPROFOR role. Designation of Security Council safe areas would have to be done with the clear intent that they would, once established, be *enforced or defended* if need be.[63]

Expanding the Safe Areas

In line with the mission's recommendation, the following week, on 6 May 1993, the Security Council passed Resolution 824. The resolution declared Sarajevo, Tuzla, Zepa, Gorazde, and Bihac to be safe areas, along with Srebrenica. Although the resolution invoked Chapter VII, it did so, as before, only in the context of the provisions of Resolution 815, which demanded freedom of movement and security of UNPROFOR troops. The Security Council did not follow the rest of the mission's recommendation and only declared "its readiness, in the event of the failure by any part to comply . . . to consider immediately the adoption of any additional measures necessary with a view to its full implementation, including to ensure respect for the safety of United Nations personnel." This time, the Security Council authorized an increase in UNPROFOR strength, but of only fifty military observers for the purposes of monitoring the humanitarian situation in the safe areas. So while the Security Council followed the letter of the mission's recommendations, it did little in the way of following their spirit.

The Security Council may have been counting on the success of the ongoing peace negotiations to help ease the pressure. At the beginning of May, Bosnian Serb leader Radovan Karadzic, under heavy pressure from Slobodan Milosevic, and in the midst of talk from the US of air strikes, signed the Vance-Owen Peace Plan.[64] A referendum on the peace plan, held in mid-May among Bosnian Serbs, however, returned an overwhelming vote against the plan, effectively ending its viability.[65]

The rejection of the peace plan was a particularly low point in the peace negotiations. At the same time, the conflict in Bosnia entered into a new and even more violent phase with fighting breaking out in a number of areas, and new fighting beginning between Bosnian Croats and Bosnian Muslims. Added into the equation was the development of a serious rift between the United States and Europe over the proper response to the deepening conflict. Up until now, the United States had been willing and interested in allowing Europeans to take the lead on what was a European security problem. With the change of U.S. administration from President George Bush to President Bill Clinton at the beginning of the year, there came a new U.S. willingness to try to have some impact on the conflict, albeit without actually getting involved in any significant way in the conflict itself. The Clinton administration focused on a so-called "lift and strike" strategy that would, it was argued, even the military disparity between the Bosnian Muslims and the Bosnian Serbs.[66] The "lift" involved lifting the arms embargo for the Bosnian Muslims and the "strike" would use air strikes against the Serbian heavy weapons being used to bombard Sarajevo and other Bosnian towns. The proposal was not well received by European countries, especially Britain and France, or by Canada—all countries with significant numbers of troops on the ground as part of the UNPROFOR mission.[67] These countries believed that such a strategy would inevitably result in serious repercussions against vulnerable UNPROFOR personnel. The very open determination by the

United States not to commit its own ground troops to Bosnia, except to oversee a final peace settlement, exacerbated the issue.

It was in this context that the Security Council took its next action on the safe areas. It did so in spite of a speech by the UN representative for Bosnia prior to the vote that strongly criticized the safe areas concept as well as the general international approach to the conflict.[68] On 4 June 1993, the Security Council passed Resolution 836 expanding the safe area mandate. The mandate expansion required UNPROFOR troops "to deter attacks against the safe areas, to monitor the cease-fire, to promote the withdrawal of military or paramilitary units other than those of [Bosnia-Herzegovina] and to occupy some key points on the ground, in addition to participating in the delivery of humanitarian relief to the population." To fulfill these additional tasks, the Security Council requested that the secretary-general make the required appropriate adjustments or reinforcements to the UNPROFOR operation and called upon member states to contribute forces to facilitate implementation.

The resolution invokes Chapter VII but, in contrast to the previous resolutions on safe areas, that invocation is made unreservedly and without reference to Resolution 815. To implement the new functions, the resolution authorizes UNPROFOR "acting in self-defence, to take the necessary measures, including the use of force, in reply to bombardments against the safe areas by any of the parties or to armed incursion into them or in the event of any deliberate obstruction in or around those areas to the freedom of movement of UNPROFOR or of protected humanitarian convoys." The Security Council then went further to authorize member states to take "all necessary measures, through the use of air power, in and around the safe areas . . . to support UNPROFOR in the performance of its mandate" relating to the safe areas.

SUMMARY

There was little Security Council action during the winter of 1993–1994, although there was considerable activity in the conflict itself. The bombing of the marketplace in Sarajevo on 4 February 1994 spawned extensive international attention and a NATO response. The renewed attention prompted Security Council discussion in mid-February but no new resolutions were passed.

For the most part, having contracted out the air support aspect of the mandate to NATO the Security Council allowed events to take their course. This was partly the result of a deliberate decision on the part of Britain, France, and the United States to avoid discussion at the Security Council for fear that Russia would try to negate or weaken the NATO role. The Security Council did pass some resolutions during this time, but these were primarily oriented towards troop security and strength. On 31 March, in response to problems relating to a lack of cooperation with respect to the UNPROFOR mandate in Croatia, the Security Council extended the authorization for close air support to Croatia, "in defence of UNPROFOR personnel in the performance of UNPROFOR's mandate."[69] In September 1994, the Security Council took action on other aspects of the conflict, including allegations of ethnic cleansing[70] and in November it extended the authorization for the use of air power, based in Resolution 836, to Croatia.

During 1995, the Security Council, inter alia, extended the UNPROFOR mandate, authorized an increase in strength to allow for the deployment of a European rapid reaction force, and demanded respect for UNPROFOR freedom of movement, guarantees of security, and the release of UN hostages,[71] but there was no change in the nature and objectives of the mandate itself.

The overall goals of Security Council action were consistent from the beginning: sanctions on the one hand to apply pressure and punishment, and on the other, the delivery of humanitarian aid and establishment and maintenance of cease-fires to alleviate the human suffering caused by the conflict. The ban on military flights over Bosnia and the establishment of safe areas were means to that end. The various efforts to enforce safe area provisions and to ensure the freedom of movement and security of UNPROFOR troops, while they often came to seem as ends in themselves, were also means to that same end.

Although the Security Council added odds and ends of tasks and functions to the UNPROFOR mandate—many of which were never implemented[72]—this framework remained the primary focus. After Resolution 836 in June 1993, even as the war continued and even intensified, the Security Council fiddled with and added to the mandate but did not alter its basic nature.

CHARTER BASIS

Unlike the Congo situation, in dealing with Bosnia neither the secretary-general nor the Security Council seemed inclined to link mandate decisions to specific articles in the UN Charter, or to more closely define the basis for decisions relating to force beyond the general invocation of Chapter VII. The focus was on crossing the perceived line between peacekeeping and enforcement. As discussed earlier, although the situation on the ground did not meet peacekeeping criteria, the UNPROFOR operation was launched under the peacekeeping rubric. Over time, the absence of a cease-fire and consent posed increasingly significant problems for the operation. This eventually prompted the shift to a peace enforcement role for the operation, although only for specific aspects of the mandate.

The interesting choice the Security Council made was to "enforce" the humanitarian aid delivery provisions of its previous resolutions rather than to enforce the cease-fires, especially those made under formal signed agreements, which were routinely broken. This kind of response was the kind of action envisaged in the secretary-general's original peace enforcement proposal in An Agenda for Peace and, if implemented, it would have created the conditions the Security Council was looking for when it chose to use force to protect the delivery of humanitarian aid.

III. MANDATE IMPLEMENTATION

RULES OF ENGAGEMENT

The rules of engagement (ROE) for UNPROFOR reflected the original peace-keeping nature of the operation even after a more forceful approach was authorized. This continued to be the case through the duration of the operation, even though Chapter VII authorization was given for specific aspects of the mandate. As with any peacekeeping operation the primary rule is that soldiers are permitted to use force in self-defense. Therefore, under the UNPROFOR mandate, soldiers had the authority to use their weapons to defend themselves, other UN personnel, and people under their protection.[73] They were also authorized to resist attempts by forceful means to prevent the fulfillment of the mission's mandate. In addition, the ROE had a specific provision allowing for the use of weapons to resist "deliberate military or para-military incursions into the United Nations Protected Areas."[74]

In an interesting change from previous practice, the Security Council seemed to make a point of defining the use of force provisions relating to self-defense in the resolutions themselves. For example, Resolution 836, in expanding the safe area mandate, authorizes UNPROFOR troops to use force, "acting in self-defence" to reply to bombardments against the safe areas or deliberate obstruction to UNPROFOR freedom of movement in or around the safe areas. In practice, these clarifications did not represent any significant change in the existing ROE and, therefore, did not require a change in the regulations. Nor did it represent any great shift in the traditional peacekeeping practice of defining self-defense as including situations in which troops are being prohibited from implementing the mandate. Having the specific authorization contained in the Security Council resolution was, presumably, to give the point greater emphasis, if not as a signal to the warring parties, at least as a signal to the general public to give the perception of greater action.

THE NO-FLY ZONE

Having prepared in advance for the possibility of taking on the enforcement of the no-fly zone over Bosnia, NATO leaders had contingency plans already in place when Resolution 816 was passed on 31 March 1993. The NATO role was given final approval by the North Atlantic Council (NAC) on 8 April 1993 and Operation Deny Flight officially began on 12 April 1993.[75] The ROE for the operation were not designed for strenuous enforcement. The ROE restricted NATO planes from shooting down civilian aircraft or attacking ground installations even if NATO planes were being fired on. Military aircraft violating the zone were to be engaged and told to leave the zone. If they did not obey, warning shots would be fired, and if there was still no response NATO planes could then shoot down the intruder.[76] The reason for the fairly circumscribed nature of the enforcement was to avoid provoking a direct conflict with the Bosnian Serbs in order to meet the concerns of troop contributing countries who feared that stringent enforcement would result in repercussions against their troops on the ground.

A year passed before the enforcement operation resulted in the first use of force. On 28 February 1994, four NATO fighters engaged six military aircraft that were violating the no-fly zone. The six aircraft dropped their bombs while being pursued by the NATO fighters who were calling warnings to them as required by the ROE. The NATO fighters then shot down three of the aircraft. A fourth aircraft was shot down by a second set of NATO fighters.[77] This incident was the first enforcement of the no-fly zone as well as the first ever use of force by NATO forces since its creation.

In general, the enforcement of the no-fly zone was fairly successful. There continued to be, however, numerous violations of the zone by noncombat aircraft.[78] In addition, the parties to the conflict quickly caught on to NATO procedures and would use short-hop flying to thwart the ban, flying only long enough to activate a NATO response and then landing before NATO jets could respond, then starting the whole procedure all over again.[79]

HUMANITARIAN AID DELIVERY

The first instance of UNPROFOR troops using force to ensure the delivery of humanitarian aid occurred in November 1992 when French troops responded to an attack from Serbian forces in attempting to get aid through to Bosanska Krupa.[80] Overall, the actual use of force in providing "protective support" to humanitarian aid convoys was fairly minimal. This was due, in part, to a lack of resources. Although reinforcements were approved along with the new mission, they were slow to arrive and never arrived in the numbers really required. In addition, the relationship between UNPROFOR and UNHCR officials—who had been given the lead role in deciding when military protection was needed and when and where humanitarian aid would be delivered—created, on occasion, a certain level of frustration for the military.[81]

By far the most significant impediment to the delivery of humanitarian aid remained the unwillingness of the fighting groups to allow aid convoys to reach besieged areas unless it suited their overall goals. The downgrading of the original authorization of the use of force in Resolution 770—at the secretary-general's suggestion, and with the Security Council's agreement—so that the protective support mission was carried out under peacekeeping ROE meant that UNPROFOR troops continued to be dependent on the consent and cooperation of the fighting factions to permit the delivery of aid.[82] Inevitably, and especially as the war spread, this meant that humanitarian aid deliveries continued to be difficult, dangerous, or thwarted altogether. Although the humanitarian aid mission became somewhat subsumed by the safe area focus, UNPROFOR troops continued to provide convoy protection for humanitarian aid delivery through to the end of the mission.[83] During the course of the UNPROFOR operation, a total of 265,000 tonnes of aid was delivered to Bosnia.[84] This is a significant achievement given the constraints and dangers that were inherent in the delivery process.

SAFE AREAS

Whatever else the safe area concept may or may not have achieved, the decision to create six protected entities had the effect of providing an ongoing point of focus for the international media, and, therefore, western public opinion. As they suffered through the cycles of the war, these enclaves, most especially Srebrenica and Sarajevo, became symbols of the worst aspects of the conflict and in that respect they became the focal point for public pressure on policy makers.

The decision to "enforce" the safe area concept, contained in Resolution 836, occurred in the context of collapse in almost every aspect of the conflict. The Vance-Owen Peace Plan, the product of four months of intensive, difficult negotiations, was effectively dead. The conflict within Bosnia was deepening, especially as relations between the Bosnians and the Croatians were disintegrating into conflict. In addition, since January the Croatian military had been engaging in determined and ongoing incursions into the UNPAs. At the international level, the rift between the United States and Europe over the proper response to the conflict was widening and becoming increasingly public and damaging. At the same time, there was strong pressure from the publics in the west for some kind of effective response to the conflict.

In this context, Resolution 836 provided a way of giving the appearance of Security Council action. There was little in the way of initial physical support for the change in mandate. After the passage of Resolution 836, the secretary-general reported on the force requirements for the new mandate, as developed by UNPROFOR military personnel.[85] In order "to ensure full respect for the safe areas," the report estimated that an additional thirty-four thousand troops would be necessary. As an alternative, the secretary-general proposed a "light option" with a minimal troop requirement of seventy-six hundred.

While this option cannot, in itself, completely guarantee the defense of the safe areas, it relies on the threat of air action against any belligerents. Its principal advantage is that it presents an approach that is most likely to correspond to the volume of troops and material resources which can realistically be expected from Member States and which meets the imperative need for rapid deployment.[86]

The light option was a reflection, not of minimum military requirements, but of the minimum willingness of states to support, in real terms, the new set of tasks outlined in Resolution 836. In a 1999 report by Secretary-General Kofi Annan on the events surrounding the fall of Srebrenica, the secretary-general, who was then in charge of peacekeeping for the United Nations, gives a good sense of this problem.

The Secretariat informed UNPROFOR that none of the co-sponsors [of Resolution 836] was willing to contribute any additional troops for UNPROFOR, and that none of them seemed to envisage a force capable of effectively defending these areas. The Secretariat believed that there was unanimity among the co-sponsors that the extension of UNPROFOR's mandate to include a capacity to deter attack against the safe areas should not be construed as signifying deployment in sufficient strength to repel attacks by military force. UNPROFOR's major deterrent capacity, rather than being a function of military strength would essentially flow from its presence in the safe areas.[87]

The Security Council approved the light option increases to UNPROFOR strength in Resolution 844, on 18 June 1993. By 16 March 1994, almost exactly nine months later, the secretary-general reported that "even this minimum requirement [was] not met immediately by Member States. Efforts by the Secretariat to find creative solutions to the lack of equipped troops proved unavailing. . . . In the meantime, troops are being redeployed to Bosnia and Herzegovina from the UNPAs, but this threatens to reduce further the effectiveness of UNPROFOR in Croatia."[88]

USING AIR POWER

The response was not so half-hearted on the issue of using air power to back up the safe area mission. On 10 June, in response to an official UN request NATO agreed to undertake "air cover" tasks for the United Nations, the provision of which was intended to make up for the expected shortfall on the ground. "In response to UNSC Resolution 836 . . . we offer our protective airpower in case of attack against UNPROFOR in the performance of its overall mandate, if it so requests."[89] The interesting and overlooked aspect of this decision was that it extended protection not just to UNPROFOR troops in the safe areas but to UNPROFOR troops generally in the performance of their mission.

In order to preserve a UN role in decision making when it came to using air power, a "dual-key" decision-making system was established. Under this system a decision to use air power required the approval of both NATO military authorities and the UN secretary-general. A negative decision by either organization meant that air power would not be used. While this kept the United Nations in the decision-making loop, it also added to the decision-making time needed for action.

The shift to using air power was the beginning of what was to become a very high profile aspect of the mandate implementation. This use of air power also came to be easily and sometimes deliberately confused with the use of air strikes. An internal UNPROFOR memo, intended to clarify the distinctions, provides a good outline of the role of air power with respect to the safe area mandate.

In [Bosnia and Herzegovina], Close Air Support is clearly the use of air power in self-defense, not offensively. The authority to employ Close Air Support equals the authority to protect UNPROFOR and associate forces. The Force Commander's idea is that in BIH, airpower has two aspects: that of deterrence. . . . and that of actual use to save lives.[90]

Through the summer of 1993, the peace talks moved into a new phase, this time discussing the possibility of partitioning Bosnia into three separate units. At the same time, the Bosnian Serbs increased their pressure on Sarajevo. By late July, Bosnian Serb forces were moving in on Mount Igman near Sarajevo. The move prompted fears that the Bosnian Serbs were seeking to take over part of Sarajevo. The main supply route for Sarajevo also ran through the area and control of the mountain would give the Serbs a closer launching point for attacks on the city itself.[91] As the Serb pressure on Sarajevo increased, so did the U.S. pressure to use air strikes. As part of a broad policy shift on the situation in the Balkans and in response to its failure to get the arms embargo lifted for the Bosnian Muslims, the Clinton administration had moved on from its previous "lift and strike" proposal to straightforward proposals for a punitive policy of strike.[92]

The open U.S. advocacy of air strikes caused the long-standing and very contentious issue of ground versus air commitments to resurface strongly. Nothing had happened to change the basic concern of the Europeans and Canada—major troop contributors to UNPROFOR—that any significant enforcement action would lead to retaliation against UNPROFOR troops. The resentment associated with the perception that the United States was willing to risk the troops of other countries in a situation where it was unwilling to risk its own was not helped by U.S. statements that it was willing to undertake air strikes on its own, under the authority of Resolution 770.[93]

The debate came to a head at a special NAC meeting on 2 August 1993 in Brussels. After considerable discussion, the NAC decided in favor of a shift towards a wider use of air power. According to EC–negotiator David Owen, Canada "used all its unrivalled expertise of UN operations"[94] to lead the campaign to ensure that troop-contributing countries' concerns were incorporated into any resulting plan for air strikes. This had the effect of turning the debate into a U.S.–Canadian one rather than a U.S.–European one thus creating an opening for some common ground to be found. The communiqué issued after the meeting indicated NATO's decision

to make immediate preparations for undertaking, in the event that the strangulation of Sarajevo and other areas continues, including wide-scale interference with humanitarian assistance, stronger measures including air strikes against those responsible, Bosnian Serbs and others, in Bosnia and Herzegovina. These measures will be under the authority of the United Nations Security Council and within the framework of relevant U.N. Security Council resolutions, and in support of UNPROFOR in the performance of its overall mandate.[95]

The NAC instructed NATO military authorities to draw up the specifics of the arrangement in consultation with UNPROFOR. These plans were approved by the NAC on 9 August 1993. The NAC made special mention of its agreement with the UN secretary-general that "the first use of air strikes in the theatre shall be authorized by him."[96] This reinforced the dual-key system established for air cover and was a major concession to troop-contributing countries as well as being contrary to the U.S. desire to keep the decisions about when to use air power out of the UN loop. The North Atlantic Council prefaced its approval of the operational procedures with an emphasis on the nature of the decision. "The Council underlines again that the air strikes foreseen by the Council decisions of August 2 are limited to the support of humanitarian relief, and must not be interpreted as a decision to intervene militarily in the conflict."[97] A senior NATO military official quoted in the press said, "It's not a war strategy. It's a genuine attempt to put military strength in the service of diplomacy."[98]

In public statements after the NAC meeting, U.S. administration officials directly linked the air strike approval to the siege of Sarajevo, stating, for example, that if the siege did not end within a week, air strikes would be used.[99] The NAC communiqué relating to the operational procedures stated that "it is essential that the Bosnian Serbs lift without delay the siege of Sarajevo and that the heights around the city and the means of access are placed under the control of UNPROFOR."[100]

On 11 August, At the negotiations in Geneva, negotiators David Owen and Thorvald Stoltenberg[101] managed to get an agreement from the Bosnian Serbs that they would withdraw from the two mountains outside Sarajevo by the next day. This deadline was not met, but further negotiations resulted in a clearer agreement as to the requirements for withdrawal. The next day, the Serb withdrawal began and UNPROFOR personnel replaced Bosnian Serb troops. The whole changeover was carried out under ongoing NATO tests of the air power system it had put in place to enforce its decisions. This involved large numbers of low-flying overflights of NATO jets, creating an atmosphere of impending use of air strikes.

On the surface, it is difficult to escape the conclusion that the NATO threat and determination to use air power was a significant factor in achieving the Bosnian Serb pullback from their positions on Mount Igman and Mount Bjelasnica. But it is less clear what broader objective was served in the process. UN military commanders, in an unusual display of outspokenness, made clear their dislike and disapproval of the air strike option.[102] For the most part, their objections were the same as those of the troop-contributing countries who were concerned about retaliation against vulnerable UN troops on the ground. But they were also concerned about the effect of air strikes on UNPROFOR impartiality and they argued that UNPROFOR troops already operating at well below desirable numbers could be put to better use in other locations rather than taking over the Bosnian Serb positions outside Sarajevo thereby freeing up Bosnian Serb soldiers to be used elsewhere.[103]

Beyond the specific question of the Serb withdrawal from the two Sarajevo mountains is the question of the impact of the decision to threaten the use of air power on the parties to the conflict. Up until this point, the disagreement between the US and UNPROFOR troop contributors over using more forceful measures provided a fairly concrete sense of the level of permissible action on the ground. The ongoing disagreement meant an ongoing unlikelihood of international action being ratcheted up beyond the existing UNPROFOR commitment. This was effectively a "go ahead" signal to those parties intent on pursuing the conflict militarily who, therefore, had a fairly firm understanding of how far they could go without risking further international intervention. Another signal may have been sent, this time to the Bosnian government, when the decision was made to take more forceful action. The Bosnian government, perhaps feeling that the possible use of force by NATO meant there was now more to be gained militarily than in the talks, refused to participate in the Geneva peace talks until the siege of Sarajevo had ended.[104] The Bosnian government played the game as well as the others. The shift to the possibility of a more interventionist mood in the west was accompanied by a shift in the Bosnian government's military strategy.

THE SHIFT TO AIR STRIKES AND EXCLUSION ZONES

After the air strikes threat and the Serbian pullback in September, there was only one further major interchange that autumn, with respect to air strikes when in mid-October renewed Serb shelling of Sarajevo prompted a reminder that air strikes could be used to prevent another siege of Sarajevo.[105] Otherwise, international activity settled down through the rest of the autumn and early winter, the peace negotiations limped along, and the conflict continued unabated, taking a new turn with an upsurge in the actions and capabilities of Bosnian Muslim forces on the ground.[106]

Through this time the long-standing divisions among NATO members continued to simmer, prompting another major debate when NATO met in early January 1994. The communiqué resulting from the meeting reaffirmed the alliance's willingness to carry out air strikes in pursuit of the UN mandate. It made particular mention, however, of the situation at Srebrenica, where a planned UN rotation of troops was being blocked, and Tuzla where the airport was being kept closed, thereby blocking the delivery of humanitarian aid.[107] Britain and France forwarded the NATO declaration to the UN secretary-general, accompanying the declaration with proposals "about exceptional command-and-control arrangements which they thought would be appropriate for military operations specifically related to the current situation in those two safe areas."[108]

The debate on the use of air power prompted a response from the Russians who were now very concerned about the balance of decision-making power shifting too far in favor of NATO. In their démarches to the secretary-general on the subject, they restated their position that "any use of force . . . should be subject to prior consultations by the Secretary-General with the members of the Security Council and that only after such consultations should a decision be made to seek enforcement assistance from any source, including NATO."[109]

For his part, the secretary-general asked his special representative, Yasushi Akashi, to undertake an urgent study of the proposals. Akashi, after consultations with NATO and UNPROFOR officials, outlined three possible scenarios for action with respect to Srebrenica and Tuzla. The secretary-general reported that the plans provided that "air power would be used, if necessary, in self-defence against a deliberate attack upon UNPROFOR by any party. Should UNPROFOR be attacked in the implementation of the plans, I would not hesitate to initiate the use of close air support without delay."[110] The only new aspect of this statement was a clear indication on the part of the secretary-general of his willingness to authorize the use of air support with respect to the planned UN rotation at Srebrenica and Tuzla if UNPROFOR troops came under attack. However, in a new tone, which marked a shift away from the secretary-general's usual emphasis on UNPROFOR as a peacekeeping mission, the secretary-general went on to say:

It is obviously desirable that the plans should, if possible be implemented . . . by mutual agreement. The parties should, however, be aware that UNPROFOR's mandate for the safe areas has been adopted under Chapter VII of the United Nations Charter. Accordingly, UNPROFOR is not obliged to seek the consent of the parties for operations which fall within the mandate conferred upon it under Security Council resolutions 836(1993) and 844(1993).[111]

The political landscape changed entirely shortly after this general airing of the issues. On 5 February 1994, a mortar attack on a marketplace in Sarajevo resulted in sixty-eight deaths and approximately two hundred casualties. The event had a tremendous effect on international attitudes to the conflict, bringing new anguish and momentum to the various efforts to bring an end to the conflict. The next day, the secretary-general sent a request to NATO asking for urgent assistance in preparing for the use of air strikes against positions outside Sarajevo that were being used to attack the city.[112]

The secretary-general's request for NATO air strikes, a shift in the air support role that had been authorized by NATO so far, was dealt with at a meeting of the North Atlantic Council on 9 February. The NAC accepted the secretary-general's request for air strikes, to be carried out "at the request of the United Nations." But they did so in the context of an ultimatum they issued to the Bosnian Serbs. The North Atlantic Council, with a view to ending the "siege of Sarajevo . . . calls for the withdrawal, or regrouping and placing under UNPROFOR control, within ten days, of heavy weapons . . . of the Bosnian Serb forces located in an area within 20 kilometers of the centre of Sarajevo."[113]

At the same time that NATO was preparing its decisions UN officials negotiated and received agreement from the Bosnian Serbs on an exclusion zone. The NATO decision was, therefore, an endorsement of that agreement with the added enforcement provisions. The UN–brokered agreement provided a way for the Bosnian Serbs to bow out gracefully. This was significantly overshadowed, however, by the heavy media coverage of the NATO "ultimatum." The political situation was made more complicated by the fact that initial analyses of the mortar crater in the marketplace suggested that it was likely that Bosnian government forces had fired the mortar. Even a hint at this possibility in public would have thrown negotiations on all fronts into disarray. Every effort was made, therefore, to keep this information as closely guarded as possible within official circles.[114]

By 21 February 1994, the expiry of the heavy weapons deadline, the Bosnian Serb forces had complied with the exclusion zone provisions, at least to an extent that allowed Akashi and General Michael Rose, the UNPROFOR commander, to agree that the spirit of the agreement had been upheld. The Bosnian Serb compliance came late in the game and only after the irritated and sudden intervention of the Russians, whose lobbying for a new Security Council resolution was firmly denied by the United States, Britain, and France. The Russian decision, just days before the deadline, to move its UNPROFOR troops from Croatia to Sarajevo was critical to the Bosnian Serb decision to meet the deadline. David Owen provides an interesting analysis of the situation.

The Russian initiative seemed to have been taken without informing the US and without the knowledge of [Britain]. The Russians had not hidden their intense irritation at the NATO decision, from which they felt excluded. They warned that [Bosnian Serb General Ratko] Mladic would be delighted if NATO air strikes took place, since it would unite all Serbs and give him the freedom he did not currently have. . . . [S]ome said [that Bosnian Serb compliance] was a vindication of the threat of air strikes and a sign that the Bosnian Serbs would crumble under threat. I felt that it was the Russians who had taken the threat of NATO air strikes seriously and that it was their decision to move their troops to Sarajevo which had forced Mladic to act over his heavy weapons.[115]

Gorazde

Shortly afterwards, the focus shifted to the safe area of Gorazde. At the end of March, perhaps partly as a response to Bosnian Muslim attacks from the area and to test NATO resolve, the Bosnian Serbs began a bombardment of the Gorazde area. This was the first test of the safe area mandate outside of the Sarajevo context, forcing UNPROFOR to develop clear criteria for what kind of actions would generate a response. The resulting guidelines determined that, in order to prompt a response, an attack against a safe area must be unprovoked, deliberately targeted against a civilian population, and of sufficient intensity and duration to distinguish it from the usual day-to-day military skirmishes.[116]

After an initial pause in the shelling, with no NATO response, the Bosnian Serbs continued to attack Gorazde. On 10 April 1994, a day after a warning from the secretary-general to the Bosnian Serbs, General Rose requested close air support to protect UNPROFOR personnel.[117] The request was approved by Akashi, and NATO jets attacked Serbian military targets in the area that day and the next. The long-predicted Bosnian Serb retaliation came quickly. Bosnian Serb forces detained 155 UN troops, closed their access routes to Sarajevo, and cut off contact with UNPROFOR leaders. On 15 April, the Bosnian Serbs renewed their attacks on Gorazde. The Russian government, having lodged strong objections to the initial air strikes, backtracked after the renewed assault and supported the strikes.[118] On 16 April, the Serbs agreed to a cease-fire and the release of UN hostages in exchange for an end to air activity over Gorazde.[119]

On 18 April 1994, the secretary-general asked NATO officials to authorize an extension of its Sarajevo air strike authorization to the five other safe areas.[120] On 22 April, NATO officials responded positively to the secretary-general's request. In doing so, they established a heavy weapons exclusion zone around Gorazde, and authorized, in advance, a similar zone around the other safe areas if those areas came under heavy weapons attack or were threatened by such an attack. The Security Council passed Resolution 913 on the same day, demanding a cease-fire in Gorazde, a Bosnian Serb pullback from the area, and cessation of provocative military activity by all parties. The NATO decision established a deadline of 27 April for the withdrawal of Bosnian Serb heavy weapons from the exclusion zone and called on Bosnian forces not to launch offensive action from within the safe area.[121] The Bosnian Serb forces complied with the deadline and no air strikes were authorized.[122]

One of the products of this period was the creation of the Contact Group. The group's establishment recognized the importance of two critical players—Russia and the United States—both of whom were now playing a greater role at all levels, and helped bring Russia more clearly into the decision-making process.

BIHAC

In late November 1994, on the verge of another winter of conflict in the region, fighting in the Bihac area became intense. In August, Bosnian government forces finally regained the Bihac area from the rebel Muslim forces who had declared the area an autonomous province under the leadership of Fikret Abdic. This victory gave the government forces the opportunity to attempt to regain some ground with respect to Bosnian Serb forces in the area, prompting, in turn, a Bosnian Serb counteroffensive. By virtue of its location, this new fighting involved every group party to the conflict in the former Yugoslavia. Deep in western Bosnia, the Bihac fighting touched on vital interests of the Krajina-based Serbs, Croats in the same area, and the Croatian, Bosnian, and Yugoslav governments.

When the battle over Bihac intensified in mid-November, several factors worked against a concerted international response. The geography of Bihac made the creation and enforcement of an exclusion zone difficult. The Security Council had not previously defined the exact boundaries of Bihac as a safe area. As usual there was no easy agreement among the major powers as to the appropriate response, especially since the U.S. government had just announced that it would no longer enforce the arms embargo against the Bosnian government. The UNPROFOR troops on the ground were minimally armed and vulnerable.[123]

On 18–19 November, serious attacks on the city, including the use of napalm, prompted Security Council action. On 19 November, the Security Council passed Resolution 958. The resolution extended the provisions for "all necessary measures through the use of air power" from Resolution 836 to cover Croatia as well. This permitted, two days later, a NATO air attack on the runways of the Udbina airport in Croatia, which were being used as the launching point for the Serb attacks.[124] On 23 November, NATO jets fired in self-defense on a surface-to-air missile site.[125] The Bosnian Serbs again retaliated by detaining large numbers of UNPROFOR personnel and the emphasis switched back to negotiation between the parties and the UN, although fighting continued into the next year.

CEASE-FIRE

While the Bihac episode was relatively minor in the scale of UN use of force in the conflict, politically it represented a penultimate "last straw" and had important implications for international actions in the year that followed. The Bihac situation prompted a major debate among the key international players. On

25 November, the North Atlantic Council met to discuss a U.S. proposal for a much wider campaign of air strikes to be used to bring the conflict to an end. In the end, no decisions on new action were taken and the United States backed away from its proposals in order to avoid deepening the policy divisions on the issue at a time when NATO enlargement was also a critical policy issue.[126] The Bihac crisis pushed two major fault lines to a meeting point—the inherent contradictions in the safe area idea itself, and the inherent tension in a U.S. policy that advocated much stronger use of force without an accompanying willingness to risk U.S. lives. Bihac became, then, a kind of stopping point where there was a general rethinking of the entire situation. In the short term, the result was a new intensity in the focus on a comprehensive country-wide cease-fire and at the United Nations, serious talk of withdrawing the UNPROFOR mission.[127]

With the help of former president Jimmy Carter, on 23 December 1994 a four-month cease-fire agreement was signed by all of the parties to the conflict.[128] The cease-fire was mostly, though not entirely, respected and provided a breathing space for internal and external actors.[129] Rather than providing a stepping-stone to a peaceful resolution, however, the break in the fighting gave the parties to the conflict a chance to regroup and reequip for the next phase of fighting.

BACK TO SARAJEVO

During the last month of the cease-fire, the general military situation began to deteriorate. After the official end of the cease-fire, in early May the Bosnian Serbs once again began a serious shelling campaign against Sarajevo.[130] On 8 May 1994, UNPROFOR officials requested air strikes in response to Bosnian Serb shelling of the Butmir suburb of Sarajevo. The special representative of the secretary-general refused the request. The refusal prompted strong objections from the US and Britain, and the British government sent a formal letter of protest to the secretary-general.[131]

Ongoing fighting in the Sarajevo area over the next two weeks in conjunction with Bosnian Serb removal of more heavy weapons from weapons collection points, prompted another ultimatum. This time UNPROFOR called for a cease-fire by noon the next day and a return of the heavy weapons that had been removed. A second deadline for the following day was established for the removal of the heavy weapons from both sides, that had been brought into the area. When the deadline was not met, on 25 and 26 May, NATO forces conducted air strikes against ammunition depots and other military sites near the Bosnian Serb headquarters at Pale, just outside Sarajevo.[132] The strikes against the Pale targets marked the first time that force had been used against military targets other than those specifically linked to attacks in violation of the mandate and was a significant shift in UN strategy.

The Bosnian Serbs responded by declaring the United Nations an enemy, taking UNPROFOR personnel hostage (this time placing them as highly visible "human shields" at possible air target locations) attacking other safe areas (including an attack at Tuzla that killed seventy-one people), shutting down access to Sarajevo, and overtaking more weapons collection points. The hostage situation created a highly charged crisis atmosphere around the UNPROFOR operation. The idea of Sarajevo as a safe area had effectively ended with the seizure of the heavy weapons collection points. The situation of the peacekeepers, so long predicted by troop contributors, exacerbated the division between the United States and other NATO members. The United States, perhaps feeling somewhat contrite, or at least trying to appear so, seemed to be considering trying to help out on the ground, but then changed its mind.[133]

The secretary-general's report provides a good sense of the situation at that point.

Relative calm currently prevails in Sarajevo but this has been achieved at an unavoidable but high cost in detained personnel and in the complete isolation of United Nations forces in the Sarajevo area. UNPROFOR has also lost control over heavy weapons in collection points from which its personnel have been removed and is subjected to further restrictions on its freedom of movement. There has been a complete breakdown in negotiations to reopen Sarajevo airport and utilities are again being cut. . . . Finally, the ability of United Nations forces to operate effectively, efficiently and safely throughout much of Bosnia and Herzegovina, on the basis of impartiality and the consent of all parties, is now seriously compromised.[134]

THE RAPID REACTION FORCE

Once again, UN action came to a halt. There were two immediate results. First, the possibility of UN withdrawal, an idea that had been discussed in general terms since the previous autumn, now became a serious possibility. Second, France, the Netherlands, and Britain, pushed to the limit by the actions being taken against their soldiers in the field, established a rapid reaction force (RRF) and placed it at the service of UNPROFOR. The force consisted of two well-armed, mobile battalion groups. As an integral part of the UNPROFOR mission, operating under its command and ROE, the RRF was intended to overcome the inability of UNPROFOR to respond to the kind of retaliation the Bosnian Serb forces had been using against them.[135] The Security Council approved the inclusion of the RRF in UNPROFOR in Resolution 998 on 16 June 1995. Deployments of some elements of the force had already begun at that point, but it did not become fully operational until late July.

THE FALL OF THE SAFE AREAS

The safe area concept, having been previously exposed as vulnerable was now destroyed for Sarajevo. It was not long before the Bosnian Serbs moved on to the other safe areas. On 12 July, in an action that remains deeply controversial the Bosnian Serbs took control of the safe area of Srebrenica. Thousands of people fled and thousands of others were massacred by the Bosnian Serb forces.[136] On 25 July, a second safe area, Zepa, also fell to the Bosnian Serbs.[137] A very limited air strike was launched at Srebrenica as the Serbs advanced but with little effect and UN fears about the safety of UNPROFOR troops kept the response limited to that.[138] The RRF, only just operational, was not in a position to be shifted to either safe area and in any case it was not clear that the political will to do so existed. In both cases, UNPROFOR troops on the ground were small in number with only limited protection and had no choice other than to stand aside or be detained while the Serbs advanced. On 12 July, the Security Council passed Resolution 1004, calling for, inter alia, a restoration of Srebrenica as a safe area and for immediate UN access. The resolution contained no provisions for following through on the demands and had no effect.

On 21 July, the North Atlantic Council met and decided to authorize a "firm and rapid response of NATO's air power"[139] in the event of any similar moves by the Bosnian Serbs on Gorazde, the area generally considered to be the next Bosnian Serb target. By singling out Gorazde, NATO effectively doomed Zepa to defeat.[140] However, according to Richard Holbrooke, the lead U.S. negotiator, the NATO decision represented a kind of "line in the sand" for the alliance, marking a point beyond which it would not allow the Bosnian Serbs to proceed. The NATO decision had two practical effects. First, on 25 July the North Atlantic Council authorized air strikes (not air cover) in defense of Gorazde, and on 1 August, it expanded this authorization to include Sarajevo, Tuzla, and Bihac. Second, at the United Nations the secretary-general delegated his authority under the dual-key system to the UNPROFOR commander in the field, a decision intended to speed up the decision-making process with regards to the use of air cover and air strikes.[141]

Shortly after these decisions and the fall of Zepa, on 4 August the Croatian military launched Operation Storm and attacked the Krajina area at a number of points. The opening for this move was created earlier in the year. On 28 and 29 April, altercations between Serbs and Croatians on the Belgrade to Zagreb highway led to an attack on 1 May by the Croatian army on the area of the UNPA West. The Croatians very quickly had the upper hand while the Serbs retreated. The decisive Croatian action and the almost immediate collapse of Serb resistance brought an end to the idea of the invulnerability of the Serbs. Operation Storm was well planned and well executed and met with little resistance. Within a few days, the Croatians had captured the territory they wanted and halted their operation. The new conflict set off yet another wave of massive population movements in the area, this time by Serbs. An estimated one hundred and eighty thousand refugees left the region for Bosnia, eastern Slavonia, and Serbia.[142]

The territorial shifts since the end of the four-month cease-fire at the beginning of the year were significant. The changes came with a staggeringly high price in precisely the kind of population displacement, human suffering, and death that the United Nations had set out to stop. The cost to the international response was also high. Along the way, the contradictions and vulnerabilities of the UN operation had been exposed and used by the combatants, and the credibility of the mission was severely damaged.

OPERATION DELIBERATE FORCE

A number of different factors came together at this time to pave the way for a focused and sustained proactive rather than reactive use of force by the international community. The two most critical factors were the territorial shifts that occurred as a result of the fighting during the summer and a new U.S. policy with an accompanying determination to carry it out. With respect to the first factor, the various territorial gains and losses within Bosnia matched the general objectives of the parties. As a result, military pressure eased in a number of areas that had previously been in a state of high tension and the political aims of the parties were adjusted accordingly.

Earlier in the summer, the Clinton administration, having promised a contribution of U.S. troops to assist in a UN pullout if necessary, faced the prospect of having U.S. troops on the ground in Bosnia involved in a tricky and possibly costly ground war to extract UN troops during an election year. This prospect, along with public pressure and the seriousness of the rifts among NATO allies caused by its previous policies on the use of air strikes, prompted a major policy shift and new focus.[143] The new U.S. determination to get deeply involved in finding a solution to the crisis, one way or the other, brought new momentum to the whole process. Most important, the new U.S. focus brought the two streams of international response—the UNPROFOR operation and the peace negotiations—firmly together into one overall strategy and decision-making process for the first time.

On 28 August 1995, in a series of statements by U.S. officials the United States sent out a message that implied—though it did not necessarily say so explicitly—that a failure to make progress on a peace plan could result in a series of repercussions including lengthy bombing campaigns.[144] That same day, a mortar attack on the same Sarajevo marketplace that was the scene of the February 1994 bombing killed thirty-seven people and wounded eighty-eight.[145] The United Nations established very quickly that the Bosnian Serbs had launched the mortar. In response, the UNPROFOR commander in Sarajevo initiated a request for air strikes.[146] According to a later review of the events leading up to the fall of Srebrenica by Secretary-General Annan, the commander made the request and decided to turn his key in the dual-key system "without consulting his superiors in the United Nations or any of the troop contributing countries."[147] The NATO Commander agreed with the request for air strikes. Based on that dual-key authorization, on 30 August 1995, after waiting for the weather to clear, NATO launched Operation Deliberate Force. The stated objective was to: "reduce the threat to the Sarajevo Safe Area and to deter further attacks there or in any other Safe Area. We hope that this operation will also demonstrate to the Bosnian Serbs the futility of further military actions and convince all parties of the determination of the Alliance to implement its decisions."[148]

The speed and relative ease of the UN–NATO response was facilitated by the streamlining of the dual-key procedures that had occurred during the debate about Gorazde and the existing authorization for action relating to Sarajevo. It was also symptomatic of the extent to which a marketplace bombing had once again galvanized international action. The territorial shifts in the rest of Bosnia meant that, for the first time, there were no UNPROFOR troops stranded in small numbers in vulnerable locations in the countryside who were subject to Serb detention or hostage taking.[149] Around Sarajevo, the earlier Bosnian Serb raiding of the heavy weapons collection points meant that UN observers were no longer posted in those vulnerable locations.

For the United States, the marketplace bombing, so soon after its decision to take the lead on Bosnia, was seen as a deliberate personal affront. As such, it pushed the Clinton administration, already at the edge of its patience on the use of air power, to a determination to launch a sustained air campaign. Potential problems with NATO approval did not materialize. NATO secretary-general Willy Claes, having only just assumed office, agreed with the U.S. proposal for a bombing campaign and informed his colleagues of his decision, rather than calling a meeting to get their approval of his decision.[150]

The Bosnian Serbs were given a set of now familiar conditions to meet that involved a cease-fire, freedom of movement for UNPROFOR troops, the opening of the Sarajevo airport, and the withdrawal of heavy weapons from the Sarajevo exclusion zone.[151] The air strikes were put on hold from 1–4 September in order to give some time for diplomatic solutions and for the Bosnian Serbs to move the heavy weapons. When this did not happen, the NATO bombing campaign began again on 5 September.[152]

As the campaign continued, the Bosnian Serbs seemed to dig in rather than show signs of movement, prompting speculation as to how long the alliance could sustain the campaign politically and what the next step should be if the Bosnian Serbs continued to refuse to meet the conditions.[153] The Russians, as always a key actor, were firmly opposed to the bombing campaign and tried unsuccessfully to get a Security Council resolution to call an end to the bombing. Timing was also becoming an issue from a military point of view. During the second week of the campaign, NATO military officials informed the negotiating team that they were running out of so-called Option Two targets and would soon have to start retargeting Option One and Two targets or move to the much more contentious Option Three targets.[154] Just as these pressures began to make themselves felt, the Bosnian Serbs began to move. On 14 September, a three-day pause in the operation was initiated after the Bosnian Serbs agreed to meet the NATO–UN conditions. At the end of the three days, Bosnian Serb compliance was such that a further extension of seventy-two hours of the bombing pause was granted.[155]

After the three-day pause, the Bosnian Serbs were deemed to have complied with the conditions and the operation was put on hold.[156] Operation Deliberate Force involved a two-week-long bombing campaign coordinated with ground action involving the RRF. A total of three thousand five hundred and fifteen air sorties occurred on eleven days, with one thousand and twenty-six bombs dropped against military targets.[157]

While the bombing campaign was ongoing, the U.S. negotiating team, led by Holbrooke, was involved in intensive negotiations with the various parties to the conflict. On 8 September 1995, in the midst of the air campaign, the three parties agreed to the basic outlines of a settlement. Under the terms of the agreed principles, the parties agreed that Bosnia-Herzegovina would exist with its currently recognized boundaries and that as an entity Bosnia-Herzegovina would consist of two units: a Bosniac/Croat federation and the Republic of Srpska. The division of territory, to be decided, was to be based on the ratio of fifty-one to forty-nine (the federation/Republic of Srpska) as established in the Contact Group negotiations.[158]

In this context, the use of force became part of a broader strategy to bring the war to an end. Both Owen and Holbrooke maintain that the US deliberately encouraged the warring parties to engage in military action on the ground in order to bring about a territorial division that reflected the fifty-one to forty-nine split agreed to in the peace negotiations. Holbrooke maintains that he sent a very specific message to both the Bosnian and Croatian governments about continuing their offensives in early October within certain limits. He made sure the point was clear by pulling Croatian defence minister Gojko Susak aside and saying: "'Gojko, I want to be absolutely clear,' I said. 'Nothing we said today should be construed to mean that we want you to stop the rest of the offensive, other than Banja Luka. Speed is important. We can't say so publicly, but please take Sanski Most, Prijedor, and Bosanski Novi. And do it quickly, before the Serbs regroup!' "[159]

In the last stages of the fighting between Croatia and the Bosnian Serbs around Banja Luka, NATO forces did not enforce violations of the no-fly zone. According to Owen this was:

a clear indication that NATO and UN commanders did not want the military balance tilted so sharply that the Contact Group's 51-49 per cent split was put in jeopardy. These same Galeb fighter planes were also used against Bosnian government forces without NATO retaliation: another sign that a more sophisticated pressure was being applied on all parties amounting to the imposition of a settlement.[160]

On 5 October, the U.S. negotiating team announced that a full cease-fire agreement had been reached. The cease-fire was set to begin on 10 October and would last sixty days or until the completion of peace negotiations. Some last-minute military moves by the Bosnian Croats and the Bosnian Muslims delayed the cease-fire for forty-eight hours,[161] but thereafter the cease-fire held. A full-scale peace conference began at the Wright-Patterson Air Force Base in Dayton, Ohio, involving all of the parties. A final accord, the General Framework Agreement for Peace in Bosnia and Herzegovina, was signed three weeks later on 21 November 1995.[162]

IV. ISSUES

OPERATIONAL ISSUES

Troop Numbers

UNPROFOR suffered from beginning to end from insufficient troop contributions.[163] This had a significant limiting effect on the ability of the troops to carry out their mission. The inability of the secretary-general to muster sufficient troops to ensure mandate fulfillment reflected the basic political dilemma of the Yugoslav crisis—states wanted the conflict stopped and resolved but did not want to be physically part of that process. The secretary-general's reports through the crisis give evidence of the ongoing difficulties experienced by the Secretariat in trying to solicit sufficient troops and equipment.

The most blatant example of this problem and its repercussions was the Security Council decision, after already having approved an expanded mandate, to approve the so-called light option for augmenting UNPROFOR for the purposes of carrying out the new safe area mandate. The light option number simply represented the maximum troop commitment the Secretariat thought it would be able to obtain at that time and even that proved to be problematic.[164] The scale of difference between that option—seventy-six hundred—and what was thought necessary for fulfilling the mandate properly—thirty-four thousand—suggests that the eventual fall of the safe areas was entirely predictable. Even when the mandate and the ROE gave UN troops the ability to use force, they could not be expected to use force to attempt to fulfill the mission mandate when they were out-numbered and out-gunned by the parties to the conflict. Media coverage of instances in which UN troops did nothing or were made hostages while the conflict raged contributed to a general public misunderstanding of the mission and pressure for increased use of force rather than highlighting the need for greater resources.

The critical actor in this respect was the United States. Initially, the United States believed that the Europeans could and should take the lead on dealing with the Yugoslav situation through the various institutions they had available to them. As it became evident that this approach was not working, and as events in Bosnia deteriorated, the United States became more involved in the efforts to bring the conflict to an end. While there was some sense of relief about U.S. involvement, and the greater involvement of NATO that came with it, the increased participation of the US in the various aspects of the conflict management process was very much a mixed blessing. On the one hand, the United States was the most vocal advocate of stronger action, on the other, it criticized Europe's handling of the conflict, criticized the actions of the UN commanders in the field, and remained steadfastly unwilling to consider contributing U.S. ground troops to the operation. U.S. experience in Somalia along with a visceral political fear of another Vietnam fed that unwillingness. The hands-in, feet-off approach of the United States eventually produced an emphasis on the use of air power. It also exacerbated a deep divide between them and the troop-contributing countries. This division over the role and extent of the use of force had significant repercussions for how the mission was carried out.

Command and Control

The dual-key system was established to keep the UN connected to the decision making on when force was to be used. Any decision to use force, in the form of air power, had to be approved by both the NATO commander and by the UN secretary-general. The system was a set-up for criticism of the UN who inevitably became the scapegoat when the use of air power was requested but refused. The system also contributed to an unavoidable time lag in decision making, which meant that by the time a decision to use air power was taken, the targets in question might have moved, stopped firing, or the weather might have closed in, thus making a response impossible in a reasonable time frame.

Nonetheless, the system was important in maintaining the link between the UN and NATO on use of force decision making. Over time, operational considerations outweighed political needs and contributed to a streamlining of the dual-key system. The more streamlined the dual-key system became, however, the more the decision-making base for the use of force shifted to NATO officials. This shift had a variety of implications for the UNPROFOR operation. Once the decision to use air power was made, the operation, at least the air operation, effectively became a NATO one with limited UN input into decision making. In his report on Srebrenica, the secretary-general indicates that this very outcome was one of the reasons the United Nations was so hesitant about authorizing the use of air power, noting that "once the 'key' was turned 'on' we did not know if we would be able to turn it 'off.' "[165]

Like the situation in Somalia, the longer the conflict went on the greater the number of actors that became involved at both the political and military levels. This complicated the decision-making environment. By the end of the conflict, NATO, the United States, and Britain, France, and the Netherlands in the form of the rapid reaction force, had joined the UN as key decision makers, all with their own agendas in the conflict. The decision making was further complicated by the disconnect between Security Council resolutions that over time, expanded the use of force authorization and added mandate tasks without a commensurate addition of military support, and decisions made by UNPROFOR commanders in the field based on what they might best be able to achieve given the resources they had at hand and the constraints of the environment in which they were operating. This disconnect was further exacerbated by the debate over the use of air power, which UNPROFOR commanders and troop-contributing countries tended to oppose because of concern for the repercussions for their troops on the ground. All of these factors put tremendous pressure on the unity of effort of the operation.

MANDATE ISSUES

Mandate Contradictions

Having established the criteria for recognition with respect to Croatia and Slovenia, the EC and then the UN had little choice but to recognize Bosnia-Herzegovina when it met the same criteria. The acceptance of Bosnia-Herzegovina as an independent state created a contradiction in the UN approach. With recognition and UN membership, Bosnia-Herzegovina was entitled to all of the protections provided by the UN Charter, and yet the United Nations continued to approach the conflict as if it was an internal one, an approach that required it to maintain impartiality in its dealings with the various groups—some of them clearly external actors—engaging in the conflict. Full-scale enforcement, with no necessity for impartiality, was always an option after Bosnia-Herzegovina received international recognition and was accepted as a member state of the United Nations—an option the Security Council never contemplated.

The one overriding characteristic of the Security Council approach to the conflict is that it was completely and consistently reactive. There was never any attempt within the Security Council to develop an overall consistent strategy for the conflict itself. Instead, mandates were passed and new tasks were added as events, such as the two marketplace bombings and the resulting public outcry, created pressure for action. This created a very unstable and contradictory structure of tasks. Some tasks were unimplementable and for others implementation was never even attempted.

Nowhere were the mandate complications and contradictions more evident than in the Security Council's safe area policy. In a war about territory and who lives on it, the safe areas protected populations of one of the parties to the conflict and not of others, and made a clear association of territory with that population. They protected some towns and some civilians while leaving the rest of the country "unprotected." The policy was dependent on the compliance of the warring parties and the willingness of the international community to provide sufficient troops and resources for implementation. Neither condition was forthcoming, nor, it could be argued, was there a reasonable expectation of either condition being met at the time the mandates were passed. Therefore, when force was used to enforce these mandates, it should not have been a surprise that it resulted in the mission being compromised and stalemated.

Chapter VII Syndrome

In the initial phases of the conflict, the Security Council was quite careful about its invocations of Chapter VII, and when it expanded its definition of when force might be used, within the concept of self-defense, it did so in carefully detailed ways. In early 1993, though, the Security Council began a pattern of invoking Chapter VII virtually automatically. In part, this was a response to the pressure of events on the ground. It was also, though, a way of dealing with the divergence of views about what kind of action should be taken between troop-contributing countries and nontroop-contributing countries. As a result, the UNPROFOR mandate became "rhetorically more robust than the Force itself."[166]

The continued use of Chapter VII authorizations contributed to a degree of public misperception (inside and outside Bosnia) about the extent to which UN-PROFOR troops were mandated to use force. This was a misperception that the Security Council played into. Invoking Chapter VII gave an impression of a strong response while simultaneously creating false expectations of action. In these situations, it is the passage of the mandate itself rather than the follow-up action that gets public attention. Press reports rarely cover things like the secretary-general's reports that clearly point out mandate contradictions or problems with implementation. This was a high-risk response, since the mandate contradictions and additions, compounded by persistent undermanning and under-equipping problems, created serious credibility problems for the United Nations and almost brought about the complete failure and withdrawal of the mission. By failing to back up its Chapter VII invocations with concrete support of the mandate's implementation, the Security Council contributed to a serious disintegration of UN credibility that extended well beyond the Balkans.

Security Council Choices

One of the fundamental characteristics of a peace enforcement operation is the importance of maintaining UN impartiality. This is in contrast to full-scale enforcement in which UN actions are directed against a clearly identified aggressor state or party. Since peace enforcement operations tend to occur in high-tension situations or where fighting is ongoing, this presents a very fine line to be walked for the operation.

In the case of Bosnia, several factors turned that fine line into a tightrope. In Bosnia, aid tended to benefit Bosnian Muslims, as those most in need, more than any other party and aid was certainly portrayed in that light in the western press. In a conflict in which civilians were almost a unit of exchange, aid, because it benefited those civilians, was equally political. The parties to the conflict used humanitarian aid and its delivery as a form of local power. Allowing or preventing the delivery of aid became part and parcel of the general strategy of conflict in given instances. The very concept of safe areas, which protected populations that were primarily Bosnian Muslim, fed into rather than diminished this equation.

The Security Council strategy reflected an early and unchanging decision to try to alleviate the worst civilian consequences of the conflict, while steering clear of trying to deal with or stop its basic cause—the conflict itself. Rather than acting as a forum for leading the international response to a threat to international peace and security, the Security Council became a kind of caretaker of the civilian victims of the war. Even in that sense its actions may have been counterproductive. The secretary-general's report on Srebrenica notes that during the eighteen months of maximum Security Council activity on Bosnia, "Bosnian Serb forces operated almost unchecked; by the time the confrontation line stabilized, in mid-1993, approximately two million people, or one half of the total population of Bosnia and Herzegovina, had fled their homes or been expelled."[167]

The Security Council deliberately chose to enforce measures whose purpose was to alleviate suffering, rather than to enforce any of the agreed to but violated cease-fires. The enforcement of an agreed cease-fire would not have required a shift to full-scale Chapter VII enforcement. Had such a decision been made and been accompanied by the kind of physical, financial, and political backing given to the Implementation Force (IFOR) and Stabilization Force (SFOR) operations that came after the Dayton peace agreement, it might have created the temporary political breathing space needed to provide for serious negotiation that UNPRO-FOR was first established to create. The decision not to enforce something as fundamental to the peace process as a cease-fire sent a signal to warring parties about Security Council attitudes and expectations, making it clear that cease-fire infringements were less important than the blocking of humanitarian aid.

But the Security Council did remain consistent in its focus on the humanitarian consequences of the conflict and this made it possible for the United Nations to stay on the tightrope of impartiality it created for itself in Bosnia, if only just. Specifically, the Security Council established clear objectives, however questionable, and UNPROFOR was able to direct its efforts, to the extent it was able, towards their implementation. Like the Katangese gendarmes just prior to the final UN military push in the Congo, the Bosnian Serbs handed the United Nations an opportunity for military action by shelling the Sarajevo marketplace. This act made it possible for the United Nations to carry out Operation Deliberate Force as an operation that was technically seeking to compel compliance with the Security Council mandate and thereby avoid allegations that it was taking a military initiative with a view to forcing a solution to the conflict.

By sticking to the humanitarian aspects of the conflict in its mandates and mandate enforcement, the Security Council also—deliberately—created a certain distance between UN involvement in the peace negotiations, in their various forms, and the UN response to the conflict. With the direct involvement of the United States (driven by the fear of being drawn into a ground operation to facilitate the withdrawal of a failed operation) in both the peace negotiations and the use of force decision making, those two aspects were brought much more firmly together than they had been previously, with a cease-fire and eventual peace treaty as a result.

NOTES

1. For a general description of Yugoslavia during this time period, see Susan L. Woodward, *Balkan Tragedy* (Washington D.C.: Brookings, 1995). See also S/23169, Annex V, "Note on economic difficulties being experienced by Yugoslavia," 25 October 1991, which, inter alia, says that "in the 1980s, growth slowed and eventually declined; through the 1980s, unemployment was about 15–20 per cent and inflation was close to 100 per

cent per year. Economic stagnation and frustration inevitably exacerbated political tensions."

2. "Slovenes Vote Decisively for Independence from Yugoslavia," *New York Times*, 24 December 1990, A4.

3. For events leading up to the independence declarations, see Woodward, *Balkan Tragedy*; "The Conflict in Yugoslavia—A Chronology," in Daniel Bethlehem and Marc Weller, eds., *The "Yugoslav" Crisis in International Law: General Issues, Part I*, Cambridge International Documents Series, vol. 5 (Cambridge: Cambridge University Press, 1997); and Laura Silber and Allan Little, *The Death of Yugoslavia* (London: Penguin, 1995).

4. On 15 May 1991, Serbia prevented the planned rotation of the collective presidency to the Croatian representative, Stipe Mesic, creating a constitutional crisis. "Rotation of Yugoslav Leaders Blocked by Dominant Region," *New York Times*, 16 May 1991, A1, A14.

5. See, for example, Celestine Bohlen, "Yugoslav Army Says It Will Quell Ethnic Clashes," *New York Times*, 7 May 1991, A8; See also Silber and Little, *Death of Yugoslavia*, 81; and "Chronology," Bethlehem and Weller, *The "Yugoslav" Crisis in International Law*, xxiv-xxv.

6. The troika included the past, present, and future presidents of the Council of Ministers of the EC. At this time, this involved the foreign ministers of Luxembourg, Italy, and the Netherlands.

7. The agreement was signed on the island of Brioni and is known as the Brioni Agreement.

8. Woodward, *Balkan Tragedy*, 169.

9. "More Yugoslavs Roll Into Croatia: Civilian Leader Ponders His Role," *New York Times*, 19 August 1991, A3; "Fighting May Unravel Yugoslav Truce," *New York Times*, 24 August 1991, A3.; and "Fighting Rages on in Croatia," *Financial Times*, 23 August 1991, A5. For more details of the escalation of the fighting, see *Keesing's Record of World Events* (September 1991): 38420–38421.

10. John Tagliabue, "Capital of Croatia under Attack As Yugoslav Accord Breaks Down," *New York Times*, 18 September 1991, A1, A7.

11. Most European states had a vested interest in avoiding the dissolution of the state of Yugoslavia on the basis of national or religious groupings for fear of setting precedents that could be followed by groups in their own or neighboring states.

12. For an overview of the European efforts, see Woodward, *Balkan Tragedy*; and David Owen, *Balkan Odyssey* (London: Indigo, 1996).

13. S/23060, 23 September 1991.

14. S/23169, 25 October 1991.

15. Chuck Sudetic, "Shelling of Besieged Yugoslav Port Is Intensified," *New York Times*, 13 November 1991, A12; Chuck Sudetic, "House-to-House Fighting in Croatian City Nears End," *New York Times*, 14 November 1991, A8.

16. "Declaration on Yugoslavia," S/23203, 8 November 1991.

17. See for example, Olivia Ward, "Oil Embargo on Yugoslavia Stalled at U.N.," *Toronto Star*, 21 November 1991, A17.

18. The secretary-general raised the issue with Security Council members in informal consultations on 15 November and asked Cyrus Vance to raise the issue with the parties to the conflict. See S/23239, 24 November 1991. Leonard Doyle, "Seizing the Initiative, UN Chief Pushes Forward to Secure Peacekeepers for War-torn Yugoslavia," *Ottawa Citizen* (from the *Independent*), 16 November 1991, 2.

19. S/23240, 26 November 1991.

20. Security Council Resolution 724, 15 December 1991.

21. Security Council Resolution 727, 8 January 1992.

22. Security Council Resolution 740, 7 February 1992.

23. S/23592, 15 February 1992.

24. Ibid., para. 28.

25. Ibid., para. 28, 29.

26. The outline of the plan is contained in S/23280, "Annex 3," 11 December 1991.

27. Lord Carrington, letter to Hans van den Broek, EC Council of Foreign Ministers, December 1991.

28. In an initial letter to the head of the EC, the foreign minister for the Netherlands, Secretary-General Pérez de Cuéllar quoted "high-level interlocutors" as describing recognition as a "potential time bomb." Javier Pérez de Cuéllar, letter to His Excellency, Mr. H. van den Broek, Minister for Foreign Affairs of the Kingdom of the Netherlands, 10 December 1991. In response, German foreign minister Genscher wrote, inter alia, that "the Serbian leadership together with the Yugoslav National Army bear the main responsibility for the non-compliance in Croatia with the cease-fire . . . To refuse recognition to those republics which desire their independence must lead to a further escalation of the use of force by the National Army which would construe it as a validation of its policy of conquest." See letter dated 13 December 1991, (courtesy translation). Secretary-General Pérez de Cuéllar replied that "early selective recognitions . . . could have grave consequences for the Balkan region as a whole, and it would seriously undermine my own efforts and those of my Personal Envoy to secure the conditions necessary for the deployment of a peace-keeping operation in Yugoslavia." Letter from Secretary-General Javier Pérez de Cuéllar to His Excellency, Mr. Hans-Dietrich Genscher, Vice-Chancellor and Minister for Foreign Affairs of the Federal Republic of Germany, 14 December 1991.

29. Stephen Kinzer, "Slovenia and Croatia Get Bonn's Nod," New York Times, 24 December 1991, A3.

30. Most Serbian citizens of the republic boycotted the referendum.

31. Security Council Resolution 749, 7 April 1992.

32. S/23900, 12 May 1992, para. 5.

33. S/24075, 6 June 1992, para. 4.

34. Security Council Resolution 762, 30 June 1992, increased UNPROFOR strength by sixty military observers and one hundred and twenty civilian police. Security Council Resolution 764, 13 July 1992, approved an expansion of the total needed to implement the Sarajevo airport aspect of the operation from an original eleven hundred to sixteen hundred.

35. Under the Lisbon Agreement, signed on 18 March 1992, the leaders of the three main groups in Bosnia agreed to recognize Bosnia's borders and to a single state that would be divided into three nations. Izetbegovic, the leader of the Bosnian delegation, reneged on the agreement almost as soon as he returned to Bosnia.

36. The ICFY officially began on 3 September 1992 in London. For detailed discussion see Owen, Balkan Odyssey, 32–93.

37. "U.S. Hints at Bosnian Intervention," Globe and Mail, 7 July 1992, A1; Craig R. Whitney, "Leaders in Munich Warn Rival Force in Bosnian Strife," New York Times, 8 July 1992, A1; and Paul Bedard, "7 Richest Nations Threaten Force," Washington Post, 8 July 1992, 1.

38. S/23900, 12 May 1992, para. 25.

39. Ibid., para. 12, 27.

40. Ibid., para. 30; and S/24000, 26 May 1992, para. 21.

41. Security Council Resolution 770, 13 August 1992.

42. Michael R. Gordon, "NATO Seeks Options to Troop Plan in Bosnia," *New York Times*, 14 August 1992, A6.

43. S/PV.3106, 13 August 1992, emphasis added. For the later responses from U.S. General Colin Powell, the Chairman of the Joint Chiefs of Staff, see Michael R. Gordon, "Powell Delivers a Resounding No on Using Limited Force in Bosnia," *New York Times*, 28 September 1992, 1, A5; and Colin L. Powell, "Why Generals Get Nervous," *New York Times*, 8 October 1992, A35.

44. S/24540, 10 September 1992.

45. Ibid., para. 3.

46. Ibid., para. 9.

47. Michael R. Gordon, "U.S. Says Serbian Warplanes Use Relief Flights as 'Cover,' " *New York Times*, 11 September 1992, A10.

48. Paul Lewis, "Bosnian Serbs' Forces Agree to Grounding of Military Planes," *New York Times*, 14 October 1992, A10. Also see, S/24783, 9 November 1992, which lists twenty-four known violations of the ban between 22 October and 4 November.

49. By 17 March 1993, there had been four hundred and sixty-five recorded violations of the no-fly zone. Security Council, *Statement by the President*, 17 March 1993.

50. Security Council Resolution 816, 31 March 1993.

51. U.S. Secretary of State, Lawrence Eagleburger, "Time to Consider Tougher Measures in Former Yugoslavia," *Text*, U.S. Embassy, Ottawa, Canada, 17 December 1992; Paul Lewis, "U.N. about to Step up Action on Serbia," *New York Times*, 18 December 1992; Blaine Harden, "U.N. General's Opposition," *Manchester Guardian Weekly*, 20 December 1992, 17; and David Binder, "U.N. and the Bosnian Foes Make New Political Attempt in Geneva," *New York Times*, 29 December 1992, A3.

52. Jeff Sallot, "NATO Officials Prepare to Enforce No-fly Zone," *Globe and Mail*, 16 December 1992, A13; Paul Lewis, "NATO to Help U.N. on Yugoslav Plans," *New York Times*, 16 December 1992, A3; "NATO Agrees to Enforce Flight Ban over Bosnia Ordered by U.N.," *New York Times*, 3 April 1993; and NATO, "NATO starts enforcement of no-fly zone," NATO Press Release, reprinted in *NATO Review* (April 1993): 5.

53. Paul Lewis, "U.N. Official Says the Serbs are Inflicting a 'Massacre,' " *New York Times*, 4 March 1993, A8; Chuck Sudetic, "Serbs Reported Willing to Allow Muslims to Leave Overrun Area," *New York Times*, 5 March 1993, A1, A8; "Local Serbs Still Thwart U.N. Evacuation of Muslims," *New York Times*, 10 March 1993, A8; and "Serbs Overrun Muslim Enclave in Bosnia's East," *New York Times*, 15 March 1993, A3.

54. For example, see John F. Burns, "U.N. General to Stay in Bosnian Town," *New York Times*, 17 March 1993, A3; and "Aid Trucks Arrive in a Bosnian Town after Serbs Yield," *New York Times*, 20 March 1993, A1.

55. In early April, an attempted UN evacuation of Muslim civilians from the town failed when a Bosnian officer refused to allow the evacuation on the grounds that it would leave the town empty and allow for a Serb takeover. See John F. Burns, "Muslim Officer Stops U.N. Evacuation of Srebrenica," *New York Times*, 5 April 1993, A3. See also "U.N. Plans to Evacuate 20,000 Besieged Muslims," *New York Times*, 6 April 1993, A14; Paul Koring, "Canadians Try to Save Town," *Globe and Mail*, 8 April 1993, A1, A13; and "UN Plans Huge Rescue Operation from Doomed Srebrenica," *Manchester Guardian Weekly*, 11 April 1993, 7.

56. Paul Lewis, "Russians Resisting Tighter Sanctions against Belgrade," *New York Times*, 9 April 1993, A1, A6; "Russia Seeks to Delay Vote on Belgrade Sanctions," *New York Times*, 12 April 1993, A8; and Elaine Sciolino, "U.S. Agrees to Delay in Voting on Serbia Sanctions," *New York Times*, 13 April 1993, A9.

57. The idea came from the experience of creating a "safe haven" for Kurds fleeing persecution and fighting in Iraq in Operation Provide Comfort.

58. Report of the Secretary-General Pursuant to General Assembly Resolution 53/35 (1998), Srebrenica Report, 15 November 1999 [hereafter cited as Srebrenica Report] para. 58.

59. See, for example, Stephen Kinzer, "Serbs Attack Muslim Stronghold in Northwest Bosnia," *New York Times*, 28 April 1993, A11.

60. S/25700, 30 April 1993, para. 18.

61. Ibid., para. 24.

62. Ibid., para. 46.

63. Ibid., para. 47, 48, emphasis added.

64. R. W. Apple, "Head Bosnia Serb, Facing U.S. Action, Signs Peace Plan," *New York Times*, 3 May 1993, A1, A11. For a detailed discussion of the Vance-Owen Peace Plan and the circumstances surrounding its signature, see Owen, *Balkan Odyssey*, especially chapter 4.

65. John F. Burns, "Nationalist Says Serbs' Rejection of Pact Means the End of Bosnia," *New York Times*, 17 May 1993, A1, A6; and "Bosnian Serbs' Leaders Meet to Ratify Vote Rejecting Peace Plan," *New York Times*, 20 May 1993, A12.

66. Michael R. Gordon, "U.S. Sees Air Raids Curbing Guns but Not Ending War," *New York Times*, 7 May 1993, A10.

67. Elaine Sciolino, "Christopher Fails to Win Consensus" *New York Times*, 7 May 1993, A12; Roger Cohen, "Europeans Reject U.S. Plan to Aid Bosnia and Halt Serbs," *New York Times*, 11 May 1993, A1, A8; and Paul Koring, "PM Opposes Bosnia Air Strike," *Globe and Mail*, 12 May 1993, 1.

68. Mr. Muhamed Sacirbey pointed out, inter alia, that "the Security Council has, at least implicitly, declared an open season on the unfortunate majority of our towns and citizens, who do not happen to fall into 'safe areas'. . . . [W]hat comfort can the citizens of Bosnia have in the resolve of the United Nations-mandated forces to defend 'safe areas'? Sarajevo suffered the heaviest shelling within the last year only after being designated a 'safe area'. Zepa has become virtually a ghost town after being shelled by Serbian forces in recognition of its designation. . . . Gorazde has been a safe area for almost two months or more, and it has not received a single relief convoy. And now, when it is being subjected to genocidal assault, not a single United Nations observer has braved Serbian obstructions to enter and fulfil this Council's mandate." See S/PV.3228, 4 June 1993, para. 4, 5.

69. Security Council Resolution 908, 31 March 1994. This resolution also approved a new series of tasks for UNPROFOR relating to the agreements signed between the Bosnian and Croatian governments and Bosnian Croatians. Known as the Framework Agreement (S/1994/255, 4 March 1994), this agreement set out the basic principles for future negotiations between the two sides on a confederation arrangement. The tasks included: monitoring a cease-fire along the confrontation lines, monitoring and establishing heavy weapons collection sites, transporting protected prisoners, and assisting in repairs to utilities. See S/1994/291, 11 March 1994, para. 14. The Security Council did not follow the secretary-general's recommendation that these new tasks "urgently" required reinforcements totalling six thousand and fifty troops, however, and the resolution emphasized the need for UNPROFOR to use its resources "in a flexible manner," authorizing a total new commitment of thirty-five hundred additional troops, with a promise of further action by 30 April 1994.

70. Resolution 941 called for an end to violations of international humanitarian law, singling out ethnic cleansing. Resolution 942 approved the territorial settlement currently under discussion and condemned the Bosnian Serb refusal to accept the settlement, expanding the sanctions against the Bosnian Serbs. Resolution 943 dealt with sanctions

against Yugoslavia. All three resolutions invoked Chapter VII and all three were passed on 23 September 1994.

71. Security Council Resolution 981, 31 March 1995, Security Council Resolution 982, 31 March 1995, Security Council Resolution 987, 19 April 1995, Security Council Resolution 988, 21 April 1995, Security Council Resolution 990, 28 April 1995, Security Council Resolution 998, 16 June 1995, and Security Council Resolution 1004, 12 July 1995.

72. For example, Resolution 838, 10 June 1993, called for international monitors to be deployed on the Croatia-Bosnia border. This was never pursued.

73. UNPROFOR Chief of Staff, *Force Commander's Policy Directive No. 13- Revised*, Headquarters UNPROFOR , Ilica Barracks, Zagreb, 24 June 1994. Also see United Nations Protection Force, *Force Commander Directive No. 01: Rules of Engagement*, HQ/UNPROFOR, Sarajevo, 24 March 1992. For an interesting example of the use of the ROE relating to being able to use force to protect people under UN protection, see "UN Hails Defiant Spanish Officer as Bosnian Hero," *Guardian*, 29 April 1993. The Spanish UNPROFOR soldier took 171 Croats fleeing Muslim militia under the protection of the "international community." A similar situation occurred during the Croatian Operation Storm in 1995 when Canadian Brigadier General Alain Forand sheltered Croatian Serbs. Interview with Canadian military personnel.

74. UNPROFOR Chief of Staff, *Force Commander's Policy Directive No. 13- Revised*, Headquarters UNPROFOR , Ilica Barracks, Zagreb, 24 June 1994. For more on the ROE, see Jane Boulden, "Rules of Engagement, Force Structure and Composition in United Nations Disarmament Operations," in *Managing Arms in Peace Processes: The Issues*, (Geneva: UN Institute for Disarmament Research, 1996) 135–168.

75. Allied Forces Southern Europe (AFSOUTH), "Operation Deny Flight," *Fact Sheet*, 13 January 1995.

76. Dick A. Leurdijk, *The United Nations and NATO in Former Yugoslavia, 1991– 1996, Limits to Diplomacy and Force* (The Hague: Netherlands Institute for International Relations, 1996) 31.

77. AFSOUTH, "Operation Deny Flight," *Fact Sheet*, 13 January 1995.

78. S/1994/300, 16 March 1994.

79. "NATO concern about No-Fly Zone Infringements," ICFY Memo, 18 December 1993.

80. Chuck Sudetic, "U.N. Troops' Role Widens in Bosnia; Aid Reaches Town," *New York Times*, 20 November 1992, A1, A8.

81. Åge Eknes, *Blue Helmets in a Blown Mission?* Research Report no. 174. (Oslo: Norwegian Institute of International Affairs, 1993) 56–62. For example, on 17 February 1993, UNHCR suspended the delivery of aid. The decision, taken without consulting any of the other UN actors, was a response to the Bosnian government's refusal to allow aid deliveries to Sarajevo until aid had reached towns in eastern Bosnia. The secretary-general overrode the decision a few days later. General Morillon reportedly overruled the decision instantly, when he was informed of it by reporters. See John F. Burns, "Most Relief Operations in Bosnia Are Halted by U.N. Aid Agency," *New York Times*, 18 February 1993, A1, A8; and Paul Lewis, "U.N. Chief, Overruling High Aide, Orders Bosnian Relief to Resume," *New York Times*, 20 February 1993, 1,2.

82. See, for example, John F. Burns, "U.N. Aid Convoy in Bosnia Blocked by Serbs for 3rd Day," *New York Times*, 17 February 1993.

83. See, for example, S/1994/300, 16 March 1994, para. 20–22. Also see United States General Accounting Office, *Humanitarian Intervention, Effectiveness of U.N. Operations in Bosnia* (Washington, D.C.: U.S. Government Printing Office, GAO/NSIAD

94-156BR, April 1994), which discusses the situation and whether or not aid was being withheld to pressure a settlement.

84. This figure represents a combined total of one hundred and seventy-five thousand tonnes of food delivered by the airlift to Sarajevo and ninety thousand tonnes brought in by road convoy. Figures from UNHCR records are quoted in William J. Durch and James A. Schear, "Faultlines: UN Operations in the Former Yugoslavia," in William J. Durch, ed., *UN Peacekeeping, American Policy and the Uncivil Wars of the 1990s* (New York: St. Martin's, 1996) 250.

85. S/25939, 14 June 1993.

86. Ibid., para. 5.

87. Srebrenica Report, para. 95.

88. S/1994/300, 16 March 1994, para. 25–26. The secretary-general added: "Before adopting resolutions requiring additional troops and equipment, the Council may therefore wish to take into account the severe difficulties which the United Nations already encounters in obtaining the military assets required for implementation of UNPROFOR's existing mandates."

89. NATO, Final Communiqué, Ministerial Meeting of the North Atlantic Council, Press Communiqué M-NAC-1(93)38, Athens, Greece, 10 June 1993.

90. UNPROFOR Interoffice memo, 29 January 1994. The criteria given to the UNPROFOR commander by the Secretariat established four circumstances for the use of air power: self-defense, in reply to bombardment of the safe areas, in response to armed incursions of the safe areas, and to neutralize attempts to obstruct UNPROFOR troops' or humanitarian convoy's freedom of movement. See Srebrenica Report, para. 111.

91. "Heavy Serb Attack on Sarajevo Stalls Effort for Renewed Talks," *Globe and Mail*, 23 July 1993, A8; John F. Burns, "3,777 Shells Hit in 16-hour Siege As Serb Pincers Close on Sarajevo," *New York Times*, 24 July 1993, 1; and "Serbs Pound a U.N. Position in Sarajevo," *New York Times*, 26 July 1993, A7.

92. See "President Clinton's Press Conference," *Weekly Compilation of Presidential Documents*, 29 (June 15, 1993): 1083. For overviews of the U.S. policy shift see Owen, *Balkan Odyssey*, especially chapter 3. Also see Richard Holbrooke, *To End a War*, (New York: Random House, 1998) and, Steven Woehrel, *Bosnia-Hercegovina: Summary of the Debate on a Unilateral Lifting of the Arms Embargo*, CRS Report for Congress, 95-477 F, 11 April 1995.

93. The US rediscovery of the broad power of Resolution 770 conveniently left aside the downgrading of the provisions found in Resolution 776.

94. Owen, *Balkan Odyssey*, 221.

95. NATO, Press Statement by the Secretary General, Brussels, 2 August 1993.

96. NATO, Decisions Taken at the Meeting of the North Atlantic Council (NAC) on 9th August 1993, Press Release (93)52.

97. Ibid.

98. Unnamed NATO official quoted in Craig R. Whitney, "NATO Allies Settle on Procedures for Air Strikes on Serbs in Bosnia," *New York Times*, 10 August 1993, A1, A2.

99. Douglas Jehl, "U.S. Turns Bosnian Threat into a Near Ultimatum," *New York Times*, 4 August 1993.

100. NAC Press Release (93)52.

101. Thorvald Stoltenberg, a former Norwegian Foreign Minister, replaced Cyrus Vance in the negotiations.

102. See, for example, the various press reports of the time. British General Vere Hayes is reported to have commented, "What does President Clinton think he is up to? Air power won't defeat the Serbs." See "UN Commanders Take up Plan to Lift Siege of Bosnia's Capital," *New York Times*, 16 August 1993, A6.

103. Owen, *Balkan Odyssey,* 222. See also, "General's Outburst Jolts Image of Alliance," *Globe and Mail,* 20 August 1993, A10, reporting on a General Francis Briquemont interview with Belgian radio.

104. Paul Lewis, "New Clashes Stall Bosnia Talk; Mediators Criticize Clinton Plan," *New York Times,* 3 August 1993, A9.

105. "U.S. Renews Warning to Serbs on Sarajevo Shelling," *New York Times,* 19 October 1993, A8.

106. See especially Owen, *Balkan Odyssey,* chapter 7.

107. Declaration of the Heads of State and Government Participating in the Meeting of the North Atlantic Council Held at NATO Headquarters, Brussels, on 10–11 January 1994, 11 January 1994.

108. S/1994/50, 18 January 1994.

109. Ibid.

110. S/1994/94, 28 January 1994.

111. Ibid.

112. S/1994/131, 6 February 1994.

113. Decisions Taken at the Meeting of the North Atlantic Council in Permanent Session, NATO Headquarters, Brussels, 9 February 1994.

114. Interview with Canadian military official. The very basic report of the UN investigation team is contained in S/1994/182, 16 February 1994. For insight into the internal balancing act this required for UN, NATO, and ICFY officials, see Owen, *Balkan Odyssey,* 280–281.

115. Owen, *Balkan Odyssey,* 287–288.

116. "UN–NATO Disagreement over the Use of Air Power" in Owen, *Balkan Odyssey,* CD-ROM version.

117. For his description of events, see General Sir Michael Rose, *Fighting for Peace,* (London: The Harvill Press, 1998) 105–107.

118. See also the Russian ambassador's statement at the Security Council vote on 21 April where he calls unequivocally for the Bosnian Serbs to withdraw from Gorazde and notes that the shelling "has no justification and runs counter to the interests of the Serbs themselves." See S/PV.3367, 21 April 1994.

119. Srebrenica Report, para. 138.

120. S/1994/466, 19 April 1994.

121. NATO, Decisions on the Protection of Safe Areas Taken at the Meeting of the North Atlantic Council on 22nd April 1994, Press Release (94)32, 22 April 1994.

122. See the secretary-general's report for details of the Gorazde operation. S/1994/600, 19 May 1994; and AFSOUTH Communiqué, 27 April 1994.

123. It was a Bangladeshi contingent based in the area. They were reportedly already on emergency rations and had only one personal weapon for every five soldiers.

124. S/1994/1389, 1 December 1994; Roger Cohen, "NATO, Expanding Bosnia Role, Strikes a Serbian Base in Croatia," *New York Times,* 22 November 1994, pp. A1, A14; NATO press release - the targets specifically excluded planes on the ground. Srebrenica Report, para. 159.

125. NATO, Press Release, 94(112), 23 November 1994.

126. "Fighting Rages As NATO Debates How to Protect Bosnian Enclave," *New York Times,* 28 November 1994, A1, A16; "U.S. Drops Talk of Using Force against Serbs," *New York Times,* 29 November 1994, A1, A16; and "U.S. Policy Shift on Bosnia Creates a Muddle with Allies," *New York Times,* 30 November 1994, A1, A16.

127. Owen, *Balkan Odyssey,* 329–331. Owen describes the Bihac crisis as "the nadir in UN–NATO and US–EU relations." Also, see Michael R. Gordon, "U.S. and Bosnia: How a Policy Changed," *New York Times,* 4 December 1994, 1, 20, for a description of U.S.

decision making based on internal documents and memos. See also the secretary-general's report at the time, which provides a thorough and devastating critique of the implementation of the safe area concept and the concept itself. See S/1994/1389, 1 December 1994.

128. Roger Cohen, "Bosnia Combatants Sign a Cease-fire But Pitfalls Remain," *New York Times*, 24 December 1994, 1, 2.

129. Fighting continued throughout this period in the Bihac area and on 1 May, the Croatian government launched Operation Flash. The operation prompted a large-scale exodus of Croatian Serbs into Bosnia, which in turn prompted an exodus of Croatians and Bosnians from the area into which the Croatian Serbs fled.

130. Small-scale fighting had begun in March before the end of the cease-fire. It included Bosnian government forces attempting to sever the Bosnian Serb lines of communication. In response, the Bosnian Serb forces retrieved some of their weapons from the UN–monitored heavy weapons collection points.

131. Owen, *Balkan Odyssey*, 346–347; and Barbara Crossette, "U.N. Overrules New Calls for Air Strikes against Serbs," *New York Times*, 9 May 1995, A8.

132. Roger Cohen, "After a 2d Strike from NATO, Serbs Detain U.N. Forces," *New York Times*, 27 May 1995, 1, 4.

133. Roger Cohen, "Allies Resolve to Bolster U.N. Peacekeeping in Bosnia; U.S. Weighs a Combat Role," *New York Times*, 30 May 1995, A1, A6; and "Washington won't Rule Out Commando Move to Free Hostages," *New York Times*, 30 May 1995, A1, A6.

134. S/1995/444, 30 May 1995, para. 15.

135. For the text of the proposal see, S/1995/470, 9 June 1995. For a description of the debate about the merits and parameters of the rapid reaction force, see Srebrenica Report, para. 214–220.

136. The UN analysis of what happened at Srebrenica can be found in Srebrenica Report. For analysis and a virtual minute-by-minute account, see David Rohde, *A Safe Area, Srebrenica: Europe's Worst Massacre since the Second World War* (London: Simon and Schuster, 1997); also see Jan Willem Honig and Norbet Both, *Srebrenica: Record of a War Crime* (London: Penguin, 1997). The actual number of people killed remains in dispute.

137. For a description of the fall of Zepa see Srebrenica Report, para. 394–402.

138. For more, see Srebrenica Report, para. 297–305.

139. Press statement on Gorazde by Secretary General Willy Claes Following North Atlantic Council meeting on 25 July 1995, NATO Press Release, reprinted in *NATO Review* (September 1995) 7.

140. The secretary-general's report on Srebrenica states: "Had the United Nations been provided with intelligence that revealed the enormity of the Bosnian Serbs' goals, it is possible, though by no means certain, that the tragedy of Srebrenica might have been averted. But no such excuse can explain our failure in Zepa. . . . Zepa was not overrun because of a lack of intelligence, but because the international community lacked the capacity to do anything other than to accept its fall as a *fait accompli*." See Srebrenica Report, para. 487.

141. Srebrenica Report, para. 412–413.

142. Figure quoted by the Stockholm International Peace Research Institute (SIPRI) in Anthony Bordon and Richard Caplan, "The Former Yugoslavia: the War and the Peace Process," in *SIPRI Yearbook 1996: Armaments, Disarmament, and International Security* (London: Oxford University Press, 1997) 208.

143. See, for example, Holbrooke, *To End a War*, 65–68. Holbrooke was the assistant secretary of state for European and Canadian Affairs at that time and became the lead U.S. negotiator in Bosnia, eventually acting as the architect of the Dayton Peace Accord.

144. Holbrooke, *To End A War*, 90–91; and Steven Greenhouse, "U.S. Officials Say Bosnian Serbs Face NATO Attack if Talks Stall," *New York Times*, 28 August 1995.

145. Roger Cohen, "Shelling Kills Dozens in Sarajevo; U.S. Urges NATO to Strike Serbs," *New York Times*, 29 August 1995, A1, A10.

146. The UNPROFOR commander in Sarajevo was temporarily the holder of the UN key in the dual-key system while the UNPROFOR force commander was away.

147. Srebrenica Report, para. 441.

148. NATO, Statement by the Secretary General of NATO, Press Release, 95(73), 30 August 1995.

149. Gorazde was the only safe area with potential vulnerability and the UNPROFOR troops stationed there had been quietly removed prior to the beginning of the operation.

150. Holbrooke, *To End a War*, 99.

151. United Nations, "Statement Attributable to the Secretary-General of the United Nations," New York, no document number, 2 September 1995.

152. Speaking at a press briefing, Admiral Leighton Smith stated: "The reason for the recommencement is that NATO and the United Nations have collectively agreed on certain conditions which must be met. Those conditions 1, were not met, and 2, certainly there was no indication that there was intent on the Bosnian Serbs' part to meet them." See Transcript of Press Conference, Admiral Leighton W. Smith, Commander in Chief Allied Forces Southern Europe, NATO Club HZ. AFSOUTH, Naples, Italy, 9 AM, 6 September 1995. See also Roger Cohen, "A NATO Deadline Passes Without Attack," *New York Times*, 5 September 1995, A1, A9; and "NATO to Intensify Use of Air Power against the Serbs," *New York Times*, 7 September 1995, A1. Holbrooke says that the decision to restart the bombing campaign had to overcome tremendous resistance from within NATO as well as from U.S. military officials. The proresumption side won out after Bosnian Serb general Mladic sent a letter threatening to widen the conflict and attack other safe areas. See Holbrooke, *To End a War*, 118, 131–132.

153. See, for example, "NATO Commanders Face Grim Choices," *New York Times*, 14 September 1995, A1, A10.

154. Option Three targets involved, inter alia, Bosnian Serb troop concentrations. See Holbrooke, *To End a War*, 146.

155. AFSOUTH, Joint Statement by Admiral Leighton W. Smith and Lt. General Bernard Janvier, Extension of Suspension of NATO Air Strikes, Press Release, 94-42, Naples, 17 September 1995. "It is our common judgement that the Bosnian Serbs have shown a substantial start towards withdrawing their heavy weapons beyond the limits of the exclusion zone. Other terms of the agreement have also been met. . . . It must be completely understood that the Bosnian Serbs must fully respect their commitments during this additional 72-hour pause or the air strikes will resume." See also AFSOUTH, Transcript, Admiral Leighton Smith, Press Conference, 1500 (Naples time) 15 September 1995; Elaine Sciolino, "Serbs, Complying with Deal Forged by U.S. Begin Moves to Lift Siege of Sarajevo," *New York Times*, 16 September 1995, 1, 5; and "Serbs Start Their Exit for Arms At Sarajevo," *New York Times*, 16 September 1995, 4.

156. AFSOUTH, Joint Statement by Admiral Leighton W. Smith, Commander in Chief Allied Forces Southern Europe, and Lt. General Bernard Janvier, Force Commander, United Nations Peace Force, Press Release, 95-43, Naples, 21 September 1995.

157. NATO, Operation Deliberate Force, Backgrounder, November 1995. The operation was NATO's largest combat operation ever. For more details on the military aspects

of the operation, see the AFSOUTH press conference transcripts of the time, available on the NATO web site.

158. The text of the accord is reprinted by the *New York Times*. See "Details of the Accord: Division Within Unity," *New York Times*, 9 September 1995, 4. See Holbrooke, *To End a War*, 133–141, for a description of the negotiations leading to this agreement.

159. Holbrooke, *To End a War*, 166. This was not necessarily a policy agreed to or known by the full Clinton administration as Holbrooke later found out. See 172–173.

160. Owen, *Balkan Odyssey*, 364.

161. Ibid., 367; Holbrooke, *To End a War*, 203–207; Srebrenica Report, para. 464.

162. The General Framework Agreement for Peace in Bosnia and Herzegovina, 21 November 1995. The agreement is also known as the Dayton Peace Accord. Also see Elaine Sciolino, "Accord Reached to End the War in Bosnia; Clinton Pledges U.S. Troops to Keep Peace," *New York Times*, 22 November 1995, A1, A10.

163. For a chart of the various member state contributions over the course of the mission, see William J. Durch, ed., *UN Peacekeeping, American Policy, and the Uncivil Wars of the 1990s* (New York: St. Martin's, 1996) 239.

164. The secretary-general said of the light option: "Its principal advantage is that it presents an approach that is most likely to correspond to the volume of troops and material resources which can realistically be expected from Member States." See S/25939, 14 June 1993.

165. Srebrenica Report, para. 482.

166. Ibid., para. 43.

167. Ibid.

Chapter 6

Conclusion

The three case studies provide a good cross section of experience from which to draw some lessons for future decision making. The case studies demonstrate that peace enforcement is not an easy or straightforward undertaking for the United Nations. The complexity of peace enforcement operations creates difficult, sometimes intractable dilemmas at the operational and mandate levels. The situation on the ground is highly changeable. Political and military support from member states is equally changeable. The risks of failure are high.

Indeed, each of these cases prompted major, highly divisive crises for the United Nations. In the case of the Congo, the operation created a major political rift with the Soviet Union, a financial crisis (from which the organization has never fully recovered), and the death of the secretary-general shook the organization deeply. The whole experience brought about a pause in the authorization of new operations. Equally, the sequence of events that led to the disbanding and withdrawal of the UN Operation in Somalia II (UNOSOM II), encouraged a general hesitation to consider new operations. The UNOSOM II experience strongly contributed to the nonrenewal of Boutros Boutros-Ghali as secretary-general and was a significant factor in the Security Council's resistance to becoming significantly involved in Rwanda in the early stages of the crisis there. The possibility of the withdrawal of the operation in Bosnia, the deep political divide between troop-contributing countries and those advocating greater use of force, and the images of helpless peacekeepers being held hostage and, in Srebrenica, standing by while the Bosnian Serbs engineered the evacuation and disappearance of its male citizens, have had a serious impact on UN credibility.

I. OPERATIONAL ISSUES

RULES OF ENGAGEMENT

Rules of engagement (ROE) are the guidelines for troops as to how force will or will not be used in the field. As such, they represent an even clearer indication of how force will be used than that found in the mandate. Self-defense remains the bedrock of peace enforcement operations, even when the use of force beyond self-defense is authorized. When the Security Council added on the use of force authorization to existing mandates, Security Council members often made it clear in statements associated with the passage of the resolution, or in the resolution itself, that force should only be used for the authorization specified and only as a last resort, when all other options had been exhausted.

The case studies indicate that there is not as direct a correlation between the authorization of force beyond self-defense and changes in the ROE as one might expect. In all cases, even when the use of force aspect of the mandate was strengthened there was little, if any, change in the ROE. Although this is due, in part, to the fact that the initiation of force remained a last resort option, it is also connected to troop and equipment constraints in the field. Even when the Security Council changes a mandate to a more forceful authorization, commanders in the field are not able or willing to upgrade their ROE or change their overall approach if they are undermanned and underarmed. Troop strength, along with the nature of the force authorization, is an important factor in determining how the use of force authorization will be used in the field.

THE EFFECTS OF CHRONIC UNDERSUPPORT

In examining the case studies, problems of undersupport are a consistent theme. The lack of troops and equipment directly affected military choices in the field. In Bosnia, the UN Protection Force's (UNPROFOR) role in protecting the safe areas and humanitarian aid was severely compromised by inadequate troop numbers and equipment. In Somalia, the UNOSOM II operation experienced similar problems. In some instances, UN troops were only able to provide for their own protection. The UN Operation in the Congo (ONUC) experienced troop-shortage problems that affected its overall operation, although, in contrast to Bosnia and Somalia, the needed troops were eventually forthcoming. This trend of undersupport applies to the ongoing, day-to-day running of the operations. Specific circumstances may override this trend, either when a sudden crisis occurs in an operation (e.g., the provision of the rapid reaction force for Bosnia), or when the very nature of the mission generates strong commitments as with the Unified Task Force (UNITAF). Indeed, by demonstrating what can be achieved when sufficient political will and resources are employed, the UNITAF experience drives home the fact that undersupport has a negative impact on a mission.

In all three of the cases, the United Nations found itself operating in situations of ongoing conflict. Chronic undersupport of these operations, therefore, increases the likelihood of incidents and operational crises that may be debilitating to the operation and to UN credibility. The undersupport phenomenon feeds a self-reinforcing cycle. By definition, the risk that force will be used or required in peace enforcement operations is higher than it is in traditional peacekeeping operations. Undersupport of peace enforcement operations increases that risk since parties to the conflict will correctly calculate that UN troops will be unable or unwilling to respond with force to violations or provocations if they are out-numbered and outgunned. When these types of problems arise in the operation, they may result in member states withdrawing their troop contingents or create resistance to further troop contributions from member states, thus entrenching the undersupport situation. All of this puts the UN operation in a position of weakness that encourages the parties to the conflict to put pressure on the op-eration, thereby increasing the risk of problems yet again.

To some extent, there is a link here with the political sensitivity of these op-erations. In all three cases, member states threatened to pull out, did pull out, or declined to become involved because they did not accept the tactics or policies being pursued. However, even taking that factor into consideration, the exami-nation of the Bosnia and Somalia experiences suggests that there is a finite pool of resources in the international community for these types of operations. The UN operations in both Somalia and Bosnia were products of new post–Cold War attitudes about the United Nations, including a general willingness that the United Nations be used in these situations. If in these circumstances a more ro-bust military commitment could not be generated, then it is unlikely that it can be generated in times when there is less of a general commitment to UN opera-tions.

All UN operations are dependent on member states to provide troops, equip-ment, and transport. But peace enforcement operations, by virtue of the fact that force might be used, have more significant resource requirements than peace-keeping operations. It is not surprising, therefore, that in each of the case studies examined here, the role of the United States as a provider of resources and trans-portation capabilities was important to the operations at critical moments. And in general, it is fair to say that in the post–Cold War era the United Nations has been reliant on the United States and other permanent members for both political and military resources in major operations.

In Bosnia, U.S. unwillingness to become involved in any significant way on the ground meant that the operation had to struggle with significantly less than it required to implement the mandate. Once the US became politically focused on the conflict, and then only because of the prospect of having to become involved on the ground, the politics of the operation changed significantly, with Opera-tion Deliberate Force and a peace accord being the result. In Somalia, the U.S. involvement in the hunt for Mohammad Farah Aidid changed the nature and the context of the UNOSOM II operation. And the eventual U.S. announcement that it would be pulling out of the operation prompted a series of similar announce-ments from troop-contributing states who were unwilling to remain involved in the operation without U.S. military and political support.

The power of U.S. involvement and the UN reliance on the United States for military support in peace enforcement operations creates a situation in which decisions made by the United States, for or against involvement, and the nature of U.S. involvement, can have a more significant impact on the outcome of the mission than any action or decision taken by the United Nations. This situation constrains UN decision making, and makes it vulnerable to vicissitudes of U.S. decision making. An operation or a conflict that might otherwise be left unattended might suddenly become a key operation for the United Nations. An ongoing operation might suddenly experience a crisis that results in a sudden withdrawal of support from member states, all beyond UN control. Over time, this vulnerability and the resulting inconsistency in the UN approach has the potential to create political problems for the United Nations as states may come to believe that UN actions are an extension of U.S. policy, or at least that the United Nations is only capable and willing to undertake significant action in crises when the United States is involved, with all the political baggage that that implies. Recent UN experience in East Timor and Sierra Leone provide positive counterbalancing examples to this trend. In the case of Sierra Leone, for example, the quick intervention of British troops saved the UN operation from collapse.[1]

COMMAND AND CONTROL

By virtue of their multinational composition, all UN operations must deal with a variety of command and control issues and complications. In peace enforcement operations, the decision-making environment can be even more complex because of the involvement of other actors. In Somalia and Bosnia, for example, other national and organizational actors became part of the command and control environment, complicating the situation for the decision makers and also for the states or groups that the operation was meant to assist.

In Somalia, U.S. troops, who remained under U.S. (not UN) command, engaged in operations without always notifying or discussing the operations with the UN command in advance. This situation opened up the possibility that the U.S. operations might, as they sometimes did, undermine or counteract UN efforts, and that the United States might draw the United Nations into situations that it had not and would not have created. For the warring groups and citizens of Somalia, the distinction between UN and U.S. actions was not always evident. It was inevitable and understandable that many Somalis saw the various UN and U.S. activities as all part of the same operation.

In Bosnia, the involvement of NATO forces and of the rapid reaction force from Britain, France, and the Netherlands created similar coordination problems. In Bosnia, though, an effort was made to ensure that decision making was a joint process and coordinated. The dual-key system of decision making for the use of air cover and air strikes was established precisely for these purposes. The dual-key system, however, demonstrated the disadvantages involved in coordinating decision making in this way. Because a decision required approval by both NATO and the UN officials, and because of the United Nations' own multiparticipant decision making structure, the dual-key, decision-making process required considerable time to complete. Often by the time a decision was made it was too late to actually implement it because the original situation had changed or ceased to exist.

These issues have an impact on perceptions about the credibility and impartiality of the operation. The actions of U.S. troops in Somalia, not constrained by the need to act impartially, and the sense that the UN operation was being run by the United States contributed to the perception that the UN operation was not at all impartial. This, in turn, encouraged or reinforced decisions by various groups to cease cooperation with the United Nations or to actively work against it. In Bosnia, the constraints of the dual-key, decision-making process and the resulting lack of UN response in different situations contributed to the perception that the United Nations was unwilling to follow through on its commitments. This undermined the credibility of the operation, created frustration inside and outside the mission, and encouraged all of the parties to factor the assumption that the United Nations was unlikely to respond into their decisions about what they could and could not do without generating an international response. This encouraged rather than discouraged the warring parties to consider taking stronger military actions and actions that contravened the UN mandate.

II. MANDATE ISSUES

SECURITY COUNCIL CHOICES

The most interesting common characteristic of these case studies is that in each case the use of force authorization was associated with an attempt to deal with the effects of the conflict rather than the conflict itself. In the Congo, the initial impetus for the operation was to deal with the destabilizing effects of the quick shift to independence and the resulting Belgium intervention. Force was later authorized to provide for the withdrawal of foreign mercenaries and to prevent civil war. In Somalia, the United Nations' initial involvement was entirely driven by the need to address the serious humanitarian crisis in the country. Only later, after the humanitarian situation was under control, did the Security Council, prompted by the new Clinton administration, authorize the UNOSOM II operation. UNOSOM II was intended to broaden the secure delivery of humanitarian aid to the entire country and to carry out various military and political tasks aimed at facilitating political reconciliation. In Bosnia, the driving force behind the use of force mandate was the desire to ameliorate the humanitarian consequences created by the conflict. All of the Security Council's decisions in Bosnia, including and especially the creation of the safe areas, were oriented towards this end.

All three cases involved situations that were internal rather than external in nature, where a state was in some form of collapse. In the Congo and Somalia, the United Nations was also dealing with an absence of government. In all three situations, the conflict was ongoing in spite of cease-fire commitments from the warring parties. The mandates of all three operations included humanitarian and political assistance tasks of some kind. In the Congo, one of the main objectives of the mandate was the reestablishment of law and order in the country. In Bosnia and Somalia, humanitarian and political assistance were major aspects of the mission. In all three, the protection of civilians and of UN personnel was a major function of the operation.

This is not to suggest that peace enforcement operations can only be used in these types of situations, but it does indicate that when the Security Council has chosen to undertake this kind of operation it has been in response to a certain type of conflict situation. This suggests that peace enforcement operations may be something the Security Council turns to when full-scale enforcement is not an option, either because of political considerations or because of the nature of the situation, and when peacekeeping is not or can not work, but when there is a strong desire and pressure to respond in some fashion.

The three case studies provide three different examples of how the Security Council comes to authorize a peace enforcement operation. In Bosnia and in the Congo, the development of a mandate for peace enforcement was a transitional, evolutionary process. The authorization of the use of force beyond self-defense came after the operation was already in place. The Security Council's response to each crisis initially took the form of a peacekeeping operation. Over time, as the situations deteriorated the Security Council moved the operation up the spectrum from peacekeeping to peace enforcement. UNOSOM II was preceded by the barely formed UNOSOM I operation and the UNITAF operation. The Security Council response to Somalia, therefore, ultimately resulting in the creation of UNOSOM II, was also a progressive, evolutionary process. In all three instances, the decision to engage in peace enforcement came as part of previous and ongoing involvement in the conflict or situation.

CHAPTER VII AUTHORIZATION

In each case, the use of force was authorized in order to send a clear signal of Security Council resolve about key aspects of the mandate. It was not expected that force would necessarily be instantly or automatically employed. The Security Council and the secretary-general hoped that force would not be used at all. For UN troops on the ground, the use of force authorization changed relatively little in operational terms. Self-defense and a general peacekeeping approach remained the foundation of the operations. Overall, the case studies reveal a general reticence about using force by those in the field. Even when force was authorized in specific circumstances and even when the use of force would have been justified, the actual use of force remained a last resort, used only when all the alternatives had failed.

By contrast to the careful, almost agonized debate over Chapter VII authorization during the Congo crisis, the use of the Chapter VII authorization in Bosnia and Somalia came about fairly readily with some but not extensive discussion of its implications. This is partly a reflection of the times. Both the Bosnian and Somali operations came about in the post–Cold War environment, at a time when there was a general sense that the United Nations could and should be used more proactively. This atmosphere, which disappeared very promptly when things started to go wrong in Somalia, contributed to the Security Council's willingness to approve and to accept the authorization of force beyond self-defense without extensive debate about its implications for the conflict or its implications for the mandate and the operation on the ground.

In the case of Bosnia, though initially the Security Council circumscribed its Chapter VII authorizations fairly carefully, the Security Council quickly came to authorize Chapter VII with a certain degree of automaticity. That automaticity contributed to an undermining of Chapter VII authorization as a signal of seriousness and resolve given the disconnect between the tasks and wordings of Security Council mandates and what was happening in the field. As secretary-general Kofi Annan's report on Srebrenica indicates, the tendency of the Security Council to use the Chapter VII authorization had as much to do with the rift between those who wanted stronger action and those with troops on the ground as it had to do with sending a signal of seriousness.[2] In Bosnia, the Chapter VII authorization was made more hollow by the willingness of the Security Council to invoke Chapter VII even when it knew that the troop and equipment reinforcements needed to make the mandate viable would not be forthcoming, either from themselves or other member states. The Security Council decision to go with the so-called light option for protection of the safe areas—an authorization of troops less than one quarter of the number believed to be required as a minimum—provides the most blatant example of the Security Council's willingness to make authorizations and commitments knowing that it is unlikely that the military capability needed to fulfill the mandate will be forthcoming.

MANDATE CONSTRAINTS

In each case, the nature of peace enforcement—more than peacekeeping, less than full-scale enforcement—meant that there were some very fine lines associated with the mandate. For example, in Bosnia there was a distinction between air cover (used only in self-defense) and air strikes. In Somalia, there was the distinction between forceful measures being used by UNOSOM II troops with respect to the disarmament provisions of the mandate in contrast to the use of force being taken by U.S. troops in an effort to find and arrest Aidid. During the ONUC operation, there was the question of what kind of action qualified as preventing civil war as opposed to bringing an end to Katangan secession by using force. These kinds of distinctions are a function of the circumscribed nature of the authorization to use force and the need for UN troops to maintain impartiality. However, they add a significant level of difficulty to operational decision making and the implementation of the mandate. They are also difficult distinctions to convey to the populations being affected by the conflict. In their mind, air power is air power. Why would it be used in one case and not in another? Why would an authorization to use force to prevent civil war not mean the ability to use force to end the secession of Katanga? How are the troops using force to find Aidid any different from those using force to search for concealed weapons at a radio station?

By contrast, the warring groups seem to quickly grasp the limits of the UN mandates and the ability and willingness of UN troops to enforce them. Bosnia provides the best example of the extent to which warring factions will push and exceed the limits imposed by the United Nations when such actions further their own objectives. All of the parties to the conflict recognized quite quickly how far they could go in terms of their actions without generating a UN response, and all of the parties incorporated that knowledge into their plans and used it to further their own goals wherever possible.

In authorizing future operations, both of these issues need to be taken into account. There is no way around either problem; both are a function of a situation in which a conflict is ongoing or in transition. Given that the mandate constraints may create a situation in which UN credibility in the field is undermined, albeit by incorrect perceptions, the Security Council should consider undertaking a stronger public relations effort when it comes to peace enforcement mandates. In particular, the provision of public explanations of the operational implications of their mandates might help guard against misunderstandings and false expectations in the populations affected by the mandate, as well as among UN member states. For its own part, when considering peace enforcement mandates the Security Council should take into consideration the fact that the mandate is likely to be severely tested by the parties to the conflict. This was a phenomenon in all three cases. Any time peace enforcement is authorized, therefore, the Security Council should authorize sufficient force and resource strength to ensure the mission will be able to withstand such tests, and it should be prepared for the fact that force will indeed be used. The simple physical presence of UN troops, even with a peace enforcement mandate, does not carry sufficient moral weight to make up for the absence of strength in numbers and resources in these situations.

III. DOES PEACE ENFORCEMENT WORK?

There remains the basic question driving the overall analysis presented here. Does peace enforcement work? Is this a useful and viable way to deal with issues of international peace and security? At the heart of this question is the question as to whether it is possible to act impartially in situations when force might be used. Any time that force is used to compel compliance with some aspect of a Security Council mandate, it means that force is being used against one or more parties to the conflict. Does this not, in and of itself, mean that impartiality is not possible when force is being used, and, therefore, that peace enforcement is inherently impossible?

Clearly, Secretary-General Boutros-Ghali believed that it is possible to use force and remain impartial given his proposal for peace enforcement units in *An Agenda for Peace*. The Security Council has authorized peace enforcement on sufficient occasions, including after the experiences of Bosnia and Somalia, to suggest that they believe it is possible. Though Dag Hammarskjöld worried about the implications of the use of force for impartiality, he never argued against the authorization of force beyond self-defense on the grounds that it was not possible to mix the two.

What have we learned from the three situations in which force has actually been used? To reiterate the distinction made in the introduction, impartiality is applied at two separate levels. Whether or not the Security Council mandate for an operation is impartial is a separate question from whether or not that mandate is implemented impartially. A helpful analogy here is that of the judicial system. At one level, a judge or jury makes a judgment about a particular case and what should be done about it. Other actors in the judicial system (e.g. the prison system) undertake the implementation of that judgment, separately and impartially. At issue here is the question of whether or not the implementation of a peace enforcement mandate occurs impartially, that is without prejudice to the parties to the conflict. This is separate from the nature of the mandate itself and whether or not it is impartial.

Some argue that it is simply not possible to be impartial in a situation of on-going conflict because the very fact of involvement will inevitably affect the positions of the parties. There is no escaping the fact that the involvement of the United Nations in these situations alters the equation of the conflict. The United Nations becomes a participant in the conflict, with its own political goals associated with the pursuit of international peace and security. Nonetheless, it remains possible that the implementation of measures taken in pursuit of those goals can be impartial. Whatever one might think about the decision to create safe areas or to establish a no-fly zone in Bosnia, it can be argued that the use of force to compel compliance with that mandate was impartial in the sense that the military means being used to achieve that objective were directed solely at ensuring compliance with the Security Council mandate.

While it may be theoretically possible to be impartial when using force beyond self-defense, is it actually doable? Unfortunately, the case studies provide no clear answers to this question. In terms of outcomes, the failure of the UNO-SOM II operation and the withdrawal of the mission stands in contrast to the eventual end to the fighting and agreement on a peace accord in both Bosnia and the Congo, and the success of the UNITAF operation. The wide variety of variables involved in each of the conflicts makes it difficult to develop any sense of whether or not there was something inherent in the conflicts themselves that contributed to the different outcomes.

From the perspective of the nature of the international involvement, there is one clear difference between what happened in Somalia and what happened in Bosnia and the Congo. In the latter two cases, when the operations faltered, international political attention and will became focused and determined to bring the crisis to an end. That focus and determination resulted in further political and military resources being dedicated to the operation and the political peace processes associated with them. In Somalia, the opposite happened. The international community, led by the United States, decided to disengage rather than pursue the Security Council's objectives with any vigor.

Peace enforcement situations impose serious constraints on the UN operation. Intuitively, the authorization of the use of force suggests a greater freedom of action for the UN mission. In fact, the authorization of force provides more rather than fewer constraints. The requirement of impartiality imposes strict limitations on how and when force can be used. The fear of crossing the line into outright enforcement played a major role in all three of the case studies. All three cases experienced situations in which a decision to use force would have taken the operation across that line. The problem is that sometimes the maintenance of impartiality can become an end in itself or a cover for an unwillingness to take firmer action. It is difficult to argue that the maintenance of impartiality is a good thing if all that is being achieved is avoidance of the failure of the mission or avoidance of taking more significant action. The events of Srebrenica provide the most glaring example of this. As the secretary-general said in his report about Srebrenica, the errors in judgment associated with Srebrenica were "rooted in a philosophy of impartiality and non-violence wholly unsuited to the conflict in Bosnia."[3]

This, in turn, raises the question as to whether or not peace enforcement is a desirable tool for dealing with international peace and security. As the case studies indicate, regardless of the goals being pursued, the involvement of the United Nations in these situations does have an impact on the conflict and does change the course of events. That impact, however, is not always predictable or desirable. In all three cases, even after UN involvement, a large number of lives were lost, populations displaced and territory destroyed. To what end? In Bosnia and in the Congo, the United Nations eventually helped bring an end to the fighting and facilitated the development of a peace accord. But the costs were high and the conflicts protracted. Somalia remains a country in conflict, without a viable government and so fragile that another humanitarian or ecological crisis seems almost certain.

The Security Council and UN member states must, therefore, take into consideration that in becoming involved in these situations, the United Nations can have a negative influence as easily as it can have a positive one. Given that these operations are inherently high risk and the potential costs are high, the Security Council should focus on enforcing issues relating to the conflict itself (e.g. cease-fires or peace agreements), rather than the effects of the conflict. If it can not agree to do so, the focus on the effects of the conflict is an imperfect and problematic compromise. Militarily, the case studies present a very consistent message for decision makers inside and outside of the Security Council that peace enforcement requires a consistent and serious commitment of resources. These are not situations in which half measures can be expected to generate success.

IV. ISSUES FOR FUTURE STUDY

UNDERSUPPORT

It is difficult to underestimate the impact of providing these operations with less than the minimum requirement for resources and sufficient numbers of adequately trained and equipped personnel. This is an issue that touches on all aspects of the operation. The case studies indicate that hoping that the simple moral weight of the presence of UN troops will act as a deterrent or will eliminate the need to take stronger action does not work. There would be considerable value, therefore, in research on how this chronic problem could be overcome, both in terms of designing Security Council mandates and in terms of member state contributions. If peace enforcement is to continue to be a tool used by the United Nations, resolution of this problem is a minimum requirement.

CONTRACTING OUT

One way of easing the undersupport problem may be to consider contracting out the peace enforcement operation to a regional organization or group of states, something that has been tried with greater frequency in recent years. This is not a suitable option in all cases. Nonetheless, in some situations this might be a reasonable and efficient alternative. Further study needs to be undertaken about the implications of taking this route, in particular, the implications of the shift in the balance of the decision making about the use of force to an organization or group of states other than the United Nations.

PEACE ENFORCEMENT WITHOUT FORCE

In order to fully understand why and under what circumstances peace enforcement works best, a study of examples of peace enforcement operations that did not involve sustained military operations should be undertaken. This would provide a fuller picture of the peace enforcement equation than is presented here and provide a good comparison to these three case studies in order to generate some firm conclusions about what does and does not work.

SECURITY COUNCIL ACCOUNTABILITY

A number of the issues raised in this book relate to the question of Security Council accountability. Further study on this broad question would be useful. First, some form of linkage between the passage of Security Council mandates and the commitment of resources may help ameliorate the undersupport problem. Second, finding a way to establish some sort of Security Council accountability for the nature of the mandate would help to avoid the problems posed by ambiguous or contradictory mandates. This might prevent the accretion of mandate tasks, often contradictory and often never fulfilled, that occurred in Bosnia, and prevent the kinds of problems associated with the mandate in Somalia. At minimum, an ongoing check of how and whether the Security Council mandate is being implemented on the ground could contribute to better Security Council decision making as the operation progresses. The possibility that greater accountability might result in considerably less UN involvement in conflicts is one argument against greater Security Council accountability. This does not negate the need to study the possibility given that it could contribute to more effective Security Council involvement in future conflicts.

The problems associated with these issues are a result of the setting aside of the Chapter VII provisions of the charter that occurred when Cold War politics took hold of the Security Council. The machinery envisaged in the charter—a Military Staff Committee to advise on and oversee UN military operations, and Article 43 agreements to ensure that the United Nations had sufficient troops and resources available to it—were it put to work, would go some distance to eliminating the problems just discussed. Member states, particularly the permanent members, have become so accustomed to working without these mechanisms and without mandate and resource accountability that the likelihood they would ever be willing to accept the constraints they see as inherent in these mechanisms (or their equivalent) is almost zero. Even in the initial post–Cold War period, when enthusiasm for the United Nations and its potential was at its highest, the secretary-general's proposal to reconsider Article 43 agreements generated absolutely no response. A full return to the charter mechanisms is thus unlikely, but the lessons of the UN experiences in operations such as those examined in this book may yet provide an important stepping-stone to improving the UN efforts in future.

NOTES

1. On 15 September 1999, in Resolution 1264, the Security Council authorized the creation of an Australian-led multinational force to restore peace and security in East Timor. Shortly, thereafter, on 25 October 1999 in Resolution 1272 the Security Council also authorized the creation of the UN Transitional Administration in East Timor (UN-TAET) to oversee and facilitate the transition to a newly elected independent government. Both operations had Chapter VII authorization. The UN Mission in Sierra Leone (UNAMSIL) was created by Security Council Resolution 1270 on 22 October 1999. The Security Council later added more tasks to the mandate under a Chapter VII authorization in Resolution 1289 on 7 February 2000. In the spring of 2000, a number of peacekeepers were killed and taken hostage when some of the warring groups returned to fighting. With the mission on the verge of collapse, Great Britain sent troops to Sierra Leone under national command in order to restore stability and assist the UN operation. As of November 2000, the situation was stable but tenuous.

2. Report of the Secretary-General Pursuant to General Assembly Resolution 53/35 (1993), Srebrenica Report, para. 43.

3. Ibid., para. 499.

Bibliography

UN DOCUMENTS AND PUBLICATIONS

Bosnia

Security Council Debates

S/PV.3106, 13 August 1992.
S/PV.3111, 2 September 1992.
S/PV.3113, 9 September 1992.
S/PV.3119, 6 October 1992.
S/PV.3146, 3 December 1992.
S/PV.3189, 30 March 1993.
S/PV.3191, 31 March 1993.
S/PV.3228, 4 June 1993.
S/PV.3344, 4 March 1994.
S/PV.3356, 31 March 1994.
S/PV.3367, 21 April 1994.

Security Council Resolutions

Resolution 713, 25 September 1991.
Resolution 721, 27 November 1991.
Resolution 724, 15 December 1991.
Resolution 727, 8 January 1992.
Resolution 740, 7 February 1992.
Resolution 743, 21 February 1992.
Resolution 749, 7 April 1992.
Resolution 752, 15 May 1992.
Resolution 753, 18 May 1992.
Resolution 754, 18 May 1992.
Resolution 755, 20 May 1992.

Resolution 757, 30 May 1992.
Resolution 758, 8 June 1992.
Resolution 760, 18 June 1992.
Resolution 761, 29 June 1992.
Resolution 762, 30 June 1992.
Resolution 764, 13 July 1992.
Resolution 769, 7 August 1992.
Resolution 770, 13 August 1992.
Resolution 776, 14 September 1992.
Resolution 777, 19 September 1992.
Resolution 779, 6 October 1992.
Resolution 781, 9 October 1992.
Resolution 786, 10 November 1992.
Resolution 787, 16 November 1992.
Resolution 795, 11 December 1992.
Resolution 798, 18 December 1992.
Resolution 802, 25 January 1993.
Resolution 807, 19 February 1993.
Resolution 808, 22 February 1993.
Resolution 816, 31 March 1993.
Resolution 817, 7 April 1993.
Resolution 819, 16 April 1993.
Resolution 820, 17 April 1993.
Resolution 821, 28 April 1993.
Resolution 824, 6 May 1993.
Resolution 827, 25 May 1993.
Resolution 836, 4 June 1993.
Resolution 838, 10 June 1993.
Resolution 842, 18 June 1993.
Resolution 844, 18 June 1993.
Resolution 845, 18 June 1993.
Resolution 847, 30 June 1993.
Resolution 855, 9 August 1993.
Resolution 857, 20 August 1993.
Resolution 859, 24 August 1993.
Resolution 869, 30 September 1993.
Resolution 870, 1 October 1993.
Resolution 871, 4 October 1993.
Resolution 877, 21 October 1993.
Resolution 900, 4 March 1994.
Resolution 908, 31 March 1994.
Resolution 913, 22 April 1994.
Resolution 914, 27 April 1994.
Resolution 936, 8 July 1994.
Resolution 941, 23 September 1994.
Resolution 942, 23 September 1994.
Resolution 943, 23 September 1994.
Resolution 947, 30 September 1994.
Resolution 958, 19 November 1994.
Resolution 959, 19 November 1994.
Resolution 967, 14 December 1994.

Resolution 970, 12 January 1995.
Resolution 981, 31 March 1995.
Resolution 982, 31 March 1995.
Resolution 983, 31 March 1995.
Resolution 987, 19 April 1995.
Resolution 988, 21 April 1995.
Resolution 990, 28 April 1995.
Resolution 998, 16 June 1995.
Resolution 1004, 12 July 1995.
Resolution 1010, 10 August 1995.
Resolution 1023, 22 November 1995.
Resolution 1025, 30 November 1995.
Resolution 1031, 15 December 1995.
Resolution 1037, 15 January 1996.
Resolution 1088, 12 December 1996.

Security Council Statements

S/24510, 2 September 1992.
S/26716, 9 November 1993.
Security Council, *Statement by the President*, 17 March 1993.

Secretary-General Reports

S/23169, 25 October 1991.
S/23280, 11 December 1991.
S/23363, 5 January 1992.
S/23513, 4 February 1992.
S/23592, 15 February 1992.
S/23777, 2 April 1992.
S/23844, 24 April 1992.
S/23900, 12 May 1992.
S/24000, 26 May 1992.
S/24049, 30 May 1992.
S/24075, 6 June 1992.
S/24100, 15 June 1992.
S/24188, 26 June 1992.
S/24221, 1 July 1992.
S/24263, 10 July 1992.
S/24333, 21 July 1992.
S/24353, 27 July 1992.
S/24353/Add. 1, 6 August 1992.
S/24540, 10 September 1992.
S/24600, 28 September 1992.
S/24767, 5 November 1992.
S/25000, 21 December 1992.
S/25221, 2 February 1993.
S/25248, 8 February 1993.
S/25264, 10 February 1993.
S/25479, 26 March 1993.
S/25555, 8 April 1993.

S/25668, 26 April 1993.
S/25777, 15 May 1993.
S/25939, 14 June 1993.
S/25993, 24 June 1993.
S/26018, 1 July 1993.
S/26099, 13 July 1993.
S/26310, 16 August 1993.
S/26470, 20 September 1993.
S/26483, 22 September 1993.
S/1994/131, 6 February 1994.
S/1994/154, 10 February 1994.
S/1994/291, 11 March 1994.
S/1994/300, 16 March 1994.
S/1994/333, 24 March 1994.
S/1994/555, 9 May 1994.
S/1994/600, 19 May 1994.
S/1994/1067, 17 September 1994.
S/1994/1389, 1 December 1994.
S/1995/38, 14 January 1995.
S/1995/222, 22 March 1995.
S/1995/444, 30 May 1995.
S/1995/755, 30 August 1995.
S/1995/987, 23 November 1995.
S/1995/1031, 13 December 1995.

Letters and Note Verbale

S/23239, 24 November 1991.
S/23240, 26 November 1991.
S/24549, 12 September 1992.
S/24783, 9 November 1992.
S/24870, 30 November 1992.
S/24900, 7 December 1992.
S/24900/Add. 39, 27 April 1993.
S/25670, 27 April 1993.
S/25800, 19 May 1993.
S/25824, 22 May 1993.
S/26468, 30 September 1993.
S/1994/50, 18 January 1994.
S/1994/94, 28 January 1994.
S/1994/159, 11 February 1994.
S/1994/182, 16 February 1994.
S/1994/217, 25 February 1994.

*Organization of Security and Cooperation in Europe and European Community
Declarations (as UN Documents)*

S/23060, 23 September 1991.
S/23155, 21 October 1991.
S/23203, 8 November 1991.
S/23906, 12 May 1992.

S/24306, 17 July 1992.
S/24364, 31 July 1992.
S/24399, 10 August 1992.

Joint Statements (as UN Documents)

S/25487, 29 March 1993.
S/25659, 26 April 1993.
S/25663, 26 April 1993.

NATO Statements and Decisions (as UN Documents)

S/1994/466, 19 April 1994.
S/1994/495, 22 April 1994.
S/1994/498, 22 April 1994.

Other

S/25130, 20 January 1993 (Report of the Special Commission of Inquiry into the Assassination of Mr. Hakija Turajlic, Deputy Prime Minister of Bosnia and Herzegovina, on 8 January 1993).
S/25700, Report of the Security Council Mission Established Pursuant to Resolution 819 (1993), 30 April 1993.
S/26726, 12 November 1993 (United Nations Protection Force Incident Report, Incident at Rajlovac, 8 November 1993).
S/26742, 13 November 1993 (Report on the Attack on Two United Nations Convoys Near Novi Travnik on 25 October 1993).
S/1995/470, 9 June 1995 (Proposed Rapid Reaction Force for the United Nations Protection Force).

Congo

Security Council Debates

S/PV.873, 13 July 1960.
S/PV.884, 8 August 1960.
S/PV.885, 8 August 1960.
S/PV.887-889, 21-22 August 1960.
S/PV.912-920, December 1960.
S/PV.935, 15 February 1961.
S/PV.941, 20 February 1961.
S/PV.942, 20 February 1961.

Security Council Resolutions

Resolution 143, 14 July 1960.
Resolution 145, 22 July 1960.
Resolution 146, 9 August 1960.
Resolution 161, 21 February 1961.

Resolution 169, 24 November 1961.

Secretary-General Reports and Documents

S/4382, 13 July 1960.
S/4387, 14 July 1960.
S/4389, 18 July 1960.
S/4417, 6 August 1960.
S/4768, 14 March 1961.
S/4771, 20 March 1961.
S/4841, 20 June 1961.
S/4923, 13 August 1961.
S/5038, 21 December 1961.
S/5053, 9 January 1962.
S/5053/Add. 14, 11 January 1963.
S/5240, and Add. 1, 4 February 1963.

Other Reports

A/5069, 24 April 1962.
S/4451, Observations by Special Representative of the Secretary-General in the Congo on the report by Major-General Alexander, 21 August 1960.
S/4761, Report of the Special Representative to the Secretary-General, 8 March 1961.
S/4791, Report of the Special Representative to the Secretary-General, 15 April 1961.
S/4940/Add. 1–19, Report of the Officer-in-Charge of the United Nations Operation in the Congo to the Secretary-General relating to the implementation of part A, operative paragraph 2, of Security Council Resolution S/4741 of 21 February 1961, 14 September 1961, 6 October 1961.
S/4964, Report of the Commission of Investigation on Lumumba's Death, 11 November 1961.
S/5025, Note verbale dated 11 December 1961 from the Representative of Belgium to the Secretary-General transmitting communications from the Minister for Foreign Affairs of Belgium; and replies dated 8 and 15 December 1961 by the Secretary-General, 15 December 1961.
S/5053/Add. 8, Report to the Secretary-General from the Officer-in-Charge of the United Nations Operation in the Congo relating to the implementation of the Security Council Resolutions S/4741 of 21 February 1961 and S/5002 of 24 November 1961, 19 February 1962.
S/5053/Add. 14, Report to the Secretary-General from the Officer-in-Charge of the United Nations Operation in the Congo relating to the implementation of the Security Council Resolutions S/4741 of 21 February 1961 and S/5002 of 24 November 1961, 11 January 1963.
S/5053/Add.15, Report to the Secretary-General from the Officer-in-Charge of the United Nations Operation in the Congo relating to the implementation of Security Council resolutions S/4741 of 21 February 1961 and S/5002 of 24 November 1961, 30 January 1963.
ST/SGB/ONUC/1, Regulations for the United Nations Force in the Congo, 1960.

Somalia

Security Council Debates

S/PV.3145, 3 December 1992.
S/PV.3188, 26 March 1993.
S/PV.3229, 6 June 1993.

Security Council Resolutions

Resolution 733, 23 January 1992.
Resolution 746, 17 March 1992.
Resolution 751, 24 April 1992.
Resolution 767, 27 July 1992.
Resolution 775, 28 August 1992.
Resolution 794, 3 December 1992.
Resolution 814, 26 March 1993.
Resolution 837, 6 June 1993.
Resolution 865, 22 September 1993.
Resolution 878, 29 October 1993.
Resolution 885, 16 November 1993.
Resolution 886, 18 November 1993.
Resolution 897, 4 February 1994.
Resolution 923, 31 May 1994.
Resolution 946, 30 September 1994.
Resolution 953, 31 October 1994.
Resolution 954, 4 November 1994.

Secretary-General Reports

S/23693, 11 March 1992.
S/23829, 21 April 1992.
S/24343, 22 July 1992.
S/24451, 12 August 1992.
S/24480, 24 August 1992.
S/24480/Add. 1, 28 August 1992.
S/24859, 27 November 1992.
S/24992, 19 December 1992.
S/25168, 26 January 1993.
S/25354, 3 March 1993.
S/26022, 1 July 1993.
S/26317, 17 August 1993.
S/26738, 12 November 1993.
S/1994/12, 6 January 1994.
S/1994/614, 24 May 1994.
S/1994/839, 18 July 1994.
S/1994/977, 17 August 1994.
S/1994/1068, 17 September 1994.
S/1994/1166, 14 October 1994.
S/1994/1245, 3 November 1994.

S/1995/231, 28 March 1995.

General Assembly Resolutions

Resolution 1471 (ES-IV), 20 September 1960.

Other Reports and Letters

Letters from the Chargé d'Affaires A. I. of the Permanent Mission of Somalia to the United Nations Addressed to the President of the Security Council:

   S/23507, 3 February 1992.
   S/23763, 27 March 1992.
   S/23957, 19 May 1992.
   S/25014, 24 December 1992.

Letters from the Secretary-General to the President of the Security Council:

   S/24179, 25 June 1992.
   S/24859, 27 November 1992.
   S/24868, 30 November 1992.

Reports from UNITAF Commander to the Security Council:

   S/24976, 17 December 1992.
   S/25126, 19 January 1993.

S/26351, Report of an Investigation into the 5 June 1993 attack on United Nations forces in Somalia by Professor Tom Farer, 24 August 1993.

S/1994/653, Report of the Commission of Inquiry Established Pursuant to Security Council Resolution 885 (1993) to Investigate Armed Attacks on UNOSOM II Personnel Which Led to Casualties Among Them, 1 June 1994.

OTHER UN DOCUMENTS AND PUBLICATIONS

A/3943, Summary Study of the Experience Derived from the Establishment and Operation of the Force: Report of the Secretary-General, 9 October 1953.
S/1995/1, Supplement to An Agenda for Peace, 3 January 1995 (also issued as A/50/60).
S/25859, Note by the President of the Security Council, 28 May 1993.
S/PV.3046, 31 January 1992.
Boutros-Ghali, Boutros. *An Agenda for Peace.* New York: United Nations, 1992 (also issued as A/47/277).
————. *Report of the Work of the Organization from the Forty-seventh to the Forty-eighth Session of the General Assembly.* New York: United Nations, DPI/1420, September 1993.
International Court of Justice. *Certain Expenses of the United Nations.* 20 July 1962.

Letter from Secretary-General Javier Pérez de Cuéllar to His Excellency, Mr. Hans-Dietrich Genscher, Vice-Chancellor and Minister for Foreign Affairs of the Federal Republic of Germany, 14 December 1991.

Pérez de Cuéllar, Javier. *Anarchy or Order, Annual Reports, 1982-1991*. New York: United Nations, 1991.

Report of the Secretary-General Pursuant to General Assembly Resolution 53/35 (1998), Srebrenica Report, 15 November 1999.

Security Council Resolution 929, 22 June 1994.

Security Council Resolution 940, 31 July 1994.

Security Council Resolution 1244, 10 June 1999.

Security Council Resolution 1272, 25 October 1999.

Security Council Resolution 1289, 7 February 2000.

Security Council Resolution 1291, 24 February 2000.

"Summary of the Experience Derived from the Establishment and Operation of the Force: Report of the Secretary-General," A/3943, 9 October 1958.

United Nations. *The Blue Helmets: A Review of United Nations Peace-keeping*. New York: United Nations, 1990.

———. *Repertory of Practice of United Nations Organs*. vol. 2. New York: United Nations, 1982.

———. *The United Nations and Somalia, 1992-1996*. New York: United Nations, 1996.

United Nations Department of Peace-keeping Operations. *Comprehensive Report on Lessons-learned from United Nations Operation in Somalia, April 1992–March 1995*. Life and Peace Institute, Sweden, Friedrich Ebert Stiftung, Germany, Norwegian Institute of International Affairs, Lessons-learned Unit, December 1995.

UNOSOM II. Appendix 6 to Annex C to UNOSOM II OPLAN 1, Rules of Engagement (ROE), Mogadishu, 021200C, May 1993.

UNPROFOR. *Force Commander Directive No. 01: Rules of Engagement*, HQ/UNPROFOR, Sarajevo, 24 March 1992.

UNPROFOR. Interoffice Memo (to ICFY), 29 January 1994 (subject: air power (general information)).

UNPROFOR, Chief of Staff. *Force Commander's Policy Directive No. 13— Revised*, Headquarters UNPROFOR, Ilica Barracks, Zagreb, 24 June 1994.

UNIDIR. *Managing Arms in Peace Processes: Croatia and Bosnia-Herzegovina*. Geneva: United Nations, 1995.

———. *Managing Arms in Peace Processes: The Issues*. Geneva: United Nations, 1995.

———. *Managing Arms in Peace Processes: Somalia*. Geneva: United Nations, 1995.

GOVERNMENT DOCUMENTS

Commission of Inquiry into the Deployment of Canadian Forces to Somalia, *Dishonoured Legacy: The Lessons of the Somalia Affair*. Ottawa: Government of Canada, 1997.

———. *Information Legacy: A Compendium of Source Material from the Commission of Inquiry into the Deployment of Canadian Forces to Somalia*. Ottawa: Government of Canada, 1997.

United Kingdom, Ministry of Information. *The First to be Freed: The Record of the British Military Administration in Eritrea and Somalia, 1941–1943*. London: His Majesty's Stationery Office, 1944.

United Kingdom. *The Covenant of the League of Nations with a Commentary Thereon*. Miscellaneous no. 3. London: His Majesty's Stationery Office, June 1919.

United States, Agency for International Development Bureau for Humanitarian Response, Office of U.S. Foreign Disaster Assistance. *Somalia—Civil Strife.* Situation Report #1, Fiscal Year (FY) 1995, 30 December 1994.

United States, Army-Air Force Center for Low Intensity Conflict. *White Paper: An Analysis of the Application of the Principles of Military Operations other than War (MOOTW) in Somalia.* DSN 574–5805, February 1994.

United States General Accounting Office. *Humanitarian Intervention, Effectiveness of U.N. Operations in Bosnia.* Washington, D.C.: Government Printing Office, GAO/NSIAD 94-156BR, April 1994.

United States, Joint Warfighting Center. *Joint Task Force Commander's Handbook for Peace Operations.* 28 February 1995.

Wider Peacekeeping, Army Field Manual. Vol. 5, *Operations Other than War*, part 2. London: Her Majesty's Stationery Office, 1995.

Woehrel, Steven. *Bosnia-Hercegovina: Summary of the Debate on a Unilateral Lifting of the Arms Embargo.* CRS Report for Congress, 95-477 F, 11 April 1995.

EUROPEAN COMMUNITY AND PEACE PROCESS DOCUMENTS

Allied Forces Southern Europe. "Operation Deny Flight." *Fact Sheet*, 13 January 1995.

International Conference on the Former Yugoslavia. "NATO concern about No-Fly Zone Infringements." Memo, 18 December 1993.

Lord Carrington letter to Hans van den Broek, EC Council of Ministers, December 1991.

Note of Lord Owen's Reaction to UN Secretary-General's Attitude to Implementing the Vance-Owen Plan, 3 March 1993.

Notes of Conversations at the Hague on the Evening of Monday 4 November 1991, written by J. P. Kavanagh, 4 November 1991.

"Options for Offensive Air Operations to 'Level the Playing Field' against the Bosnian Serb Army." Memo from Brigadier Graham Messervy-Whiting, Lord Owen's military adviser, 18 April 1993.

Report from Ambassador Wijnaendts on his seventh mission, Bzvertrouwelijk, 2 November 1991.

NATO DOCUMENTS

Declaration of the Heads of State and Government Participating in the Meeting of the North Atlantic Council Held at NATO Headquarters, Brussels, on 10–11 January 1994, 11 January 1994.

Decisions Taken at the Meeting of the North Atlantic Council in Permanent Session, NATO Headquarters, Brussels, 9 February 1994.

Decisions Taken at the Meeting of the North Atlantic Council on 9th August 1993. Press Release (93)52, 9 August 1993.

Decisions Taken on the Protection of Safe Areas Taken at the Meeting of the North Atlantic Council on 22nd April 1994. Press Release (94)32, 22 April 1994.

Ministerial Meeting of the North Atlantic Council, M-NAC-1(93)38, Athens, Greece, 10 June 1993.

NATO. Press Release (94)112, 23 November 1994.

NATO Starts Enforcement of No-fly Zone. NATO Press Release, reprinted in *NATO Review* (April 1993): 5.

Press Statement by the Secretary-General, Brussels, 2 August 1993.

Press Statement on Gorazde by Secretary-General Willy Claes Following North Atlantic Council Meeting on 25 July 1995. NATO Press Release, reprinted in *NATO Review* (September 1995): 7.

Press Statement Issued Jointly by UN and NATO. Press Release· (94)103, 28 October 1994.

Statement by the Secretary-General of NATO. Press Release (95)73, 30 August 1995.

Transcript, Admiral Leighton Smith, Press Conference, 1500 (Naples time) 15 September 1995.

Transcript of Press Conference, Admiral Leighton W. Smith, Commander in Chief Allied Forces Southern Europe. NATO Club HZ. AFSOUTH, Naples, Italy, 9 AM, 6 September 1995.

AFSOUTH COMMUNIQUÉS

AFSOUTH Communiqué, 27 April 1994.

Joint Statement by Admiral Leighton W. Smith and Lt. General Bernard Janvier, Extension of Suspension of NATO Air Strikes. Press Release 95-42, Naples, 17 September 1995.

Joint Statement by Admiral Leighton W. Smith, Commander in Chief Allied Forces Southern Europe and Lt. General Bernard Janvier, Force Commander, United Nations Peace Force, Press Release, 95-43, Naples, 21 September 1995.

ARTICLES

"Address to the Nation on Somalia." *Weekly Compilation of Presidential Documents* 29 (October 7, 1993): 2022-2025.

African Rights. "Somalia, Operation Restore Hope: A Preliminary Assessment." *Press Release* (1 May 1993).

Albright, Madeline. "Yes, There Is a Reason to Be in Somalia." *Backgrounder*, 93-25, U.S. Embassy, Ottawa, Canada, 11 August 1993.

Amer, Ramses. "The United Nations' Reactions to Foreign Military Interventions." *Journal of Peace Research* 31, no. 4 (1994): 425–444.

Berkowitz, Bruce D. "Rules of Engagement for U.N. Peacekeeping Forces in Bosnia." *Orbis* (Fall 1994): 635–646.

Blechman, Barry M. "The Intervention Dilemma." *Washington Quarterly*. (Summer 1995): 63–73.

Bloomfield, Lincoln, ed. "International Force—A Symposium." *International Organization* 17, no. 2 (Spring 1963).

Bolton, John R. "Wrong Turn in Somalia." *Foreign Affairs* 73, no. 1 (January/February 1994): 56–66.

Borchard, Edwin. "The Impracticability of 'Enforcing' Peace." *Yale Law Journal* 55 (1946): 966–973.

Boutros-Ghali, Boutros. "Empowering the UN." *Foreign Affairs* (Winter 1992–1993): 89–102.

Bryden, Matthew. "Somalia: The Wages of Failure." *Current History* (April 1995): 145–151.

Childers, Erskine. "Gulf Crisis Lessons for the United Nations." *Bulletin of Peace Proposals* 23, no. 2 (1992): 129–138.

Clark, Jeffrey. "Debacle in Somalia." *Foreign Affairs* 72, no. 1 (1993): 109–123.

Claude, Inis. "The Blueprint." *International Conciliation,* no. 532 (March 1961): 325–355.

———. "United Nations Use of Military Force." *Journal of Conflict Resolution* 7, no. 2 (June 1963).

Clemons, Elgin. "No Peace to Keep: Six and Three-quarters Peacekeepers." *New York University Journal of International Law and Politics* 26, no. 1: 107–141.

Crocker, Chester A. "The Lessons of Somalia, Not Everything Went Wrong." *Foreign Affairs* (May–June 1995): 2–8.

Daniel, Don, and Bradd Hayes. "Securing Observance of UN Mandates through the Employment of Military Force." *International Peacekeeping* 3, no. 4 (Winter 1996): 105–125.

Dobbie, Charles. "A Concept for Post-Cold War Peacekeeping." *Survival* 36, no. 3 (Autumn 1994): 121–148.

Draper, G.I.A.D. "The Legal Limitations upon the Employment of Weapons by the United Nations Force in the Congo." *International Comparative Law Quarterly* 12 (April 1963): 387–413.

Eagleburger, Lawrence. "Time to Consider Tougher Measures in Former Yugoslavia." *Text,* U.S. Embassy, Ottawa, Canada, 17 December 1992.

Farrell, Theo. "Sliding into War: The Somalia Imbroglio and US Army Peace Operations Doctrine." *International Peacekeeping* 2, no. 2 (Summer 1995): 194–214.

Fitzmaurice, G. G. "The Foundations of the Authority of International Law and the Problem of Enforcement." *Modern Law Review* 19, no. 1 (January 1956): 1–13.

"Frustration and Anxiety at UN as US Puts Somalia Operation on 6-month Notice." *International Documents Review* 4, no. 35 (1993): 1–2.

Goulding, Marrack. "The Evolution of United Nations Peace-keeping." *International Affairs* 69, no. 3 (1993): 451–464.

Gow, James. "Deconstructing Yugoslavia." *Survival* 33, no. 4 (July–August 1991): 291–311.

Halderman, John W. "Legal Basis for United Nations Armed Forces." *American Journal of International Law* 56, (1962): 971–996.

Higgins, Rosalyn. "The New United Nations and Former Yugoslavia." *International Affairs* 69, no. 3 (1993): 465–483.

Hoar, Joseph P. "A CINC's Perspective." *Joint Forces Quarterly* (Autumn 1993): 56–63.

Howe, Jonathon T. "The United States and United Nations in Somalia: The Limits of Involvement." *Washington Quarterly* 18, no. 3 (1995): 49–62.

James, Alan. "The Congo Controversies." *International Peacekeeping* 1, no. 1 (Spring 1994): 44–58.

———. "Internal Peace-keeping, A Dead End for the UN?" *Security Dialogue* 24, no. 4 (1993).

Lorenz, Col. F. M. "Forging Rules of Engagement: Lessons Learned in Operation United Shield." *Military Review* (November-December 1995): 17–25.

———. "Law and Anarchy in Somalia." *Parameters* 23, no. 4 (Winter 1993–94): 27–41.

———. "Rules of Engagement in Somalia: Were They Effective?" Staff Judge Advocate, I Marine Expeditionary Force, Camp Pendleton, California, no date.

MacInnis, Major-General John A. "The Rules of Engagement for U.N. Peacekeeping Forces in Former Yugoslavia: A Response." *Orbis* (Winter 1995): 97–100.

Maren, Michael. "Somalia: Whose Failure?" *Current History* (May 1996): 201–205.

McDougal, Myres S., and F. P. Feliciano. "Legal Regulation of Resort to International Coercion: Aggression and Self-Defense in Policy Perspective." *Yale Law Journal* 68, no. 6 (May 1959): 1057–1165.

Menkhaus, Ken. "Getting out vs. Getting through: U.S. and U.N. Policies in Somalia." *Middle East Policy* 3, no. 1 (1994): 146–162.

"Message to the Congress Transmitting a Report on Somalia." *Weekly Compilation of Presidential Documents* 29 (October 13, 1993): 2065-2066.

Miller, Andrew S. "Universal Soldiers: U.N. Standing Armies and the Legal Alternatives." *Georgetown Law Journal* 81 (March 1993): 773–828.

Miller, E. M. "Legal Aspects of the United Nations Action in the Congo." *American Journal of International Law* 55, (1961): 1–28.

Omaar, Rakiya. "Somaliland: One Thorn Bush at a Time." *Current History* (May 1994): 232–236.

———. "Somalia: At War with Itself." *Current History* (October 1991): 230–234.

Picco, Giandomenico. "The U.N. and the Use of Force, Leave the Secretary General out of It." *Foreign Affairs* 73, no. 5 (September–October 1994): 14–18.

Possony, Stefan T. "Peace Enforcement." *Yale Law Journal* 55 (1946): 910–949.

"President Clinton's Press Conference." *Weekly Compilation of Presidential Documents* 29 (June 15, 1993): 1083.

"The President's Radio Address." *Weekly Compilation of Presidential Documents* 29 (June 12, 1993): 1070.

Reisman, W. Michael. "Peacemaking." *Yale Journal of International Law* 18 (1993): 415–423.

Roberts, Adam. "The Crisis in UN Peacekeeping." *Survival* 36, no. 3 (Autumn 1994): 93–120.

Sahnoun, Mohamed M. "Prevention in Conflict Resolution: The Case of Somalia." *Irish Studies in International Affairs* 5 (1994): 5–13.

Samatar, Abdi Ismail. "Destruction of State and Society in Somalia: Beyond the Tribal Convention." *Journal of Modern African Studies* 30, no. 4 (1992): 625–641.

Samatar, Said. "Somalia: A Nation in Turmoil." *A Minority Rights Group Report* (August 1991): 19-20.

Schacter, Oscar. "Legal Issues at the United Nations." *Annual Review of United Nations Affairs* (1960-1961): 142–149.

Stevenson, Jonathan. "Hope Restored in Somalia?" *Foreign Policy* no. 91 (Summer 1993): 138–154.

Tulumello, Andre. "Rethinking Somalia's Clanism." *Harvard Human Rights Journal* 6 (Spring 1993): 230–234.

Urquhart, Brian. "For a UN Volunteer Military Force." *New York Review of Books,* 10 June 1993, 3–4.

White, Nigel D. "U.N. Peacekeeping - Development or Destruction?" *International Relations* 12, no. 1 (April 1994): 129–158.

BOOKS, BOOK CHAPTERS AND MONOGRAPHS

Abdi, Said Y. "Decolonization in the Horn and the Outcome of Somalia Aspirations for Self-determination." In *The Decolonization of Africa: Southern Africa and the Horn of Africa.* Paris: UN Educational, Scientific, and Cultural Organization, 1981.

Abi-Saab, Georges. *The United Nations Operation in the Congo, 1960–1964.* Oxford: Oxford University Press, 1978.

Africa Watch. *A Government at War with Its Own People: Testimonies about the Killings and the Conflict in the North.* New York: Africa Watch, 1990.

Allard, Kenneth. *Somalia Operations: Lessons Learned*. Washington, D.C.: National Defense University Press, 1995.

Ayoob, Mohammed. *The Horn of Africa: Regional Conflict and Super Power Involvement*. Canberra Papers on Strategy and Defence, no. 18. Canberra: Australian National University, 1978.

Bayne, E. A. *Four Ways of Politics*. New York: American Universities Field Staff, 1965.

Bentley, David, and Robert Oakley. *Peace Operations: A Comparison of Somalia and Haiti*. Carlisle, Pa.: U.S. Army War College, May 1995.

Bethlehem, Daniel, and Marc Weller, eds. *The "Yugoslav" Crisis in International Law: General Issues, Part I*. Cambridge International Documents Series. Vol. 5. Cambridge: Cambridge University Press, 1997.

Boland, Frederick H., Thomas M. Franck, Ernest A. Gross, and Oscar Schachter. *The Legal Aspects of the United Nations Action in the Congo*. The Hammarskjöld Forums, Working Paper 525/62/2, Association of the Bar of the City of New York, April 1962.

Borden, Anthony, and Richard Caplan. "The Former Yugoslavia: The War and the Peace Process." In *SIPRI Yearbook 1996: Armaments, Disarmament, and International Security*. London: Oxford University Press, 1997.

Boulden, Jane. *Prometheus Unborn: The History of the Military Staff Committee*. Aurora Papers 19. Ottawa: Canadian Centre for Global Security, 1993.

———. "Rules of Engagaement, Force Structure and Composition in United Nations Disarmament Operations." In *Managing Arms in Peace Processes: The Issues*. Geneva: UN Institute for Disarmament Research, 1996.

Bowett, Derek W. *United Nations Forces*. London: Stevens, 1964.

Brownlie, Ian. *International Law and the Use of Force by States*. Oxford: Clarendon, 1963.

Burns, Arthur Lee, and Nina Heathcote. *Peace-keeping by U.N. Forces from Suez to the Congo*. London: Pall Mall, 1963.

Burns, E. L. M., *Between Arab and Israeli*. Toronto: Clark, Irwin, 1962.

Chopra, Jarat, Åge Eknes, and Toralv Nordbø. *Fighting for Hope in Somalia*. Peacekeeping and Multinational Operations, no. 6. Oslo: Norwegian Institute of International Affairs, 1995.

Clark, Jeffrey. *Famine in Somalia and the International Response: Collective Failure*. Issue Paper, Washington, D.C.: U.S. Committee for Refugees, November 1992.

Clarke, Walter, and Jeffrey Herbst. *Learning from Somalia*. Boulder, Colo.: Westview, 1997.

Cohen, Herman J. "Intervention in Somalia." In Allan E. Goodman, ed., *The Diplomatic Record 1992–1993*. Boulder: Westview Press, 1995.

Cordier, A., and M. Harrelson, eds. *Public Papers of the Secretaries-General of the United Nations*. Vol. 6, *U Thant, 1961–1964*. New York: Columbia University Press, 1976.

Cox, David. *Exploring an Agenda for Peace: Issues Arising from the Report of the Secretary-General*. Aurora Papers 20. Ottawa: Canadian Centre for Global Security, 1993.

Damrosch, Lori Fisler, ed. *Enforcing Restraint: Collective Intervention in Internal Conflicts*. New York: Council on Foreign Relations, 1993.

Damrosch, Lori Fisler, and David J. Scheffer, eds. *Law and Force in the New International Order*. Boulder, Colo.: Westview, 1991.

Durch, William J., ed. *The Evolution of UN Peacekeeping*. New York: St. Martin's, 1993.

———, ed. *UN Peacekeeping, American Policy, and the Uncivil Wars of the 1990s*. New York: St. Martin's, 1996.

Eknes, Åge. *Blue Helmets in a Blown Mission? UNPROFOR in Former Yugoslavia.* Research Report no. 174. Oslo: Norwegian Institute of International Affairs, December 1993.

Evans, Gareth. *Cooperation for Peace: The Global Agenda for the 1990s and Beyond.* St. Leonards: Allen & Unwin, 1993.

Ferencz, Benjamin B. *Enforcing International Law—A Way to World Peace.* New York: Oceana Publications, 1983.

Frye, William R. *A United Nations Peace Force.* New York: Oceana Publications, 1957.

Goldman, Kjell. *Peace-keeping and Self-defence.* Monograph no. 7. Paris: International Information Center on Peace-keeping Operations, March 1968.

Goodrich, Leland M., Edvard Hambro, and Anne Simons. *Charter of the United Nations Commentary and Documents.* New York: Columbia University Press, 1969.

Gordon, King. *The United Nations in the Congo.* New York: Carnegie Endowment for International Peace, 1962.

Goulding, Marrack. "Current Rapid Expansion Unsustainable Without Major Changes." In *Keeping the Peace in the Post–Cold War Era, A Report to the Trilateral Commission.* The Triangle Papers 43. New York: Trilateral Commission, 1993.

Hansch, Steve, Scott Lillibridge, Grace Egeland, Charles Teller, and Michael Toole. *Lives Lost, Lives Saved: Excess Mortality and the Impact of Health Interventions in the Somalia Emergency.* Washington, D.C.: Refugee Policy Group, November 1994.

Hempstone, Smith. *Katanga Report.* London: Faber and Faber, 1962.

Henkin, Louis, et al. *Right v. Might, International Law and the Use of Force.* New York: Council on Foreign Relations, 1991.

Hess, Robert L. *Italian Colonialism in Somalia.* Chicago: University of Chicago Press, 1996.

Higgins, Rosalyn. *The Development of International Law through the Political Organs of the United Nations.* London: Oxford University Press, 1963.

———. *United Nations Peacekeeping 1946-1967, Documents and Commentary.* Vol. 1, *The Middle East.* Oxford: Oxford University Press, 1969.

———. *United Nations Peacekeeping 1946-1967, Documents and Commentary.* Vol. 2, *Asia.* Oxford: Oxford University Press, 1970.

———. *United Nations Peacekeeping 1946-1967, Documents and Commentary.* Vol. 3, *Africa.* Oxford: Oxford University Press, 1980.

Hilderbrand, Robert C. *Dumbarton Oaks: The Origins of the United Nations and the Search for Postwar Security.* Chapel Hill: University of North Carolina Press, 1990.

Hindmarsh, Albert E. *Force in Peace.* Cambridge: Harvard University Press, 1933.

Hirsch, John L., and Robert B. Oakley. *Somalia and Operation Restore Hope.* Washington, D.C.: United States Institute for Peace, 1995.

Holbrooke, Richard. *To End a War.* New York: Random, 1998.

Honig, Jan Willem, and Norbert Both. *Srebrenica: Record of a War Crime.* London: Penguin, 1996.

Horn, Major-General Carl von. *Soldiering for Peace.* London: Cassel, 1966.

Hoskyns, Catherine. *The Congo: A Chronology of Events, January 1960–December 1961.* Chatham House Memoranda. London: Royal Institute of International Affairs, May 1962.

———. *The Congo since Independence, January 1960 to December 1961.* London: Oxford University Press, 1965.

International Peace Academy. *Peacemaking and Peacekeeping for the Next Century.* International Peace Academy Report of the Twenty-fifth Vienna Seminar. New York, International Peace Academy, 1995.

James, Alan. *The Role of Force in International Order and United Nations Peace-keeping*. Report of a Conference at Ditchley Park. Ditchley Park: The Ditchley Foundation, 16-19 May 1969.

Johnston, Harry, and Ted Dagne. "Congress and the Somali Crisis." In Walter Clarke and Jeffrey Herbst, eds., *Learning from Somalia*. Boulder, Colo.: Westview, 1997.

Johnstone, Ian. *Aftermath of the Gulf War: An Assessment of UN Action*. Occasional Paper Series. New York: International Peace Academy, 1994.

Kalb, Madeleine. *Congo Cables*. New York: Macmillan, 1982.

Knock, Thomas J. *To End All Wars, Woodrow Wilson and the Quest for a New World Order*. New York: Oxford University Press, 1992.

Kyle, Keith. *The UN in the Congo*. Occasional Paper 2. INCORE, Coleraine: University of Ulster, 1995.

Larus, Joel. *From Collective Security to Preventive Diplomacy*. New York: Wiley, 1965.

Lefever, Ernest W. *Crisis in the Congo: A United Nations Force in Action*. Washington, D.C.: Brookings, 1965.

Legum, Colin. *Congo Disaster*. London: Penguin, 1961.

Leurdijk, Dick A. *The United Nations and NATO in Former Yugoslavia, 1991–1996: Limits to Diplomacy and Force*. The Hague: Netherlands Institute of International Relations, 1996.

Lewis, Ian M. *A Pastoral Democracy*. London: Oxford University Press, 1982.

Lyons, Terrence, and Ahmed I. Samatar. *Somalia, State Collapse, Multilateral Intervention and Strategies for Political Reconstruction*. Washington, D.C.: Brookings, 1995.

Mackinlay, John, and Jarat Chopra. *A Draft Concept of Second Generation Multinational Operations 1993*. Providence, R.I.: Brown University, 1993.

Malcolm, Noel. *Bosnia: A Short History*. London: Papermac, 1996.

Markakis, John. *National and Class Conflict in the Horn of Africa*. Cambridge: Cambridge University Press, 1987.

Mayall, James, ed. *The New Interventionism, 1991–1994*. Cambridge: Cambridge University Press, 1996.

Metz, Helen Chapin, ed. *Somalia: A Country Study*. Washington, D.C.: Federal Research Division, Library of Congress, 1993.

Mezerick, Avrahm G. *Congo and the United Nations*. New York: International Review Service, 1960.

Morrison, Alex, Douglas A. Fraser, and James D. Kiras. *Peacekeeping with Muscle: The Use of Force in International Conflict Resolution*. Toronto: Canadian Peacekeeping, 1997.

Northedge, F. S. ed. *The Use of Force in International Relations*. London: Faber and Faber, 1974.

O'Brien, Conor Cruise. *To Katanga and Back*. London: Hutchinson, 1962.

Ottaway, Marina. *Soviet and American Influence in the Horn of Africa*. New York: Praeger, 1982.

Owen, David. *Balkan Odyssey*. London: Indigo, 1996.

Parkhurst, E. Sylvia. *Ex-Italian Somaliland*. New York: Greenwood, 1951.

Pugh, Michael, ed. *The UN, Peace and Force*. London: Frank Cass, 1997. (The same text is also published as a full issue of *International Peacekeeping* 3, no. 4 [Winter 1996].)

Rikhye, Indar Jit. *The Theory and Practice of Peacekeeping*. London: Hurst, 1984.

———. *Military Adviser to the Secretary-General*. London: Hurst, 1993.

Roberts, Adam. *Humanitarian Action in War*. Adelphi Paper 305. London: International Institute for Strategic Studies, 1996.

Rohde, David. *A Safe Area, Srebrenica: Europe's Worst Massacre since the Second World War*. London: Simon and Schuster, 1997.

Roper, John. "The Return of Collective Security and the Expansion of United Nations Tasks." In *Keeping the Peace in the Post-Cold War Era, A Report to the Trilateral Commission*. The Triangle Papers 43. New York: Trilateral Commission, 1993.

Rose, General Sir Michael. *Fighting for Peace*. London: Harvill, 1998.

Russell, Ruth B. *A History of the United Nations Charter*. Washington, D.C.: Brookings, 1958.

————. *United Nations Experience with Military Forces: Political and Legal Aspects*. Washington, D.C.: Brookings, August 1964.

Sahnoun, Mohamed. *Somalia: The Missed Opportunities*. Washington, D.C.: United States Institute for Peace, 1994.

Samatar, Said S. *Somalia: A Nation in Turmoil*. London: Minority Rights Group, August 1991.

Schacter, Oscar. "Authorized Uses of Force by the United Nations and Regional Organizations." In Lori Fisler Damrosch and David J. Scheffer, eds., *Law and Force in the New International Order*. Boulder, Colo.: Westview, 1991.

A "Seamless" Transition: United States and United Nations Operations in Somalia—1992–1993, Parts A and B, CO9-96.1324.0, CO9-96-1325.0. Case Program, John F. Kennedy School of Government, Harvard University, 1996.

Seiple, Chris. *The U.S. Military/NGO Relationship in Humanitarian Interventions*. Carlisle, Pa.: U.S. Army War College, 1996.

Seyersted, Finn. *United Nations Forces in the Law of Peace and War*. The Hague: A. W. Sijthoff-Leyden, 1966.

The Shorter Oxford English Dictionary on Historical Principles. 2 vols. Oxford: Clarendon, 1996.

Silber, Laura, and Allan Little. *The Death of Yugoslavia*. London: Penguin, 1995.

Simmonds, R. *Legal Problems Arising from the United Nations Military Operations in the Congo*. The Hague: Martinus Nijhoff, 1968.

Smith, Hugh, ed. *Peacekeeping: Challenges for the Future*. Canberra: Australian Defence Studies Centre, 1993.

Sommer, John G. *Hope Restored? Humanitarian Aid in Somalia, 1990–1994*. Washington, D.C.: Refugee Policy Group, November 1994.

Stone, Julius. *Aggression and World Order*. Berkeley: University of California Press, 1958.

————. *Legal Controls on International Conflict*. London: Stevens, 1959.

Sutterlin, James S. *The United Nations and the Maintenance of International Security, A Challenge to be Met*. New York: Praeger, 1995.

Thakur, Ramesh, and Carlyle A. Thayer, eds. *A Crisis of Expectations: UN Peacekeeping in the 1990s*. Boulder, Colo.: Westview, 1995.

Thant, U. *A View from the UN*. New York: Doubleday, 1978.

Tharoor, Shashi. *Peace-keeping: Principle, Problems, and Prospects*. Strategic Research Department Research Report 9-93. Newport, R.I.: Center for Naval War Studies, U.S. Naval War College, 1993.

Urquhart, Brian. *Hammarskjöld*. New York: Norton, 1994.

Wainhouse, David W. *International Peace Observation*. Baltimore: Johns Hopkins University Press, 1966.

Washington Center of Foreign Policy Research. *The Future Character and Role of Peace Observation Arrangements under the United Nations*. Apps. 1 and 3. Washington, D.C.: 1964.

Westcott, Jan. *The Somalia Saga: A Personal Account, 1990–1993*. Washington, D.C.:
    Refugee Policy Group, November 1994.
White, Nigel D. *The United Nations and the Maintenance of International Peace and
    Security*. Manchester: Manchester University Press, 1990.
Woodward, Susan L. *Balkan Tragedy*. Washington, D.C.: Brookings, 1995.

Index